John Disturnell

Across the continent

John Disturnell

Across the continent

ISBN/EAN: 9783337257361

Printed in Europe, USA, Canada, Australia, Japan

Cover: Foto ©Andreas Hilbeck / pixelio.de

More available books at **www.hansebooks.com**

Across the Continent.

DISTURNELL'S

DISTANCE TABLES;

OR,

Travellers' Pocket Companion,

GIVING THE

Great Lines of Travel Across the Continent.

ALSO, CONTAINING A LIST OF ALL THE

RAILROADS IN THE UNITED STATES AND CANADA,

WITH OTHER USEFUL INFORMATION RELATING TO

STEAMSHIP LINES, TELEGRAPH LINES, ETC.

PRICE, 50 CENTS.

PHILADELPHIA:
PUBLISHED BY W. B. ZIEBER,
106 SOUTH THIRD STREET,
And for Sale by the AMERICAN NEWS COMPANY, 121 Nassau Street, New York,
and Booksellers and News Agents.
1871.

THIS Work is prepared and presented to the Public, owing to the great importance of the Line of Railroads crossing the Continent from different points of our extended country. The completion of the Union Pacific Railroad and Central Pacific Railroad, in May, 1869, forming a Through Line of Travel from Ocean to Ocean, was a bright event that will be forever remembered by the American public. Since that period, the Southern Pacific Railroad and Northern Pacific Railroad, have both been commenced, the one to terminate at the Pacific Ocean in Southern California, and the other to extend from the head of Lake Superior to Puget Sound, in Washington Territory—thus affording an International communication from Ocean to Ocean, *via* the St. Lawrence River.

The Eastern Cities that are mostly interested at this time in these great works, and from whence connecting Railroads diverge, are Baltimore, Washington, Philadelphia, New York and Boston; while other cities in the Valley of the Mississippi and on the shores of the Great Lakes, will be alike benefitted.

The Baltimore and Ohio Railroad, Pennsylvania Central Railroad, Erie Railway of New York, the Boston and Albany, and New York Central Railroads, and the Grand Trunk Railway of Canada, and their connections, form the first great links in this Continental Line of Travel, extending from the Atlantic to CHICAGO, ST. LOUIS and OMAHA, and from thence, crossing the Rocky Mountains, to the Pacific Ocean. The recent completion of the Kansas Pacific Railroad, extending Westward to DENVER, Colorado, forms another great Through Route of Travel.

From the principal Seaports on both Oceans, Lines of Steamers run to Europe on the East, and Asia on the West, thus encircling the World as with a band of iron—carrying civilization and commerce to every part of the inhabitable globe. These modes of communication, in connection with Ocean Lines of Telegraph, form the most important era in the World's history, and will, no doubt, tend to civilize and benefit the whole human family.

TO THE MANAGERS OF RAILROAD AND STEAMSHIP LINES.

YOUR favorable attention is respectfully called to the above Work which contains much valuable information required by the Travelling Public, giving reliable DISTANCE TABLES on all the TRUNK RAILWAYS extending from the Atlantic to the Pacific Ocean, and a Complete List of RAILROADS in the UNITED STATES and CANADA, Etc.

TERMS.

The Work will appear early in March, 1871, and be Revised from time to time, as New Editions are called for. It contains about 150 pages, and will be neatly bound in muslin; Retail Price, 50 Cents, from which a liberal deduction will be made when ordered in large quantities, either for sale or distribution. No better Advertising medium for Railroad Companies, Steamship Companies, and Land Agencies can be desired,—*Price per Page, Twenty Dollars.*

Address, J. DISTURNELL,

No. 17 South Sixth Street, (up stairs,)

PHILADELPHIA.

CONTENTS.

	PAGE.
TRUNK RAILWAYS	5–6
Distances from New York & Washington	7–8
Distances to Foreign Ports	9
Distances from Chicago & St. Louis	10
Distances Around the World	11
Table of Altitudes and Distances Across the Continent	12
CONDENSED TABLES OF DISTANCES.	
Baltimore to St. Louis, S. Francisco, &c.	13
Baltimore to Chicago, Omaha, &c.	14
Philadelphia to Chicago, S. Franc'o, &c.	14
Philadelphia to St. Louis, Denver, &c.	14
N. York to Pittsburgh, S. Francisco, &c.	15
N. York to Chicago, S. Francisco, &c.	15
New York to Buffalo, St. Louis, &c.	16
Boston to Chicago, San Francisco, &c.	17
Boston to Chicago, Puget Sound, &c.	17
Northern Pacific Railroad Route	18
Lake Superior to Puget Sound	18
Portland to Montreal, Chicago, &c.	18
Washington to Philadelphia, New York, Boston, Portland, &c.	19–20
Washington and Baltimore to St. Louis, &c.	21–22
St. Louis to Kansas City, Denver, &c.	23–24
Denver to Cheyenne, Wyoming Territory,	24
Baltimore to St. Louis, Kansas City, &c.	25–26
Baltimore to Pittsburgh, St. Louis, &c.	27
Philadelphia to Indianapolis, St. Louis, &c.	28
Philadelphia to Chicago, Omaha, &c.	29–30
Philadelphia to Columbus, St. Louis, &c.	31–32
New York to Pittsburgh, Chicago, Omaha, &c.—Allentown Line,	33–34
Philadelphia to Erie, Duluth & St. Paul, via Lakes Huron and Superior	35–36
New York to Buffalo, Niagara Falls, &c.	37–38
New York to Toledo, Quincy, St. Louis, &c.	39–40
New York to Williamsport and Erie, Pa.	41
New York to Detroit, Chicago, &c.	42–43
New York to Indianapolis and St. Louis	44
St. Louis to Springfield, State Line and Fort Scott, Kan	45
St. Louis to Kansas City, Ottumwa and Omaha	46–47
Boston to Detroit, Milwaukee, &c.	48–49
Boston to Detroit, Chicago and Omaha	50–51
Omaha to Cheyenne, Utah, S. Francisco, &c.	52–53
Central Pacific Railroad	54
Boston to Buffalo, Toledo, Chicago, Omaha and San Francisco	55–56
Buffalo to Toledo and Chicago	57
Cleveland to Columbus, Cincinnati, Indianapolis and St. Louis	58–59
Toledo to Quincy, St. Louis and Keokuk	60
Hannibal and Quincy to St. Joseph and Kansas City	61
Chicago to Alton and St. Louis	62
Chicago to Quincy and St. Joseph	63
Chicago to Burlington and Omaha	64
Chicago to Cairo and St. Louis	65
Cairo to Dubuque, &c., via Illinois Central Railroad	66
Chicago to Dubuque and Sioux City, Iowa.	67
Chicago to Madison and St. Paul	68
Milwaukee to Prairie du Chien, St. Paul, &c.	69
Cincinnati to Indianapolis and Chicago	70
Portland to Montreal, Quebec, Toronto and Detroit	71
Buffalo to Goderich, Can.	72
St. Louis to Dubuque, St. Paul, &c., via Mississippi River	73–74
RAILROADS IN THE UNITED STATES AND CANADA—Finished and in Progress of Construction	75–88
Tonnage of the United States	89
Variation of Time in Crossing the Continent	90

4   CONTENTS.

	PAGE.
Commencement of Railroads in the United States—Early History, &c	91-92
Railroad Statistics—Length, Cost, &c.	93
RAILROAD SYSTEM OF THE UNITED STATES AND CANADA—GREAT TRUNK RAILWAYS	94
Baltimore and Ohio—Pennsylvania Central—Erie Railway	94
Hudson River—New York Central—Boston and Albany	95
New York and Oswego Midland	95
Chesapeake and Ohio	95
Grand Trunk of Canada	95
Trunk Railways—Union Pacific, &c.	96
Toledo, Wabash and Western—Chicago, Burlington and Quincy	96

TRUNK RAILWAYS—Continued.	PAGE.
Burlington and Missouri River—Chicago and Northwestern—Chicago, Rock Island and Pacific	97
Pacific—North Missouri	98
Atlantic and Pacific—Kansas Pacific, &c	99
Union Pacific—Denver & Rio Grande	100
St. Paul and Sioux City	101
Lake Superior and Mississippi	102-104
St. Paul and Pacific—Northern Pacific—Table of Distances, &c	105-106
Southern Pacific, &c	107-108
Railroad Companies in New York	109
Telegraph Companies in New York	110

ADVERTISEMENTS.

	PAGE.
Pennsylvania Central Railroad	111-115
Philadelphia and Erie Railroad	116-118
New York and Philadelphia Railroad	119
Northern Central—Baltimore to Williamsport, Elmira, &c	120
Allentown Line—New York to Pittsburgh, &c	34
Erie Railway—New York to Buffalo, &c.	38
Illinois Central Railroad	121-122
Chicago, Burlington and Quincy R. R.	123-124
Chicago, Rock Island & Pacific R. R.	125-126
Chicago, Alton and St. Louis Railroad	127
Chicago and Northwestern Railroad	128

	PAGE.
Cleveland, Columbus, Cincinnati and Indianapolis Railroad	129
Burlington and Missouri River Railroad.	130
North Missouri Railroad	131-132
Pacific Railroad of Missouri	133
Kansas Pacific Railway	134-135
Atlantic and Pacific Railroad—Land Department	136-137
Union Pacific and Central Pacific Railroads	138-140
Northern Pacific Railroad—Land Dep't.	141-144
GRAND PLEASURE EXCURSION—1871	145-146
HOTELS—Life Insurance Company	147-152

TRUNK RAILWAYS,

Forming Through Lines of Travel from the Atlantic to the Pacific Ocean, via the Southern Pacific*, Kansas Pacific, Union Pacific, or Northern Pacific Railroad*.

RAILWAYS.	FROM	TO	MILES
ATLANTIC AND PACIFIC	St. Louis, Mo.	State Line	330
Laclede and Fort Scott	Lebanon, Mo	Fort Scott, Kan	110
Van Buren Branch*	Pierce City, Mo	Van Buren, Ark	125
BALTIMORE AND OHIO	Baltimore	Wheeling, W. Va.	379
Parkersburg Division	Grafton, W. Va	Parkersburg, "	104
Central Ohio Division	Bellaire, Ohio	Columbus, O	137
Lake Erie Division	Newark, Ohio	Sandusky, O	116
Boston and Albany	Boston	Albany	200
Boston and Maine	Boston	Portland, Me	111
BURLINGTON AND MISSOURI RIVER.	Burlington, Iowa	Omaha, Neb	296
Nebraska Division*	Plattsmouth, Neb	Lincoln, Neb	55
CENTRAL PACIFIC	Ogden, Utah	Sacramento	743
Central Branch Union Pacific*	Atchison, Kan	Waterville	100
Central New Jersey, (Allentown Route)	New York	Harrisburg, Pa	182
Chicago, Alton and St. Louis	Chicago	St. Louis	280
CHICAGO, BURLINGTON AND QUINCY	Chicago	Quincy, Ill	263
Burlington Branch	Galesburg, Ill	Burlington, Iowa.	43
Galesburg and Peoria	Peoria, Ill	Galesburg, Ill	53
CHICAGO AND NORTHWESTERN	Chicago	Clinton, Iowa	138
Iowa Division	Clinton, Iowa	Omaha, Neb	354
Galena Division	Chicago	Freeport, Ill	121
Milwaukee Division	Chicago	Milwaukee	85
CHICAGO, ROCK ISLAND AND PACIFIC	Chicago	Rock Island	182
Iowa Division	Davenport, opp. R. I.	Omaha, Neb	313
Cincinnati, Ham. & Dayton and Dayton & Mich.	Cincinnati	Detroit	267
Cincinnati, Richmond and Chicago	Hamilton, O	Chicago	294
Cleveland, Columbus, Cincinnati & Indianapolis	Cleveland	Columbus	138
" " " "	Crestline, O	Indianapolis	207
Cleveland and Pittsburgh	Pittsburgh	Cleveland	150
Des Moines Valley	Keokuk, Iowa	Sioux City Junct.	244
Denver Pacific	Denver, Col	Cheyenne, Wy. Tr	106
Detroit and Milwaukee	Detroit, Mich	Grand Haven	189
ERIE—Main Line	New York	Dunkirk, N. Y	460
Rochester Division	Corning, N. Y	Rochester	94
Buffalo Division	Hornellsville	Buffalo	91
Atlantic and Great West. Division	Salamanca, N. Y	Cincinnati	448
GRAND TRUNK—Main Line	Portland, Me	Montreal, Canada	297
Quebec Division	Richmond, Can	Quebec, Canada	97
Montreal to Toronto	Montreal, Can	Toronto, Canada	333
Toronto to Sarnia	Toronto, Can	Point Edward	168
Point Edward to Detroit	Point Edward	Detroit	73
GREAT WESTERN OF CANADA	Suspension Bridge	Detroit	230
Toronto Branch	Hamilton, Canada	Toronto	39
HANNIBAL AND ST. JOSEPH	Hannibal, Mo	St. Joseph	206
Quincy Branch	Quincy, Ill	Palmyra, Mo	15
Kansas City and Cameron Branch	Cameron, Mo	Kansas City	55
HUDSON RIVER	New York	Albany	145

* Unfinished.

5

RAILWAYS.	FROM	TO	MILES
ILLINOIS CENTRAL—Chicago Division	Chicago	Cairo, Ill	365
Northern Division	Dubuque	Centralia, Ill	345
Iowa Division	Dubuque, Iowa	Sioux City	326
Cedar Falls and Minnesota Division	Waterloo	Mona, Iowa	75
Indianapolis, Bloomington and Western	Indianapolis	Peoria, Ill	212
Indianapolis, Cincinnati and La Fayette	Cincinnati	La Fayette	179
Indianapolis and St. Louis	Indianapolis via Alton	St. Louis	261
Kansas City, St. Joseph and Council Bluffs	Kansas City, Mo	Council Bluffs	200
KANSAS PACIFIC	Kansas City, Mo	Denver, Col	638
Leavenworth Branch	Lawrence	Leavenworth	34
LAKE SHORE AND MICHIGAN SOUTHERN	Buffalo, N. Y	Cleveland, O	183
Toledo Division	Cleveland	Toledo	113
Michigan Southern Division	Toledo, O	Chicago	244
Lake Superior and Mississippi	Duluth, Minn	St. Paul	155
Little Miami	Columbus, Ohio	Cincinnati	120
Marietta and Cincinnati	Parkersburg, W. Va	Cincinnati	205
Michigan Central	Detroit, Mich	Chicago	284
MILWAUKEE AND ST. PAUL	Milwaukee, Wis	Prarie du Chien	194
Iowa and Minnesota Division	McGregor, Iowa	St. Paul	212
La Crosse Division	Milwaukee	La Crosse	195
NEW YORK CENTRAL	Albany	Buffalo	297
" " "	Rochester	Niagara Falls	77
New York, New Haven, Hartford & Springfield	New York	Springfield, Mass.	136
New York and Philadelphia Line	New York	Philadelphia	90
NORTH MISSOURI	St. Louis	Kansas City, Mo..	272
North Branch	Moberly, Mo	Ottumwa, Iowa	130
St. Louis, C. B. and Omaha*	Brunswick, Mo	Omaha, Neb	188
St. Joseph Division	R. & L. Junction	St. Joseph, Mo	72
Northern Central	Baltimore	Sunbury, Pa	138
NORTHERN PACIFIC*	Duluth, Minn		
OHIO AND MISSISSIPPI	Cincinnati	St. Louis	340
PACIFIC (of Missouri)	St. Louis, via Ks. City	Atchison, Kan	330
PENNSYLVANIA CENTRAL	Philadelphia	Pittsburgh	354
Philadelphia and Erie	Sunbury, Pa	Erie, Pa	288
Philadelphia, Wilmington and Baltimore	Philadelphia	Baltimore	98
Pittsburgh, Fort Wayne and Chicago	Pittsburgh	Chicago.	468
Pittsburgh, Cincinnati and St. Louis	Pittsburgh	Columbus, O	193
St. Louis, Vandalia, T. H. and Indianapolis	Indianapolis	St. Louis	238
ST. PAUL AND PACIFIC*	St. Paul, Minn	Wilmar, Minn	105
Branch Line	St. Anthony, Minn	Sauk Rapids	68
St. Paul and Sioux City*	St. Paul, Minn	Madelia, Minn	100
Southern Pacific*	(See Atlan. & Pacific)		
SOUTHERN TRANS-CONTINENTAL*	Texana, Texas	El Paso	
Toledo, Peoria and Warsaw	Logansport, Ind	Warsaw, Ill	227
TOLEDO WABASH AND WESTERN	Toledo, Ohio	Quincy, Ill	476
St. Louis Division	Decatur, Ill	St. Louis	104
Hannibal Branch	Bluffs Station	Hannibal, Mo	48
Moberly Branch	Hannibal	Moberly, Mo	70
Keokuk Branch	Clayton, Ill	Keokuk, Iowa	42
UNION PACIFIC	Omaha, Neb	Ogden, Utah	1032
Utah Central	Ogden, Utah	Salt Lake City	40
WESTERN PACIFIC	Sacramento, Cal	San Francisco	138

* Unfinished.

DISTANCES FROM NEW YORK AND WASHINGTON

TO THE

PRINCIPAL CITIES IN THE UNITED STATES.

CITIES.	MILES. FROM N. Y.	FROM W.	CITIES.	MILES. FROM N. Y.	FROM W.
ALBANY, N. Y.	145	375	CONCORD, N. H.	279	509
Alexandria, Va.	238	8	Covington, Ky.	745	614
Alleghany City, Pa.	433	376	Cumberland, Md.	366	200
Alton, Ill.	1,060	974			
ANNAPOLIS, Md.	228	42	Davenport, Iowa	1,084	1,028
Ann Arbor, Mich.	716	732	Dayton, Ohio.	760	606
Appalachicola, Flor.	1,370	1,140	DENVER, Col.	1,942	1,842
ATLANTA, Geo.	955	725	DES MOINES, Iowa	1,259	1,203
Atchison, Kan.	1,360	1,284	Detroit, Mich.	678	695
Auburn, N. Y.	328	416	Dover, N. H.	306	536
AUGUSTA, Me.	404	634	DOVER, Del.	156	158
Augusta, Geo.	904	674	Dubuque, Iowa	1,088	1,034
AUSTIN, Texas.	2,043	1,813	Duluth, Minn.	1,505	1,457
Baltimore, Md.	188	40	Easton, Pa.	75	210
Bangor, Me.	477	707	Elizabeth, N. J.	15	216
Bath, Me.	376	606	Elmira, N. Y.	272	298
Baton Rouge, La.	1,620	1,390	Erie, Pa.	486	469
Binghamton, N. Y.	215	357	Evansville, Ind.	1,020	857
BOISE CITY, Idaho	2,884	2,824	Fall River, Mass.	180	410
BOSTON, Mass.	234	466	Fond du Lac, Wis.	1,082	1,022
Bridgeport, Conn.	59	287	Fort Wayne, Ind.	763	694
Bristol, R. I.	215	439	FRANKFORT, Ky.	900	742
Brooklyn, N. Y.	1	232	Frederick, Md.	252	83
Buffalo, N. Y.	442	447	Freeport, Ill.	1,030	965
Burlington, Vt.	305	535			
Burlington, Iowa	1,122	1,053	Galena, Ill.	1,082	1,016
			Galveston, Texas	1,817	1,587
Cairo, Ill.	1,150	1,009	Georgetown, D. C.	232	2
Cambridge, Mass.	236	468	Grand Rapids, Mich.	836	853
Camden, N. J.	87	141	Green Bay, Wis.	1,200	1,088
CARSON CITY, Nev.	2,850	3,004			
Charleston, S. C.	822	592	Hamilton, Ohio.	730	641
Charlestown, Mass.	236	468	HARRISBURG, Pa.	182	126
Chattanooga, Tenn.	980	750	HARTFORD, Conn.	112	345
CHEYENNE, Wy. Ter	1,910	1,850	Hudson, N. Y.	118	348
Chicago, Ill.	900	844			
Cincinnati, Ohio.	744	612	INDIANAPOLIS, Ind.	838	722
Cleveland, Ohio.	581	516	Iowa City, Iowa	1,200	1,082
COLUMBUS, Ohio	624	535			
COLUMBIA, S. C.	753	523	JACKSON, Miss.	1,297	1,097
			JEFFERSON CITY, Mo.	1,179	1,079

7

CITIES.	MILES. FROM N. Y.	FROM W.
Jersey City, N. J............	1	229
Kansas City, Mo............1,372		1,226
Key West, Flor............1,587		1,357
Knoxville, Tenn............ 744		514
La Crosse, Wis............1,200		1,128
Lancaster, Pa............ 260		123
LANSING, Mich............ 785		747
Lawrence, Kan............1,400		1,277
Leavenworth, Kan............1,393		1,265
Lexington, Ky............ 903		713
LINCOLN, Neb............ .1,472		1,417
Little Rock, Ark............1,287		1,087
Louisville, Ky............ 947		747
Lynchburg, Va............ 404		174
Macon, Geo............1,121		891
MADISON, Wis............1,049		976
Marietta, Ohio............ 580		418
Memphis, Tenn............1,135		937
Milwaukee, Wis............ 996		931
Minneapolis, Minn............1,360		1,297
Mobile, Ala............1,316		1,086
MONTGOMERY, Ala............1,130		900
MONTPELIER, Vt............ 306		536
NASHVILLE, Tenn............1,085		777
New Albany, Ind............ 903		751
Newark, N. J............ 9		222
New Brunswick, N. J...... 32		200
Newburgh, N. Y............ 60		290
NEW HAVEN, Conn........ 76		308
New London, Conn......... 126		358
NEW ORLEANS, La........1,490		1,260
NEWPORT, R. I............ 162		402
NEW YORK,.................. 0		230
Norfolk, Va............ 466		236
Ogden, Utah............2,424		2,471
OLYMPIA, Wy. Ter.........3,300		3,400
Omaha, Neb............1,392		1,337
Oshkosh, Wis............1,100		1,039
Ogdensburg, N. Y........ 394		622
Oswego, N. Y............ 285		473
Paterson, N. J............ 17		246

CITIES.	MILES. FROM N. Y.	FROM W.
Peoria, Ill............1,072		938
PHILADELPHIA............ 90		140
Pittsburgh, Pa............ 432		375
Portland, Me............ 344		570
Portland, Or............3,850		3,790
Portsmouth, N. H............ 294		524
Poughkeepsie, N. Y........ 75		306
PROVIDENCE, R. I............ 193		423
Quincy, Ill............1,170		1,076
Racine, Wis............ 967		907
RALEIGH, N. C............ 546		316
Reading, Pa............ 128		157
RICHMOND, Va............ 361		131
Rochester, N. Y............ 372		396
Rock Island, Ill............1,083		1,027
Rutland, Vt............ 239		469
Sacramento, Cal............3,176		3,173
Saginaw, Mich............ 850		797
St. Anthony, Minn............1,360		1,297
St. Joseph, Mo............1,385		1,260
St. Louis, Mo............1,150		954
St. Paul, Minn............1,350		1,287
Salem, Mass............ 250		484
SALEM, Or............3,800		3,739
Sandusky, Ohio............ 660		577
SALT LAKE CITY, Utah...2,464		2,511
San Francisco, Cal.........3,286		3,250
Santa Fé, N. M............2,300		2,106
Savannah, Geo............ 928		698
Schenectady, N. Y......... 162		394
Selma, Ala............1,112		882
Sitka, Alaska............4,810		4,750
Springfield, Mass......... 138		371
SPRINGFIELD, Ill............1,062		963
Staunton, Va............ 388		158
Steubenville, Ohio 474		418
Syracuse, N. Y............ 291		437
Tallahassee, Flor............1,191		961
Taunton, Mass............ 210		457
Terre Haute, Ind............ 900		795
Toledo, Ohio............ 742		630
TOPEKA, Kan............1,530		1,307

CITIES.	MILES. FROM N. Y.	FROM W.	CITIES.	MILES. FROM N. Y.	FROM W.
Trenton, N. J	60	172	Wilmington, N. C	711	381
Troy, N. Y	150	382	Winona, Minn	1,240	1,162
Tucson, Ariz	2,889	2,659	Worcester, Mass	192	426
Utica, N. Y	249	472	Xenia, Ohio	660	490
Vicksburg, Miss	1,542	1,312			
Virginia City, Mont	2,937	2,837	Yancton, Dak	1,500	1,404
			York, Pa	250	98
Washington, D. C	230	0	Ypsilanti, Mich	708	724
Wheeling, W. Va	522	402			
Wilmington, Del	116	110	Zanesville, Ohio	600	476

DISTANCES TO FOREIGN PORTS

FROM

NEW YORK AND NEW ORLEANS, BY WATER.

CITIES.	MILES. FROM N. Y.	FROM N. O.	CITIES.	MILES. FROM N. Y.	FROM N. O.
Amsterdam	3,500	4,710	Lisbon	3,175	4,500
Aspinwall	2,320	1,300	London	3,350	5,100
Barbadoes	1,900	1,200	Liverpool	3,200	4,950
Batavia	13,000	12,000	Madras	11,850	11,250
Bermudas	660	1,600	Malta	4,325	5,720
Bordeaux	3,300	4,600	Manilla	13,675	13,000
Bombay	11,575	10,800	Monrovia	3,825	4,900
Buenos Ayres	7,100	6,380	Naples	4,330	5,725
Calcutta	12,500	12,000	Panama	2,350	1,300
Canton	14,000	13,000	Pekin	15,000	14,000
Cape Horn	8,120	7,300	Pernambuco	4,760	3,900
Cape of Good Hope	6,830	6,200	Rio de Janeiro	3,850	5,100
Constantinople	5,140	6,400	San Francisco via Pana.	5,860	4,850
Copenhagen	3,640	5,800	Sandwich Islands	15,000	14,000
Dublin	3,225	5,000	St. Petersburg	4,420	6,250
Gibraltar	3,300	4,700	Singapore	12,700	11,800
Halifax	612	2,500	Smyrna	5,000	6,310
Hamburg	3,775	5,500	Stockholm	4,000	6,000
Havana	1,420	610	Trieste	5,130	6,500
Havre	3,150	5,400	Valparaiso	9,750	9,000
Kingston	1,640	1,000	Vera Cruz	2,250	830
Lima	11,310	10,750	Yokohama	13,000	12,000

DISTANCES FROM CHICAGO AND ST. LOUIS,

BY THE MOST DIRECT ROUTES.

CITIES.	FROM C.	FROM ST. L.	CITIES.	FROM C.	FROM ST. L.
ALBANY, N. Y.	818	1,026	MADISON, Wis.	138	418
Alton, Ill	257	23	Marquette, Mich	437	717
Baltimore, Md	802	928	Memphis, Tenn	600	400
Bloomington, Ill	126	154	Milwaukee, Wis	85	365
BOSTON, Mass	1,018	1,226	Montgomery, Ala	941	895
Buffalo, N. Y.	540	728	Montreal, Can	843	1,056
Burlington, Iowa	208	200	Nashville, Tenn	485	455
Cairo, Ill	365	200	New Orleans	1,365	1,200
Cheyenne, Wy. Ter	1,008	1,016	NEW YORK.	898	1,088
CHICAGO	0	280	Niagara Falls, N. Y.	515	750
Cincinnati, O.	294	340	Norfolk, Va.	950	975
Cleveland, O.	357	545	Omaha, Neb	497	800
COLUMBUS, O.	296	427	Ottumwa, Iowa	285	383
CONCORD, N. H.	1,197	1,392	PHILADELPHIA	823	975
Davenport, Iowa	183	243	Pittsburgh	468	620
DENVER, Col.	1,120	910	Portland, Me	1,123	1,331
Des Moines, Iowa	357	325	Quincy, Ill.	263	160
Detroit, Mich	284	497	RICHMOND, Va.	982	1,004
Dubuque, Iowa	188	350	Rochester, N. Y	590	797
Duluth, Minn.	600	880	Rock Island, Ill	182	242
Effingham, Ill.	199	99	SACRAMENTO, Cal.	2,272	2,260
Erie, Pa.	452	640	St. Joseph, Mo	473	305
Evansville, Ind	388	125	ST. LOUIS	280	0
Freeport, Ill	121	314	St. Paul	448	728
Fort Wayne.	148	338	Salt Lake City,	1,580	1,570
Galesburg, Ill	164	160	SAN FRANCISCO.	2,410	2,400
Hannibal, Mo	283	140	Savannah, Geo.	1,260	1,240
HARRISBURG, Pa.	717	868	SPRINGFIELD, Ill.	185	95
INDIANAPOLIS	193	238	Terre Haute, Ind	183	166
JACKSON, Miss	869	698	Toledo, O	244	432
Jefferson City, Mo	405	125	TOPEKA, Kan	590	340
Kansas City, Mo	522	272	Toronto, Can	510	723
Keokuk, Iowa	270	160	Urbana, O	292	379
Lawrence, Kan	560	310	Vicksburg, Miss	1,000	800
Leavenworth, Kan	514	309	WASHINGTON, D. C	842	950
LITTLE ROCK, Ark	710	590	Wheeling, W. Va.	435	564
Louisville, Ky	296	276	Zanesville, Ohio	380	486

	STATUTE MILES.	TIME.
NEW YORK to CHICAGO, Illinois.............*Railroad.*	900	1¼ Days.
CHICAGO to SAN FRANCISCO, California..............*Railroad.*	2,410	5¼ "
SAN FRANCISCO to YOKOHAMA, Japan...............*Steamship.*	4,816	21 "
YOKOHAMA to HONG KONG, China....................*Steamship.*	1,670	6 "
HONG KONG to CALCUTTA, India........................*Steamship.*	3,500	14 "
CALCUTTA to BOMBAY..*Railroad.*	1,229	2 "
BOMBAY to CAIRO, Egypt...................................*Steamship.*	3,800	14 "
CAIRO to MARSEILLES, France.........................*Steamship.*	1,700	4 "
MARSEILLES to HAVRE, France.........................*Railroad.*	575	1½ "
HAVRE to NEW YORK ....*Steamship.*	3,150	10 "
Total	**23,750**	**79** Days.

☞ Making 5,114 Miles by Railroad, and 18,636 Miles by Steamship.

DISTANCE AROUND THE WORLD IN GEOGRAPHICAL MILES,
COMMENCING AT THE MERIDIAN OF GREENWICH, ENGLAND.

	DEGREES.		GEO. MILES.	
WEST COAST OF AFRICA, crossing Atlantic Ocean...To	50	West.		3,000
MOUTH OF THE AMAZON RIVER to the Pac. Coast... "	80	"	1,800	4,800
GALAPAGOS ISLANDS, Pacific O., (under the Equator) "	90	"	600	5,400
GALAPAGOS ISLANDS, to CHRISTMAS ISLAND, P. O. "	160	"	4,200	9,600
CHRISTMAS ISLAND to KINGSMILL GROUP, P. O..... "	180	"	1,200	10,800
KINGSMILL GROUP to PAPUA or NEW GUINEA, P. O. "	140	East.	2,400	13,200
NEW GUINEA to the MOLUCCAS ISLANDS, Pacific O. "	130	"	600	13,800
MOLUCCAS to the CELEBES, Pacific Ocean............ "	120	"	600	14,400
CELEBES to BORNEO..................................... "	118	"	120	14,520
ISLAND OF BORNEO...................................... "	108	"	600	15,120
BORNEO to SUMATRA, (West Coast) .... "	100	"	480	15,600
SUMATRA to the EAST COAST OF AFRICA, Indian O. "	40	"	3,600	19,200
EAST COAST OF AFRICA to Meridian of Greenwich.. "	0	"	2,400	21,600

NOTE.—The *Land* passed in going around the World, under the Equator, being about 5,600 Geographical Miles, and the *Water* 16,000 Miles; making a total of about 24,000 English Statute Miles.

TABLE OF ALTITUDES AND DISTANCES

ACROSS THE CONTINENT.

CITIES, &C.	ALT. FT.	MILES.	CITIES, &C.	ALT. FT.	MILES.
NEW YORK	0	0	Rock Creek	6,690	2,017
HARRISBURG, Pa	320	183	Medicine Bow	6,550	2,039
Altoona, "	1,168	316	St. Mary's	6,751	2,074
Gallitzin, Alleghany Mts.	2,180	327	Rawlins	6,732	2,103
Cresson	1,996	330	Bitter Creek	6,685	2,179
Johnstown	1,184	354	Point of Rocks	6,490	2,203
PITTSBURGH, Pa	700	432	Rock Springs	6,280	2,229
Alliance, Ohio		516	Green River	6,140	2,239
Crestline, "		621	Bryan	6,340	2,252
Fort Wayne, Ind		752	Church Buttes	6,317	2,281
Chicago, Ill	590	900	Fort Bridger	6,780	2,309
Rock Island "	550	1,083	Piedmont	6,540	2,324
(*Mississippi River.*)			Wahsatch, Utah	6,879	2,362
			Castle Rock	6,290	2,371
DAVENPORT, Iowa	550	1,084	Weber Canon	5,130	2,401
Iowa City, "		1,138	Devil's Gate	4,870	2,413
Des Moines	780	1,257	**Ogden.** (*R. R. Junc.*),	4,340	2,426
COUNCIL BLUFFS	966	1,390	Corinne	4,294	2,451
(*Missouri River.*)			Promontory	4,943	2,487
Omaha, Neb	966	1,394	Kelton	4,500	2,518
Elkhorn	1,150	1,423	Toano, Nev	5,964	2,609
Fremont	1,176	1,441	Tulasco	5,418	2,653
North Bend	1,260	1,456	Elko	5,030	2,701
COLUMBUS	1,432	1,486	Carlin	4,930	2,724
Lone Tree	1,686	1,526	Battle Mountain	4,534	2,790
Grand Island	1,850	1,548	WINNEMUCCA	4,355	2,844
Kearny	2,106	1,585	Humboldt	4,262	2,885
Willow Island	2,511	1,644	Wadsworth	4,104	2,980
North Platte	2,790	1,685	Reno	4,525	3,014
Roscoe	3,105	1,726	TRUCKEE, Cal	5,866	3,048
Julesburg, Col	3,500	1,771	Summit Sierras	7,042	3,063
Lodge Pole	3,800	1,791	Cisco	5,911	3,076
Sidney	4,073	1,808	Alta	3,625	3,100
Antelope	4,712	1,845	Colfax	3,448	3,114
Pine Bluffs, Wy. Ter	5,026	1,867	Auburn	1,385	3,133
Cheyenne, "	6,041	1,911	Junction, *Cal. & Or. R. R.*	189	3,150
Sherman, (Summit)	8,242	1,944	**Sacramento**	56	3,168
Red Buttes	7,336	1,959	STOCKTON	46	3,216
LARAMIE	7,123	1,967	**San Francisco**	0	3,308

13

ACROSS THE CONTINENT.

CONDENSED TABLES.

No 1.

FROM.	TO.	RAILROADS.	MILES.
Baltimore to **Parkersburg,** W. Vir., *via* Balt. & Ohio Railroad.			383
Parkersburg to Cincinnati, O., *via* Marietta & Cincinnati Railroad....			205
Cincinnati to St. Louis, Mo., *via* Ohio & Mississippi Railroad...........			340
St. Louis to Kansas City, Mo., *via* Pacific Railroad of Missouri..........			283
Kansas City or State Line to Denver, Col., *via* Kansas Pacific R. R.			638
Denver to Cheyenne, Wyoming Ter., *via* Denver & Pacific Railroad...			106
Cheyenne to Ogden, Utah, *via* Union Pacific Railroad.....................			516
Ogden to San Francisco, *via* Central Pacific Railroad.....................			881

Total Miles.. **3,352**

WASHINGTON to SAN FRANCISCO, *via* same Route...... **3,374** Miles.

No 2.

FROM.	TO.	RAILROADS.	MILES.
Baltimore to **Bellaire.** O., *via* Baltimore & Ohio Railroad.......			375
Bellaire to Columbus, *via* Central Ohio Division			137
Columbus to Indianapolis, *via* Columbus & Indiana Central R. R......			182
Indianapolis to St. Louis, *via* St. Louis, Van., T. H. & Ind. Railroad...			239
St. Louis to Kansas City, *via* North Missouri Railroad....................			272
Kansas City or State Line to Denver, *via* Kansas Pacific Railroad...			638
Denver to Cheyenne, *via* Denver & Pacific Railroad....................			106
Cheyenne to San Francisco, *via* Union Pacific & Central Railroad.....			1,397

Total Miles.. **3,346**

No. 3.

FROM.	TO.	RAILROADS.	MILES.
Baltimore to **Harrisburg.** Pa., *via*, Northern Central R. R......			85
Harrisburg to Pittsburgh, *via* Pennsylvania Central Railroad..........			249
Pittsburgh to Indianapolis, *via* Crestline, Ohio.			396
Indianapolis to St. Louis, *via* Indianapolis & St. Louis Railroad.........			262
St. Louis to Kansas City, *via* North Missouri Railroad....................			272
Kansas City to Denver, *via* Kansas Pacific Railroad.....................			638
Denver to Cheyenne, Wyoming Ter., *via* Denver & Pacific Railroad....			106
Cheyenne to San Francisco, *via* Union & Central Pacific Railroads...			1,397

Total Miles.. **3,405**

No. 4.

FROM.	TO.	RAILROADS.	MILES.
Baltimore to **Pittsburgh**, *via* Northern & Penn. Central R. R.			334
PITTSBURGH to CHICAGO, *via* Pittsburgh, F. W. & Chicago Railroad.....			468
CHICAGO to OMAHA, *via* Chicago, Rock Island & Pacific Railroad........			494
OMAHA to OGDEN, Utah, *via* Union Pacific Railroad............................			1,032
OGDEN to SACRAMENTO, *via* Central Pacific Railroad............................			743
SACRAMENTO to SAN FRANCISCO, *via* Western Pacific Railroad...........			138

Total Miles.. **3,209**

WASHINGTON to SAN FRANCISCO, *via* same Route...... **3,249** Miles.

No 5.

FROM.	TO.	RAILROADS.	MILES.
Philadelphia to **Pittsburgh**. *via* Penn. Central Railroad.......			354
PITTSBURGH to CHICAGO, Ill., *via* Pittsburgh, F. W. & Chicago R. R.....			468
CHICAGO to DAVENPORT, Iowa, *via* Chicago, R. I. & Pacific Railroad....			183
DAVENPORT to OMAHA, Neb., *via* " " "			311
OMAHA to OGDEN, Utah, *via* Union Pacific Railroad..........................			1,032
OGDEN to SAN FRANCISCO, *via* Central Pacific Railroad......................			881

Total Miles.. **3,229**

NEW YORK to SAN FRANCISCO, *via* same Route........ **3,317** Miles.

No. 6.

FROM.	TO.	RAILROADS.	MILES.
Philadelphia to **Pittsburgh**, *via* Penn. Central Railroad.......			354
PITTSBURGH to INDIANAPOLIS, *via* Columbus, Ohio......................			381
INDIANAPOLIS to ST. LOUIS, *via* Indianapolis & St. Louis Railroad........			262
ST. LOUIS to KANSAS CITY, *via* North Missouri Railroad......................			272
KANSAS CITY to DENVER, Col., *via* Kansas Pacific Railroad..............			638
DENVER to CHEYENNE, Wyoming Ter., *via* Denver & Pacific Railroad...			106
CHEYENNE to OGDEN, Utah, *via* Union Pacific Railroad......................			516
OGDEN to SAN FRANCISCO, *via* Central Pacific Railroad......................			881

Total Miles.. **3,410**

No. 7

FROM.	TO.	RAILROADS.	MILES.
Philadelphia to **Pittsburgh**, *via* Penn. Central Railroad.......			354
PITTSBURGH to COLUMBUS, Ohio, *via* Pan Handle Route....................			193
COLUMBUS to INDIANAPOLIS, " " "			188
INDIANAPOLIS to PEORIA, Ill., *via* Ind., Bloom. & Western Railroad......			212
PEORIA to BURLINGTON, Iowa, *via* Chicago, Quincy & Bur. Railroad....			96
BURLINGTON to OMAHA, Neb., *via* Burlington & M. River Railroad.....			293
OMAHA to OGDEN, Utah, *via* Union Pacific Railroad..........................			1,032
OGDEN to SAN FRANCISCO, *via* Central Pacific Railroad......................			881

Total Miles.. **3,249**

No. 8.

FROM.	TO.	RAILROADS.	MILES.
New York to **Pittsburgh,** *via* Allentown Route & Penn. R. R.			432
PITTSBURGH to CHICAGO, *via* Pittsburgh, F. W. & Chicago Railroad			468
CHICAGO to BURLINGTON, Iowa, *via* C. B. & Q. Railroad			207
BURLINGTON to OMAHA, Neb., *via* Bur. & Missouri River Railroad			293
OMAHA to OGDEN, Utah, *via* Union Pacific Railroad			1,032
OGDEN to SAN FRANCISCO, *via* Central Pacific Railroad			881

Total Miles.. **3,313**

No. 9.

FROM.	TO.	RAILROADS.	MILES.
New York to **Harrisburg,** Pa., *via* Allentown Route			182
HARRISBURG to PITTSBURGH, *via* Pennsylvania Central Railroad			249
PITTSBURGH to CHICAGO, *via* Fort Wayne Route			468
CHICAGO to DAVENPORT, Iowa, *via* Chicago, Rock Is. & Pacific R. R.			183
DAVENPORT to OMAHA, Neb., " " " " "			310
OMAHA to OGDEN, Utah. *via* Union Pacific Railroad			1,032
OGDEN to SAN FRANCISCO, *via* Central Pacific Railroad			881

Total Miles.. **3,306**

BOSTON to SAN FRANCISCO, *via* same Route............. **3,540** Miles.

No. 10.

FROM.	TO.	RAILROADS.	MILES.
New York to **Cleveland,** Ohio., *via* Erie Railroad			605
CLEVELAND to CHICAGO, *via* L. S. & Michigan Southern Railroad			357
CHICAGO to OMAHA, *via* Chicago, Rock Island & Pacific Railroad			493
OMAHA to OGDEN, *via* Union Pacific Railroad			1,032
OGDEN to SAN FRANCISCO, *via* Central Pacific Railroad			881

Total Miles.. **3,388**

No. 11.

FROM.	TO.	RAILROADS.	MILES.
New York to **Albany,** N. Y., *via* Hudson River Railroad			145
ALBANY to SUSPENSION BRIDGE, *via* New York Central Railroad			304
SUSPENSION BRIDGE to DETROIT, *via* Great Western Railroad			230
DETROIT to CHICAGO, *via* Michigan Central Railroad.			284
CHICAGO to OMAHA, *via* Chicago & Northwestern Railroad			491
OMAHA to SAN FRANCISCO, *via* Union Pacific & Central Pacific R. R.			1,913

Total Miles.. **3,367**

No. 12.

FROM.	TO.	RAILROADS.	MILES.
New York to Buffalo, via Erie Railway			423
Buffalo to Toledo, via Lake Shore & Michigan Southern Railroad....			296
Toledo to Chicago, via Southern Michigan Railroad.			244
Chicago to Omaha, via Chicago, Rock Island & Pacific Railroad			493
Omaha to Ogden, Utah			1,032
Ogden to San Francisco			881
Total Miles			**3,369**

No. 13.

FROM.	TO.	RAILROADS.	MILES.
New York to Buffalo, via Erie Railway			423
Buffalo to Toledo, Ohio, via Lake Shore Railroad.			296
Toledo to St. Louis, via Toledo, Wabash & Western Railroad			432
St. Louis to Kansas City, Mo., via North Missouri Railroad			272
Kansas City to Denver, Col., via Kansas Pacific Railroad			638
Denver to Cheyenne, Wyoming Ter., via Denver Pacific			106
Cheyenne to Ogden, Utah, via Union Pacific			516
Ogden to San Francisco, Cal., via Central Pacific			881
Total Miles			**3,464**

No. 14.

FROM.	TO.	RAILROADS.	MILES.
New York to Cleveland, via Erie Railway			605
Cleveland to Toledo, via Lake Shore Railroad			113
Toledo to Hannibal, via Toledo, Wabash & Western Railroad			464
Hannibal to Moberly, via Hannibal & Moberly R. R. (New Road)			70
Moberly to Kansas City, via North Missouri Railroad			126
Kansas City to Denver, via Kansas Pacific			638
Denver to Cheyenne, via Denver & Pacific			106
Cheyenne to Ogden, via Union Pacific			516
Ogden to San Francisco, via Central Pacific			881
Total Miles			**3,519**

No 15.

FROM.	TO.	RAILROADS.	MILES.
New York to Cleveland, Ohio, via Erie Railroad			605
Cleveland to Toledo, via Lake Shore Railroad			113
Toledo to Quincy, Ill., via Toledo, Wabash & Western Railroad			476
Quincy to Kansas City, via Hannibal & St. Joseph Railroad			226
Kansas City to Denver, Col., via Kansas Pacific			638
Denver to Cheyenne, Wyoming Ter., via Denver Pacific			106
Cheyenne to Ogden, Utah, via Union Pacific			516
Ogden to San Francisco, Cal., via Central Pacific			881
Total Miles			**3,561**

No 16.

FROM.	TO.	RAILROADS.	MILES.
Boston to **Albany,** New York, *via* Boston & Albany Railroad......			200
ALBANY to SUSPENSION BRIDGE, Can., *via* N. York Central Railroad...			304
SUSPENSION BRIDGE to DETROIT, Mich., *via* Great Western Railroad....			230
DETROIT to CHICAGO, *via* Michigan Central Railroad........................			284
CHICAGO to OMAHA, *via* Chicago & N. W. Railroad............			491
OMAHA to OGDEN, *via* Union Pacific..			1,032
OGDEN to SAN FRANCISCO, *via* Central Pacific........................			881

Total Miles..**3,422**

No 17.

FROM.	TO.	RAILROADS.	MILES.
Boston to **Buffalo.** *via* Albany, New York............................			498
BUFFALO to TOLEDO, *via* Cleveland, Ohio.........................			296
TOLEDO to CHICAGO, *via* Michigan Southern Railroad......................			244
CHICAGO to OMAHA, Neb., *via* Chicago Rock Is. & Pacific Railroad......			496
OMAHA to OGDEN, Utah, *via* Union Pacific..............			1,032
OGDEN to SAN FRANCISCO, *via* Central Pacific..........................			881

Total Miles........ ....**3,117**

No 18.

FROM	TO.	RAILROADS.	MILES.
Boston to **Albany,** *via* Springfield, Massachusetts........................			200
ALBANY to DETROIT, *via* Suspension Bridge.........			534
DETROIT to CHICAGO...			284
CHICAGO to ST. PAUL, *via* Prairie du Chien.....			448
ST. PAUL to GEORGETOWN, Minnesota, (Red River of the North).........			260
GEORGETOWN to MISSOURI RIVER, Dakota..........................			252
MISSOURI RIVER to CADOTT'S PASS, Montana............................			630
CADOTT'S PASS to COLUMBIA RIVER, Idaho.........................			440
COLUMBIA RIVER to SEATTLE, Puget Sound............................			220

Total Miles..**3,268**

No 19.

NEW YORK to ST. LOUIS, via Great Broad Gauge Route, Erie, Atlantic and Great Western Railway.

FROM.	TO.	RAILROADS.	MILES.
New York to **Salamanca,** *via* Erie Railway............................			413
SALAMANCA to CINCINNATI, *via* Erie Railway.............................			447
CINCINNATI to ST. LOUIS, *via* Ohio & Mississippi Railroad................			340

Total Miles........ ....**1,200**

No 20.

NORTHERN PACIFIC RAILROAD ROUTE.

FROM.	TO.	RAILROADS.	MILES.
New York to Chicago, *via* Pittsburgh, Pa.............			900
Chicago to St. Paul, *via* Prairie du Chien..........			448
St. Paul to Georgetown, on the Red R. of the N., *via* S. P. & P. R. R.			260
Georgetown to Missouri River, *via* Northern Pacific............			252
Missouri River to Big Horn River, Montana............			340
Big Horn River to Cadott's Pass, Montana.............			290
Cadott's Pass to Spokane River, Idaho.............			290
Spokane River to Columbia River, Idaho.............			150
Columbia River to Seattle, Puget Sound.............			220

Total Miles...**3,150**

No. 21.

LAKE SUPERIOR TO PUGET SOUND, via Northern Pacific R. R.

FROM.	TO.	ALTITUDE.		MILES.
Duluth (L. S.) to Red River of the North............		985 feet		**232**
"	To Missouri River, Dakota..............	1,800 "	253	**485**
"	To Cadott's Pass, Montana.............	6,167 "	730	**1,115**
"	To Columbia River, Idaho.............	330 "	440	**1,555**
"	To Snoqualmie Pass, Washington Ter.....	3,030 "	139	**1.694**
"	To Seattle, Puget Sound.............	0 "	81	**1,775**

Portland Branch, Missouri River to Portland, Or....**1,100** Miles.
Puget Sound Branch, Portland Or. to Puget Sound.. **140** "

No. 22.

PORTLAND to CHICAGO, via Montreal and Toronto.

FROM.	TO.	RAILROADS.	MILES.
Portland to Montreal, Canada, *via* Grand Trunk Railway........			297
Montreal to Toronto,	" " " "		333
Toronto to Detroit, Michigan,	" " "		231
Detroit to Chicago, Ill., *via* Michigan Central Railroad.............			284

Total Miles...**1,145**

Quebec to Chicago, by same Route............**1,020** Miles.

WASHINGTON TO NEW YORK, BOSTON, AND PORTLAND, Me., Via MOST DIRECT ROUTE.

Baltimore & Ohio Railroad.

MILES.	STATIONS.		MILES.
40	**WASHINGTON**, D.C.		0
34	Bladensburg, Md		6
32	Paint Branch	2	8
28	Beltsville	4	12
25	White Oak Bottom	3	15
23	Laurel	2	17
21	Savage	2	19
20	ANNAPOLIS JUNCTION	1	20
17	Jessup's	3	23
15	Dorsey's	2	25
13	Hanover	2	27
10	Elk Ridge	3	30
9	RELAY HOUSE	1	31
4	Camden Junction	5	36
0	**BALTIMORE**	4	40

☞ Connects at Baltimore with the *Northern Central Railway.*

Philadelphia, Wilmington & Baltimore Railroad.

98	**BALTIMORE**		40
89	Stemmer's Run	9	49
83	Chase's	6	55
79	Magnolia	4	59
77	Edgewood	2	61
74	Bush River	3	64
71	Perryman's	3	67
67	Aberdeen	4	71
64	Oakington	3	74
62	HAVRE DE GRACE	2	76

(Susquehanna River.)

61	PERRYVILLE	1	77
58	Principio	3	80
55	Charlestown	3	83
52	North-East	3	86
46	ELKTON	6	92
40	Newark	6	98
34	Stanton	6	104
32	Newport	2	106

MILES.	STATIONS.		MILES.
30	New Castle Junction	2	108
28	**Wilmington***, Del	2	110
26	Ellerslie	2	112
23	Bellevue	3	115
22	Holly Oak	1	116
20	Claymont	2	118
18	Linwood	2	120
16	Thurlow	2	122
15	LAMOKIN	1	123
14	Chester	1	124
11	Lazaretto	3	127
2	Gray's Ferry	9	136
0	**PHILADELPHIA**	2	138

☞ Connects at Philadelphia with the *Pennsylvania Central Railroad.*

New York and Philadelphia Railway Line.

90	**West Philadelphia**		138
80	Mantua Junction	1	139
81	Frankford	8	147
79	Tacony	2	149
67	Bristol	12	161
64	Tullytown	3	164
58	Morrisville	6	170

(Delaware River.)

57	**TRENTON**, N. J.	1	171
47	Princeton Junction	10	181
46	Plainsboro'	1	182
41	Monmouth Junction	5	187
32	**New Brunswick**	9	196
27	Metuchin	5	201
23	Uniontown	4	205
20	Rahway	3	208
15	ELIZABETH	5	213
9	**Newark**	6	219
1	**Jersey City**	8	227

(Hudson River.)

0	**NEW YORK**	1	228

* Dining Stations.

N. York & N. Haven & Hartford & Springfield R. R.

MILES.	STATIONS.		MILES.
236	**NEW YORK,**		228
234	27th Street and 4th Av...	2	230
228	Harlem	6	236
222	WILLIAMS' BRIDGE	6	242
219	Mount Vernon	3	245
216	New Rochelle	3	248
212	Mamaroneck	4	252
209	Rye	3	255
207	PORT CHESTER	2	257
204	Greenwich, Conn.	3	260
199	STAMFORD	5	265
195	Darien	4	269
191	**Norwalk**	4	273
188	Westport	3	276
184	Southport	4	280
182	Fairfield	2	282
177	**Bridgeport**	5	287
174	Stratford	3	290
172	Naugatuck Junction	2	292
169	Milford	3	295
160	**NEW HAVEN**	9	304

☞ Connects with *New Haven, New London and Stonington Railroad.*

154	North Haven	6	310
148	Wallingford	6	316
142	Meriden	6	322
135	BERLIN	7	329
124	**HARTFORD**	11	340
118	Windsor	6	346
112	Windsor Locks	6	352
110	Warehouse Point	2	354
107	Thompsonville	3	357
102	Long Meadow	5	362
98	**SPRINGFIELD*.**	4	366

Boston & Albany Railroad.

98	**SPRINGFIELD**		366
92	Indian Orchard	6	372
89	Wilbraham	3	375
83	PALMER	4	381
79	Brimfield	4	385
73	Warren	6	391
69	WEST BROOKFIELD	4	395
67	Brookfield	2	397
57	Charlton	10	407
53	Rochdale	4	411
44	**Worcester**	9	420
38	Grafton	6	426
32	Westboro'	6	432
28	Southville	4	436
24	Ashland	4	440
21	SOUTH FRAMINGHAM	3	443
5	Brighton	16	459
0	**BOSTON.**	5	464

☞ Connects with *Eastern Railroad of Massachusetts,* forming a through line of travel to Portland, Me.

Boston & Maine Railroad.

112	**BOSTON**		464
108	Medford Junction	4	468
107	Malden	1	469
105	Melrose	2	471
100	Reading	5	476
91	Ballardville	9	485
89	Andover	2	487
86	SOUTH LAWRENCE	3	490
85	NORTH LAWRENCE	1	491
84	North Andover	1	492
80	Bradford	4	496
79	HAVERHILL	1	497
75	Atkinson	4	501
71	Newton	4	505
62	EXETER	9	514
55	New Market	7	521
50	Durham	5	526
44	**Dover,** N. H.	6	532
41	Rollinsford	3	535
38	SOUTH BERWICK	3	538
34	North Berwick	4	542
23	Kennebunk	11	553
15	Biddeford	8	561
13	SACO	2	563
6	Scarsborough	7	570
0	**PORTLAND**	6	576

* Dining Stations.

FROM WASHINGTON AND BALTIMORE TO CINCINNATI AND ST. LOUIS.

Baltimore & Ohio Railroad.

MILES.	STATIONS.		MILES.
405	**WASHINGTON** ...	0	0
384	Annapolis Junction	0	21
374	RELAY HOUSE	10	31
383	**BALTIMORE**	0	0
374	Washington Junction	0	9
368	ELLICOTT CITY	6	15
363	Elysville	5	20
356	Mariottsville	7	27
351	Sykesville	5	32
340	Mount Airy	11	43
333	Monrovia	6	50
325	Frederick Junction	8	58

	Frederick (*Br. R. R.*)	4	62
319	Adamstown	6	64
314	Point of Rocks	5	69
304	Hagerstown Junction	10	79
303	Sandy Hook	1	80
302	**Harper's Ferry** ...	1	81

☞Connects with *Winchester and Potomac Railroad.*

296	Duffield's	6	87
291	Kearneysville	5	92
283	MARTINSBURG*	8	100
270	Cherry Run	13	113
261	Hancock, Md	9	122
255	Sir John's Run	6	228
250	Willett's Run	5	133
226	Little Cacapon	24	157
213	Patterson's Creek	13	170
205	**Cumberland***	8	178

☞ Connects with *Pittsburgh and Connellsville Railroad.*

MIELS.	STATIONS.		MILES.
198	Brady's Mill	7	185
182	New Creek	16	201
177	PIEDMONT	5	206
175	Bloomington	2	208
169	Frankville	6	214
163	Swanton	6	220
160	ALTAMONT	3	223
157	Deer Park	3	226
151	**Oakland**	6	232
141	Cranberry Summit	10	242
130	Rowlesburg	11	253
123	Tunnelton	7	260
117	Newburg	6	266
110	Thornton	7	273
104	**Grafton***	6	279

(To **Wheeling**, 100 Miles.)

PARKERSBURG DIVISION.

100	Webster	4	283
94	Flemington	6	289
87	Bridgeport	7	296
82	CLARKSBURG	5	301
78	Wilsenburg	4	305
68	Salem	10	315
58	Smithton	10	325
54	WEST UNION	4	329
42	Pennsboro	12	341
37	Ellenboro	5	346
32	Cornwallis	5	351
29	Cairo	3	354
22	Petrolium	7	361
20	L. F. Junction	2	363
15	Walker's	5	368
10	Kanawha	5	373
7	Claysville	3	376
0	**Parkersburg**	7	383

(*Ohio River.*)

NOTE.—Twenty-two miles further from Washington, D. C., from all the Stations after leaving the Relay House.

.* Dining Stations.

Marietta and Cincinnati Railroad.

MILES.	STATIONS.		MILES.
205	**Belpre,** Ohio	0	383
	MARIETTA	12	395
196	Scott's Landing	9	392
186	Vincent's	10	402
179	Cutler	7	409
170	New England	9	418
166	Warren's	4	422
160	**Athens**	6	428
153	Marshfield	7	435
140	Zaleski	13	448
129	HAMDEN	11	459
118	Raysville	12	470
111	Londonderry	7	477
106	Schooley's	5	482
99	**Chillicothe***	7	489
86	Frankfort	13	502
75	Greenfield	11	513
69	Monroe	6	519
63	Lexington	6	525
58	Vienna	5	530
51	Martinsville	7	537
42	BLANCHESTER	9	546
32	Spence's	10	556
26	LOVELAND	6	562
21	Montgomery	5	567
25	Madisonville	6	573
8	C. H. and D. Junction	7	580
0	**CINCINNATI**	8	588

Ohio & Mississippi Railroad.

340	**CINCINNATI**	0	588
331	Delhi	9	597
327	North Bend	4	601
320	**Lawrenceb'g** I'd.	7	608

Junction *Indianapolis and Cincinnati Railroad.*

| 316 | AURORA | 4 | 612 |
| 314 | Cochran | 2 | 614 |

MILES.	STATIONS.		MILES.
298	Milan	16	630
288	Osgood	10	640
278	Nebraska	10	650
267	NORTH VERNON	11	661

LOUISVILLE DIVISION.

N. VERNON to LOUISVILLE, 53 Miles.

| 253 | **Seymour** | 14 | 675 |

Junction *Jeff. Mad. and Ind. R. R.*

| 234 | Medora | 29 | 694 |
| 213 | MITCHELL | 21 | 715 |

Junction *Louisville, New Albany and Chicago Railroad.*

201	Huron	12	727
182	Loogootee	19	746
167	Washington	15	761
148	**Vincennes**	19	780

Junction *Evansville and Crawfordsville Railroad.*

139	Lawrenceville	9	789
127	Hadley	12	801
117	Olney	10	811
102	Clay City	15	826
86	Xenia	17	843
64	**Odin**	21	864

Crossing *Chicago Branch Illinois Central Railroad.*

| 60 | **Sandoval** | 4 | 868 |

Junction *Illinois Central Railroad.*

30	Trenton	30	898
1	**East St. Louis**	29	927
0	**ST. LOUIS**	1	928

☞ Connects with the *Atlantic and Pacific, Missouri Pacific,* and *North Missouri Railroads;* also, with Steamers running on the Lower and Upper Mississippi, to *New Orleans, St. Paul, &c.*

* Dining Stations.

23

ST. LOUIS TO KANSAS CITY, TOPEKA, DENVER, &c.

Missouri Pacific Railway.

MILES.	STATIONS.		MILES.
330	**ST. LOUIS**		0
325	Cheltenham		5
322	Laclede	3	8
320	Webster	2	10
316	Kirkwood	4	14
314	Barrett's	3	16
311	MERAMEC	3	19
304	Glencoe	7	26
300	Eureka	4	30
293	**Franklin***	7	37

Junction *Atlantic and Pacific Railway.*

285	Labadie	8	45
282	Augusta	3	48
278	South Point	4	52
275	Washington	3	55
268	Newport	7	62
263	Miller's Landing	5	67
260	Etlah	3	70
255	Berger	5	75
249	HERMANN	6	81
242	Gasconade	7	88
237	Morrison	5	93
230	Chamois	7	100
225	St. Aubert	5	105
218	Bonnot's Mill	7	112
213	Osage	5	117
205	**Jefferson City**	8	125
198	Scott	7	132
196	Elston	2	134
190	Centretown	6	140
180	California	10	150
174	Moniteau	6	156
168	TIPTON	6	162
162	Syracuse	6	168
155	Otterville	7	175
149	Smithton	6	181
141	**Sedalia***	8	189
135	Dresden	6	195
123	Knobnoster	12	207
112	WARRENSBURG	11	218

MILES.	STATIONS.		MILES.
105	Centreview	7	225
98	Holden	7	232
93	Kingsville	5	237
82	PLEASANT HILL	11	248
76	Greenwood	6	254
65	Little Blue	11	265
58	**Independence**	7	272
48	**KANSAS CITY**	10	282

Junction *Kansas City, St. Joseph and Council Bluffs Railroad.*

46	**State Line***	2	284

Junction *Kansas Pacific Railroad.*

44	**Wyandotte**	2	286
35	Pomeroy	9	295
29	Redmond	6	301
21	**Leavenworth**	8	309
18	Fort Leavenworth	3	312
14	Kickapoo	4	316
4	Sumner	10	326
0	**ATCHISON**, Kan	4	330

At Atchison connects with *Central Branch Union Pacific Railroad,* running towards Fort Kearny.

Kansas Pacific Railway.

	KANSAS CITY		282
638	**Missouri S. Line**	2	284
637	Armstrong	1	285
630	Muncy	7	292
625	Edwardsville	5	297
622	Tiblow	3	300
616	Lenape	6	306
607	Fall Leaf	9	315
602	L. & L. Junction	5	320
	(To **Leavenworth**, 34 Miles.)		
600	**Lawrence**	2	322

Junc. *Lawrence and Galveston R. R.*

590	Williamsville	10	332
587	Perryville	3	335

* Dining Stations.

MILES.	STATIONS.		MILES.	MILES.	STATIONS.		MILES.
586	Medina	1	336	316	Park's Fort	10	606
583	Newman	3	339	298	Coyote	18	624
578	Grantville	5	344	286	Buffalo	12	636
571	**TOPEKA**	7	351	274	Grinnell	12	648
561	Silver Lake	10	361	262	Carlyle	12	660
555	Rossville	6	367	252	Monument	10	670
548	St. Mary's	7	374	240	Gopher	12	682
534	WAMEGO*	14	388	233	Sheridan	7	689
528	St. George	6	394	218	WALLACE	15	704
520	MANHATTAN	8	402	209	Eagle Tail	9	713
509	Ogden	11	413	201	Monotony	8	721
503	Fort Riley	6	419	186	Arrapaho	15	736
500	**Junction City**	3	422	176	Cheyenne Wells	10	746
Junc. *Missouri, Kansas & Texas R. R.*				166	First View	10	756
488	Chapman's Creek	12	434	151	**Kit Carson**	15	771
481	Detroit	7	441	139	Wild Horse	12	783
476	Abilene	5	446	127	Aroya	12	795
467	Solomon	9	455	115	Mirage	12	807
453	SALINA*	14	469	104	HUGO	11	818
444	Bavaria	9	478		**DENVER DIVISION.**		
438	BROCKVILLE	6	484	91	Lake	13	831

SMOKY HILL DIVISION.

MILES.	STATIONS.		MILES.	MILES.	STATIONS.		MILES.
433	Rock Spring	5	489	76	Cedar Point	15	846
420	Fort Harker	13	502	72	Godfrey	4	850
415	**Ellsworth**	5	507	66	Agate	6	856
408	Black Wolf	7	514	55	Deer Trail	11	867
399	Wilson's Creek	9	523	43	Bijou	12	879
386	Bunker Hill	13	536	30	KIOWA	13	892
364	Walker's	22	558	21	Box Elder	9	901
350	HAYS	14	572	9	Schuyler	12	913
336	ELLIS*	14	586	2	Denver Pacific Junction	7	920
326	Ogallah	10	596	0	**DENVER**	2	922

☞ Connects with the *Denver Pacific Railroad.*

Stages run from DENVER to all points in Colorado and New Mexico.

DENVER to CHEYENNE, via DENVER and PACIFIC RAILWAY.

106	**DENVER,** Col		0	39	Pierce	15	67
104	Outer Depot		2	20	Carr	9	86
89	Hughes	15	17	10	Summit Siding	10	96
74	Johnson	15	32	0	**CHEYENNE,** W.T.	10	106
58	Evans	16	48				
54	GREELEY	4	52				

Junction *Union Pacific Railway.*

BALTIMORE TO WHEELING, COLUMBUS, INDIANAPOLIS, ST. LOUIS AND KANSAS CITY.

Baltimore & Ohio Railroad.

MILES.	STATIONS.	MILES.
379	BALTIMORE	0
370	Washington Junction	9
364	Ellicott City 6	15
321	Frederick Junction 43	58
	(To FREDERICK, 4 Miles)	
298	Harper's Ferry 23	81
279	MARTINSBURG* 19	100
256	Hancock, Md 23	123
201	Cumberland* 55	178
173	PIEDMONT 28	206
147	Oakland 26	232
100	Grafton* 47	279
98	Fetterman 2	281
85	Texas 13	294
82	Benton's Ferry 3	297
77	FAIRMONT 5	302
67	Farmington 10	312
60	Mannington 7	319
42	Littleton 18	337
35	Bellton 7	344
28	Cameron 7	351
11	Moundsville 17	368
4	BENWOOD 7	375
0	WHEELING 4	379
	(Ohio River.)	

CENTRAL OHIO DIVISION.

MILES.	STATIONS.	MILES.
	Benwood	0
137	BELLAIRE,* Ohio	375
128	Glencoe 9	384
125	Warnock 3	387
119	Belmont 6	393
110	Barnesville 9	402
102	Millwood 8	410
100	Salesville 2	412
93	Campbell's 7	419
85	CAMBRIDGE 8	427
76	Concord 9	436
73	Norwich 3	439
66	Sonora 7	446

MILES.	STATIONS.	MILES.
59	Zanesville* 7	453
50	Pleasant Valley 9	462
44	Black Hand 6	468
33	Newark 11	479
27	Union 6	485
22	Kirkersville 5	490
16	Columbia 6	496
10	Black Lick 6	502
0	COLUMBUS 10	512

LAKE ERIE DIVISION.

116	Newark	479
107	Louisville 9	488
102	Utica 5	493
91	Mt. Vernon 11	504
84	Frederick 7	511
74	Independence 10	521
68	Belleville 6	527
63	Lexington 5	532
54	Mansfield 9	541
42	Shelby Junction 12	553
34	Plymouth 8	561
23	Havana 11	572
19	Pontiac 4	576
15	MONROEVILLE 4	580
8	Prout's 7	587
0	Sandusky, (L. Erie). 8	595

Columbus & Indiana Central Railway.

188	COLUMBUS	512
178	Hilliard's 10	522
170	Pleasant Valley 8	530
160	Milford 10	540
141	Urbana 19	559
130	St. Paris 11	570
115	PIQUA 15	585
105	Bradford Junction 10	595
94	Greenville 11	606
83	New Madison 11	617

* Dining Stations.

MILES.	STATIONS.		MILES.	MILES.	STATIONS.		MILES.
68	**Richmond**	15	632	182	BRAZIL	4	757
53	Cambridge City	15	647	180	Newburg	2	759
44	Lewisville	9	656	178	Staunton	2	761
34	Knightstown	10	666	176	Cloverland	2	763
21	Greenfield	13	679	174	Seeleyville	2	765
11	Cumberland	10	689	166	**Terre Haute**	8	773
0	**INDIANAPOLIS**	11	700	156	Woodville	10	783

☞ Connects with Railroads running to *Chicago, Cincinnati, Louisville, &c.*

St. Louis, Vandalia, T. Haute and Indianapolis R. R.

MILES.	STATIONS.		MILES.	MILES.	STATIONS.		MILES.
239	**INDIANAPOLIS.**		700	149	Marshall	7	790
230	Bridgeport	9	709	138	Martinsville	11	891
225	Plainfield	5	714	131	Casey	7	808
222	Cartersburg	3	717	123	Greenup	8	816
221	Belleville	1	718	117	Pleasantville	6	822
229	Clayton	2	720	103	Teutopolis	14	836
214	Arno	5	735	99	EFFINGHAM*	4	840
211	Coatsville	3	728	95	Funkhouser	4	844
207	Fillmore	4	732	82	St. Elmo	13	857
201	**Greencastle**	6	738	76	Brownstown	6	863
199	Junction	2	740	68	**Vandalia***	8	871
195	Hamrick's	4	744	64	Hagerstown	4	875
192	Reelsville	3	747	58	Mulberry Grove	6	881
139	Eagle's	3	750	50	Greenville	8	889
185	Harmony	3	753	40	Pocahontas	10	899
				36	Oakdale	4	905
				31	Highland	5	908
				18	Troy	13	921
				12	Collinsville	6	927
				1	**East St. Louis**	11	938
				0	**ST. LOUIS**	1	939

ST. LOUIS to KANSAS CITY, via NORTH MISSOURI R. R.

MILES.	STATIONS.		MILES.
272	**ST. LOUIS**		0
267	Bellefontaine		5
257	Bridgton	10	15
251	**St. Charles**	6	21
238	O'Fallon	13	34
223	Millville	15	49
214	WARRENTON	9	58
204	Jonesburg	10	68
195	New Florence	9	77
189	MONTGOMERY	6	83
163	Mexico	26	109
126	**Moberly** Junction	37	146

WESTERN DIVISION.

MILES.	STATIONS.		MILES.
105	Salisbury	21	167
86	**Brunswick**	19	186
76	Miami	10	196
63	Carrollton	13	209
46	Hardin	17	226
40	R & L JUNCTION	6	232
17	Missouri City	23	255
9	N. Missouri Junction	8	263
1	HARLEM	8	271
0	**KANSAS CITY**	1	272

☞ Connects with *Kan. Pac. R. R.*

BALTIMORE TO PITTSBURGH, INDIANAPOLIS, ST. LOUIS & CHICAGO, via Pan Handle Route, & Fort Wayne Route.

Northern Central Railway.

MILES.	STATIONS.		MILES.
333	**BALTIMORE**		0
304	Parkton,		29
294	Hanover Junction	18	47
276	**York**	18	57
249	Bridgeport	27	84
248	**HARRISBURG***.	1	85

Pennsylvania Central R. R.

240	Marysville	8	93
220	Newport	20	113
199	Mifflin	21	134
187	Lewistown	12	146
175	McVeytown	12	158
162	Mount Union	13	171
151	Huntingdon	11	182
131	Tyrone	20	202
116	**Altoona***	15	217
105	Gallitzin	11	228
80	Conemaugh	25	253
78	Johnstown	2	255
60	Lockport	18	273
41	Latrobe	19	292
31	Greensburg	10	302
15	Wall's	16	318
0	**PITTSBURGH***.	15	333

☞ Connects with P., F. W. & C. R. R.

Pittsburgh, Cincinnati and St. Louis Railroad.

381	**PITTSBURGH**		333
365	Noblestown	16	349
338	**Steubenville***	27	376
320	Bloomfield	18	394
313	Cadiz Junction	7	401
304	New Market	9	410
289	Dennison	15	425
267	Oxford	22	447
257	Coshocton	10	457
243	Dresden	14	471
237	Frazeysburgh	6	477

MILES.	STATIONS.		MILES.
229	Hanover	8	485
221	**Newark***	8	493
206	Pataskala	15	408
195	Big Walnut	11	419
188	**COLUMBUS***.	7	526

☞ Connects with Railroads for *Cleveland, Cincinnati, &c.*

178	Hilliards	10	536
160	Milford	18	554
141	**Urbana***	9	573
130	St. Paris	11	584
115	Piqua*.	15	599
105	Bradford Junction	10	609
94	Greenville	11	620
68	**Richmond***	26	646
53	Cambridge City	15	661
32	Knightstown	21	682
21	Greenfield	11	693
0	**INDIANAPOL'S***	21	714

St. Louis, Vandalia, T. Haute and Indianapolis R. R.

239	**INDIANAPOLIS***		714
221	Belleville	18	732
201	**Greencastle**	20	752
182	Brazil	19	771
166	**Terre Haute***	16	787
149	Marshall	17	804
138	Martinsville	11	815
123	Greenup	15	830
117	Pleasantville	6	836
99	**Effingham***	18	854
82	St. Elmo	17	871
68	**Vandalia***	14	885
50	Greenville	18	903
31	Highland	19	922
18	Troy	13	935
1	**East St. Louis**	17	952
0	**ST. LOUIS***	1	953

To **Chicago**, *via* Pittsburgh and Fort Wayne, 802 Miles.

PHILADELPHIA TO PITTSBURGH, CRESTLINE, OHIO, INDIANAPOLIS AND ST. LOUIS.

Pennsylvania Central R. R.

MILES.	STATIONS.	MILES.
355	PHILADELPHIA	0
322	Downingtown...........	33
311	Parkesburg............11	44
286	Lancaster...........25	69
273	Mount Joy..........13	82
249	Harrisburg*........24	106
221	Newport..........28	134
200	Mifflin.............21	155
176	McVeytown..........24	179
151	Huntingdon..........25	204
131	Tyrone..........20	224
117	Altoona*...........14	238
78	Johnstown..........39	277
41	Latrobe..........37	314
31	Greensburg..........10	324
0	PITTSBURGH*..31	355

Pittsburgh, Fort Wayne and Chicago Railroad.

MILES	STATIONS	MILES
396	PITTSBURGH*..	355
370	Rochester..........26	381
366	New Brighton.......... 4	385
350	Enon..........16	401
326	Salem..........24	425
312	Alliance*...........14	439
294	Canton..........18	457
286	Massillon.......... 8	465
272	Orrville..........14	479
261	Wooster..........11	490
220	Mansfield..........41	531
207	Crestline*..........13	544

Cleveland, Columbus, Cincinnati & Indianapolis R. R.

MILES	STATIONS	MILES
207	Crestline*..........	544
202	Galion.......... 5	549
191	Caledonia..........11	560
182	Marion.......... 9	569

MILES.	STATIONS.	MILES.
168	La Rue..........14	583
161	Mt. Victory.......... 7	590
151	Rushsylvania..........10	600
142	Bellefontaine...... 9	609
130	Quincy..........12	621
120	Sidney..........10	631
102	Versailles..........18	649
94	Dallas.......... 8	657
85	Union.......... 9	666
64	Morristown..........21	687
54	Muncie..........10	697
36	Anderson..........18	712
28	Pendleton.......... 8	723
14	Oakland..........14	737
0	INDIANAP'LIS*.14	751

Indianapolis and St. Louis Railroad.

MILES	STATIONS	MILES
262	INDIANAPOLIS*	751
250	Avon..........12	763
243	Danville.......... 7	770
234	Reno.......... 9	779
223	Greencastle..........11	790
209	Carbon..........14	804
198	Grant..........11	815
190	Terre Haute*...... 8	823
178	Vermillion..........12	835
171	Paris.......... 7	842
145	Charleston..........26	868
134	Mattoon..........11	879
111	Shelbyville..........23	902
95	Pana..........16	918
67	Hillsboro..........28	946
51	Clyde..........16	962
37	Bunker Hill..........14	976
22	Alton Junction..........15	991
10	Nameoki..........12	1,003
1	East St. Louis..... 9	1,012
0	ST. LOUIS*.......... 1	1,013

Note.—This Line of Travel connects with Trains at Alliance for Cleveland, and at Crestline with Trains for Columbus, Cincinnati, &c.

FROM PHILADELPHIA TO PITTSBURGH, CHICAGO, AND OMAHA, NEBRASKA.

Pennsylvania Central R. R.

MILES.	STATIONS.		MILES.
355	**PHILADELPHIA**		0
353	Mantua Junction		2
325	Paoli	18	20
333	Westchester Intersection	2	22
322	**Downingtown***	11	33
316	COATESVILLE	6	39
311	**Parkesburg**	5	44
306	Christiana	5	49
303	Gap	3	52
297	Leaman Place	6	58
287	**Lancaster***	11	69
285	Dillerville	1	70
278	Landisville	7	77
273	**Mount Joy**	5	82
267	Elizabethtown	6	88
259	Branch Intersection	8	96
258	Middletown	1	97
249	**HARRISBURG***	9	106
241	Marysville	8	114
234	Duncannon	7	121
221	Newport	13	134
200	**Mifflin**	21	155
188	LEWISTOWN	12	167
163	Mount Union	25	192
151	**Huntingdon**	12	204
144	Petersburg	7	211
131	TYRONE	13	224
127	Tipton	4	228
117	**Altoona***	10	238
105	Gallitzin	12	250
102	Cresson	3	253
89	Summerhill	18	266
81	**Conemaugh**	8	274
78	JOHNSTOWN	3	277

MILES.	STATIONS.		MILES.
65	New Florence	13	290
54	Blairsville Branch	11	301
41	**Latrobe***	13	314
31	**Greensburg**	10	324
22	Irwin's	9	333
14	Walls	8	341
12	Brinton's	2	343
0	**PITTSBURGH***	12	355

☞ Connects with *Pittsburgh, Cincinnati and St. Louis R. R.*

Pittsburgh, Fort Wayne and Chicago Railroad.

MILES.	STATIONS.		MILES.
468	**PITTSBURGH**		355
450	Economy	18	173
442	ROCHESTER	8	381
438	New Brighton	4	385
433	Homewood	5	390
422	Enon	11	401
408	Columbiana	14	415
398	Salem	10	425
384	**Alliance***	14	439
	Junction *Cleve'd & Pittsb'gh R. R.*		
366	Canton	18	457
358	MASSILLON	8	465
344	ORRVILLE	14	479
333	Wooster	11	490
311	Londonville	22	512
292	MANSFIELD	19	531
279	**Crestline***	13	544
	Junction *C. C. C. & Ind. R. R.*		
267	Bucyras	12	556
238	FOREST	29	585
215	Lafayette	23	608
207	LIMA	8	616

* Dining Stations.

MILES.	STATIONS.		MILES.
193	Delphos.	14	630
180	Van Wert	13	643
148	**FORT WAYNE***..32		675
	☞ Connects with *Toledo, W. & W. Railroad.*		
129	Columbia	19	694
117	Pierceton	12	706
108	Warsaw.	9	715
95	Bourbon	13	728
84	PLYMOUTH*	11	739
53	Wanatah	31	770
44	VALPARAISO	9	779
24	Clarke	20	799
7	Rock Island Junction	17	816
0	**CHICAGO**	7	823

☞ Connects at Chicago with the *Chicago, Burlington and Quincy Railroad; Chicago, Rock Island and Pacific Railroad,* and the *Chicago and Northwestern Railroad,* all forming lines of travel to Omaha, Neb.; there connecting with the *Union Pacific Railroad.*

Chicago, Rock Island and Pacific Railroad.

MILES.	STATIONS.		MILES.
494	**CHICAGO**		823
487	Englewood	7	830
478	Blue Island	9	839
470	Bremen	8	847
464	Mokena.	6	853
454	JOLIET.	10	863
443	Minooka	11	874
433	Morris	10	884
423	Seneca.	10	894
418	Marseilles	5	899
410	OTTAWA	8	907
400	Utica	10	917
395	LA SALLE	5	922
394	Peru	1	923
380	**Bureau***	14	937
372	Tiskilwa	8	945
366	Pond Creek.	6	951

MILES.	STATIONS.		MILES.
358	Sheffield	8	959
348	Annawan	10	969
342	Atkinson	6	975
335	GENESEO	7	982
324	Colona	11	993
315	Moline	9	1,002
312	**ROCK ISLAND**	3	1,005

(*Mississippi River.*)

IOWA DIVISION.

MILES.	STATIONS.		MILES.
311	**DAVENPORT***..	1	1,006
299	Walcott	12	1,018
295	Fulton	4	1,022
286	Wilton	9	1,031
283	Moscow	3	1,034
278	Atalissa	5	1,039
273	West Liberty	5	1,044
257	**Iowa City**	16	1,060
242	Oxford	15	1,075
237	Homestead	5	1,080
227	**Marengo**	10	1,090
215	Victor	12	1,102
207	BROOKLYN*	8	1,110
201	Malcolm	6	1,116
192	Grinnell	9	1,125
181	Kellogg	11	1,136
172	NEWTON	9	1,145
160	Colfax	12	1,157
154	Mitchellville	6	1,163
137	**DES MOINES***..17		1,180
122	Boone	15	1,195
115	De Soto	7	1,202
102	Dexter	13	1,215
86	Casey	16	1,231
72	Anita	14	1,245
58	Atlantic.	14	1,259
39	AVOCA*	19	1,278
31	Shelby	8	1,286
20	Neola	11	1,297
4	**Council Bluffs**..16		1,313
1	Missouri River.	3	1,316
0	**OMAHA**	1	1,317

* Dining Stations.

PHILADELPHIA TO PITTSBURGH, COLUMBUS, INDIANAPOLIS AND ST. LOUIS.

Pennsylvania Central Railroad.

MILES.	STATIONS.		MILES.
355	**PHILADELPHIA**		0
322	DOWNINGTOWN		33
311	PARKESBURG	11	44
286	**Lancaster***	25	69
273	MOUNT JOY	13	82
249	**HARRISBURG***.24		106
221	NEWPORT	28	134
200	MIFFLIN	21	155
176	McVEYTOWN	24	179
151	HUNTINGDON	25	204
131	TYRONE	20	224
117	**Altoona***	14	238
78	JOHNSTOWN	39	277
41	LATROBE*	37	314
31	GREENSBURG	10	324
0	**PITTSBURGH***..31		355

☞ Connects with *Pittsburgh, Fort Wayne and Chicago Railroad*, and other Railroads diverging from Pittsburgh.

Pittsburgh, Cincinnati and St. Louis Railroad.

MILES.	STATIONS.		MILES.
193	**PITTSBURGH***		355
192	Birmingham	1	356
187	Brodhead	5	361
185	MANSFIELD	2	363
178	Oakdale	7	370
177	NOBLESTOWN	1	371
170	Bulger	7	378
166	Burgettstown	4	382
161	Hanlin's	5	387
157	Collier	4	391
150	**Steubenville***, O....	7	398
142	Alexandria Road	8	406
138	Smithfield	4	410
132	Bloomfield	6	416
130	Unionport	2	418
125	CADIZ JUNCTION	5	423
121	Fairview	4	427
116	NEW MARKET	5	432
110	Bowerstown	6	438
101	DENNISON	9	447
100	Uhrichsville	1	448
97	Trenton	3	451
89	Port Washington	8	459
83	New Comerstown	6	465
79	Oxford	4	469
75	West Lafayette	4	473
69	COSHOCTON	6	479
59	Adam's Mills	10	489
55	Dresden	4	493
49	FRAZEYSBURGH	6	499
41	Hanover	8	507
33	**Newark***	8	515
18	Pataskala	15	530
7	Big Walnut	11	541
0	**COLUMBUS***..	7	548

☞ Connects with *Cleveland, Columbus, Cincinnati & Indianapolis Railroad*, and *Little Miami Railroad*.

MILES.	STATIONS.		MILES.
188	**COLUMBUS***		448
178	Hilliards	10	558
170	Pleasant Valley	8	566
166	Unionville	4	570
160	**Milford**	6	576
155	Woodstock	5	581
150	Cable	5	586
141	**Urbana***	9	595
130	St. Paris	11	606
115	**Piqua***	15	621
109	Covington	6	627

* Dining Stations.

MILES.	STATIONS.		MILES.
105	BRADFORD JUNCTION ...	4	631
101	Gettysburg.	4	635
94	**Greenville**	7	642
83	New Madison	11	653
74	New Paris	9	662
68	**Richmond***	6	668
63	Centreville	5	673
53	**Cambridge City**	10	683
44	Lewisville	9	692
39	Dunreith	5	697
34	Knightstown	7	704
29	Charlottesville	3	707
21	GREENFIELD	8	715
17	Philadelphia	4	719
11	Cumberland	6	725
0	**INDIANAP'LIS***	11	736

☞ Connects with Railroads running *East, West, North and South.*

St. Louis, Vandalia, T. Haute and Indianapolis R. R.

MILES.	STATIONS.		MILES.
239	**INDIANAPOLIS***		736
225	Fairview	4	740
230	Bridgeport	5	745
225	Plainfield	5	750
222	Cartersburg	3	753
221	BELLEVILLE	1	754
219	Clayton	2	756
214	Amo	5	761
211	Coatsville	3	764
207	Fillmore	4	768
201	**Greencastle**	6	774
199	Junction	2	776
195	Hamrick's	4	780
192	Reelsville	3	783
189	Eagle's	3	786

MILES.	STATIONS.		MILES.
186	Harmony	3	789
182	BRAZIL	4	793
180	NEWBURG	2	795
178	Staunton	2	797
176	Cloverland	2	791
174	Seeleyville	2	801
166	**Terre Haute***	8	809
156	Woodville	10	819
149	Marshall	7	826
138	Martinsville	11	837
131	Casey	7	844
123	GREENUP	8	852
117	Pleasantville	6	858
103	Teutopolis	14	872
99	**Effingham***	4	876

Junc. *Illinois Central, Chicago Branch.*

MILES.	STATIONS.		MILES.
95	Funkhouser	4	880
82	St. Elmo	13	893
76	Brownstown	6	899
68	**Vandalia***	8	907

Crossing *Illinois Central Railroad.*

MILES.	STATIONS.		MILES.
64	Hagerstown	4	911
58	Mulberry Grove	6	917
50	Greenville	8	925
40	Pocahontas	10	935
36	Oakdale	4	939
31	Highland	5	944
18	Troy	13	957
15	Confidence	3	960
12	Collinsville	3	963
1	**East St. Louis**	11	974

(*Mississippi River.*)

0	**ST. LOUIS***	1	975

☞ Connects with *Railroads* at *St. Louis,* and with *Steamers* on the *Mississippi River.*

*Dining Stations.

NEW YORK TO HARRISBURG, PITTSBURGH, CHICAGO AND OMAHA, via ALLENTOWN ROUTE.

Central New Jersey R. R.

MILES.	STATIONS.		MILES.
182	**NEW YORK**		0
	From Foot of Liberty Street.		
181	**Jersey City**		1
178	Greenville	3	4
174	Bergen Point	4	8
169	**Elizabeth**	5	13
167	Roselle	2	15
165	Crawford	2	17
162	Westfield	3	20
160	Fanwood	2	22
158	PLAINFIELD	2	24
155	Dunnellen	3	27
151	Bound Brook	4	31
146	SOMERVILLE	5	36
145	Raritan	1	37
141	North Branch	4	41
136	WHITEHOUSE	5	46
132	Lebanon	4	50
130	Clinton	2	52
128	High Bridge	2	54
124	Spruce Run	4	58
123	JUNCTION	1	59
120	Asbury	3	62
118	Valley	2	64
115	BLOOMSBURY	3	67
113	Springtown	2	69
108	Phillipsburg	5	74
107	**EASTON** * Pa	1	75

☞ Connects with the *Lehigh Valley Railroad*, and *Lehigh and Susquehanna Railroad*.

MILES.	STATIONS.		MILES.
95	BETHLEHEM	12	87
90	**Allentown**	5	92
69	Lyons	21	113
54	**Reading**	15	128
26	LEBANON*	28	156
0	**HARRISBURG** *.26		182

☞ Connects with the *Northern Central Railway.*

Pennsylvania Central Railroad.

MILES.	STATIONS.		MILES.
248	**HARRISBURG** *.		182
240	MARYSVILLE	8	190
233	Duncannon	7	197
220	NEWPORT	13	210
199	MIFFLIN	21	231
187	LEWISTOWN	12	243
175	McVEYTOWN	12	255
162	MOUNT UNION	13	268
151	HUNTINGDON	11	279
131	TYRONE*	20	299
116	**Altoona** *	15	314
105	GALLITZIN	11	325
102	Cresson	3	328
80	CONEMAUGH	22	350
78	JOHNSTOWN	2	352
60	Lockport	18	370
56	Derry	14	384
41	LATROBE*	5	389
31	GREENSBURG	10	399
15	Wall's	16	415
6	Homewood	9	424
0	**PITTSBURGH** *..	6	430

* Dining Stations.

☞ Connects with the *Pittsburgh, Cincinnati and St. Louis Railroad,* and with other Railroads diverging from Pittsburgh.

Pittsburgh, Fort Wayne and Chicago Railroad.

MILES.	STATIONS.	MILES.
468	**PITTSBURGH*** ..	430
450	Economy.................18	448
442	ROCHESTER............. 8	456
430	NEW BRIGHTON......... 3	459
422	Enon.................17	476
405	Leetonia.............17	493
398	SALEM 7	500
384	**Alliance*** 14	514

☞Connects with *Cleveland and Pittsburgh Railroad.*

366	CANTON........18	532
358	MASSILLON 8	540
344	ORRVILLE........14	554
333	WOOSTER........11	565

MILES.	STATIONS.	MILES.
317	Lakeville...........16	581
292	MANSFIELD..........25	606
279	**Crestline*** 13	619

☞ Connects with *C. C. C.* and *Indianapolis Railroad.*

267	BUCYRUS........12	63
250	Upper Sandusky.....17	648
238	Forest 12	660
229	Washington 9	669
207	LIMA 22	691
193	Delphos.........14	705
180	Van Wert........13	718
148	**Fort Wayne*** 32	750
129	Columbia.........19	769
108	Warsaw 21	790
84	PLYMOUTH*........24	814
53	Wanatah 31	845
44	VALPARAISO....... 9	854
30	Liverpool.........14	868
9	Ill. Central R. R. Junc..21	889
0	**CHICAGO**...... 9	898

Important to Western Travellers.

ALLENTOWN LINE.

TWO EXPRESS TRAINS run DAILY to and from the WEST by this POPULAR LINE OF TRAVEL.

☞ Passengers by this Route save **60 to 100 miles**, and three hours in time, over other Lines, with but one change of cars between **New York** and **Cincinnati**, or **Chicago**, and but two changes to **St. Louis**.

SILVER PALACE CARS Daily to CHICAGO, on the Evening Train.

H. P. BALDWIN, Gen. Pass. Agent,
119 Liberty Street, NEW YORK.

FROM PHILADELPHIA to ERIE, DULUTH and ST. PAUL, via RAILROAD and STEAMBOAT ROUTE, passing through LAKES HURON and SUPERIOR.

Pennsylvania Central R. R.

MILES.	STATIONS.	MILES.
451	**PHILADELPHIA**	0
417	Downingtown*........	34
381	Lancaster*............36	70
345	**Harrisburg***.......36	106

Philadelphia and Erie R. R.

MILES.	STATIONS.	MILES.
288	Sunbury....................57	163
286	Northumberland........ 2	165
279	Lewisburg 7	172
276	Catawissa Junction..... 3	175
275	Milton 1	176
271	Watsontown............. 4	180
268	Dewart.................... 3	183
264	Montgomery............. 4	187
260	Muncy 4	191
248	**Williamsport***...12	203

☞Connects with *Northern Central Railway.*

246	Newberry 2	205
243	Linden.................... 3	208
242	Susquehanna............. 1	209
236	Jersey Shore............ 6	215
228	Wayne................... 8	223
223	Lock Haven*.......... 5	228
218	Farrandsville............ 5	233
208	Whetham..............10	243
199	North Point............. 9	252
196	Renovo*.................. 3	255
184	Keating...................12	267
178	Round Island............ 6	273
168	Driftwood................10	283

MILES.	STATIONS.	MILES.
159	Sterling 9	292
155	Cameron 4	296
150	Emporium............... 5	301
140	Beechwood...............10	311
128	St. Mary's*............12	323
119	Ridgway................. 9	332
104	Wilcox...................15	347
95	Kane* (Alt. 2,008 ft.). 9	356
90	Wetmore................. 5	361
80	Sheffield 10	371
73	Pattonia................. 7	378
66	Warren................... 7	385
61	Irvineton 5	390

Junction *Oil Creek and Allegheny River Railroad.*

58	Youngsville.............. 3	393
55	Pittsfield 3	396
45	Spring Creek............10	406
40	Columbus................ 5	411
38	**Corry*** 2	413

Junction *Atlantic and Great Western Railway.*

34	Lovell's................... 4	417
32	Concord................. 2	419
27	Union.................... 5	424
19	Waterford............... 8	432
13	Jackson's 6	438
7	Belle Valley............. 6	444
0	**ERIE*** 7	451

☞Connects with *Lake Shore R. R.*

* Dining Stations.

Lake Superior Steamboat Line.

MILES.	STATIONS.		MILES.
1,140	**ERIE, Pa**..........		451
1,045	CLEVELAND, Ohio....95		546
945	Malden, Canada.....100		646
925	DETROIT, Mich...... 20		666
	(Lake St. Clair.)		
850	Port Huron.......... 75		741
	(Lake Huron.)		
625	Point de Tour......225		966
	(St. Mary's River.)		
584	Church's Landing... 40		1,006
570	SAUT STE. MARIE... 14		1,020
564	Point Aux Pins Can. 6		1,026
530	White Fish Point... 34		1,060
	(Lake Superior.)		
450	Pictured Rocks...... 80		1,140
440	Grand Island......... 10		1,150
400	**Marquette**....... 40		1,190
320	Portage Entry........ 80		1,270

(HOUGHTON AND HANCOCK, 14 Miles.)

270	Keweenaw Point.... 50		1,320
255	Copper Harbor...... 15		1,335
239	Eagle Harbor......... 16		1,351
229	EAGLE RIVER........ 10		1,361
209	Entrance Ship Canal 20		1,381
169	ONTONAGON 40		1,421
89	La Pointe, Wis'...... 80		1,501
86	BAYFIELD 3		1,504
	(Twelve Apostle Islands.)		
6	SUPERIOR CITY 80		1,584
0	**DULUTH**, Min. 6		1,590

Lake Superior and Mississippi Railroad.

MILES.	STATIONS.		MILES.
155	**DULUTH**		1,590
151	Oneonta.................	4	1,594
137	Fond Du Lac...........	14	1,608
	(Dalles of St. Louis.)		
129	**Thompson**	8	1,616
	Junction *Northern Pacific Railroad.*		
128	JUNCTION................	1	1,617
110	Moose Lake.............	18	1,635
95	Kettle River............	15	1,650
77	**Hinckley***	18	1,668
65	Pine City...............	12	1,680
54	Rush City..............	11	1,691
42	North Branch..........	12	1,703
30	Wyoming...............	12	1,715
25	Forest Lake.............	5	1,720
17	Centreville..............	8	1,728
12	White Bear Lake......	5	1,733
	Junction *Stillwater Branch Railroad.*		
0	**ST. PAUL**..........	12	1,745

GRAND PLEASURE EXCURSION.

This Railroad and Steamboat Route forms one of the most healthy and Grand Excursions on the Continent,—passing from the Atlantic Cities through Lakes *Erie, Huron,* and *Superior,*—affording River and Lake Scenery of the most enchanting character.

Steamers of a large class run daily, during the season of Navigation, from Buffalo, Erie, Cleveland and Detroit, to the Saut Ste. Marie, Marquette and Duluth, Minn.

NEW YORK to BUFFALO, NIAGARA FALLS, &c.,
Via ERIE RAILWAY.

Erie Railway.

MILES.	STATIONS.		MILES.
447	**NEW YORK**		0
	Foot of Chambers Street, and Foot of 23d Street.		
446	**Jersey City**		1
437	Rutherfurd Park	9	10
435	Passaic	2	12
430	PATERSON	5	17
425	Ridgewood	5	22
423	Hohokus	2	24
421	Allendale	2	26
419	Ramsey's	2	28
415	SUFFERN	4	32
413	Ramapo	2	34
411	Sloatsburg	2	36
405	Southfields	6	42
401	Newburgh Junction	4	46
399	Turner's	2	48
397	Monroe	2	50
395	Oxford	2	52
393	Greycourt	2	54
387	GOSHEN	6	60
383	Hampton	4	64
380	MIDDLETOWN	3	67
376	Howell's	4	71
371	Otisville	5	76
359	**Port Jervis***	12	88
340	Shohola	19	107
336	LACKAWAXEN	4	111
330	Mast Hope	6	117
324	NARROWSBURGH	6	123
316	Cochecton	8	131
311	Callicoon	5	136
283	Hancock	28	164
270	DEPOSIT	13	177
254	Susquehanna	16	193
246	GREAT BEND	8	201
241	Kirkwood	5	206
232	BINGHAMTON	9	215
223	Union	9	224
217	Campville	6	230
210	OWEGO	7	237

MILES.	STATIONS.		MILES.
200	Smithboro	10	247
198	Barton	2	249
191	WAVERLY	7	256
186	Chemung	5	261
180	Wellsburg	6	267
173	**Elmira***	7	274
156	CORNING	17	291

ROCHESTER DIVISION, 95 Miles.

MILES.	STATIONS.		MILES.
154	Painted Post	2	293
145	Addison	9	302
140	Rathboneville	5	307
132	Cameron	8	315
124	Adrian	8	323
119	Canisteo	5	328
115	HORNELLSVILLE	4	332
107	Burns'	8	340
103	Canaseraga	4	344
98	Swain's	5	349
91	NUNDA	7	356
89	Hunt's	2	358
85	Portage	4	362
81	Castile	4	366
79	Gainesville	2	368
72	WARSAW	7	375
66	Dale	6	381
61	Linden	5	386
55	ATTICA	6	392
49	Darien	6	398
43	Alden	6	404
34	Lancaster	9	413
24	**BUFFALO**	10	423

☞ Connects with *Lake Shore R. R.*

13	Tonawanda	11	434
2	**Niagara Falls**	11	445

☞ Connects with *N. Y. Cent. R. R.*

0	SUSPENSION BRIDGE	2	447

☞ Connects with *Great Western Railway of Canada.*

To **Chicago** via Detroit, by this Route, 960 Miles.

NEW YORK to DUNKIRK, CLEVELAND, &c.

Erie Railway.

MILES.	STATIONS.		MILES.
460	**NEW YORK**		0
400	GOSHEN		60
372	**Port Jervis***	28	88
283	DEPOSIT	89	177
259	GREAT BEND	24	201
245	BINGHAMTON	14	215
223	OWEGO	22	237
186	**Elmira***	37	274
169	CORNING	17	291
128	HORNELLSVILLE	41	332
119	Alfred	9	341
110	Andover	9	350
102	Genesee	8	358
94	Phillipsville	8	366
90	Belvidere	4	370
86	Friendship	4	374
77	Cuba	9	383
65	OLEAN	12	395

MILES.	STATIONS.		MILES.
61	Allegany	4	399
52	Carrollton	9	408
49	Great Valley	3	411
46	**Salamanca**	3	414

☞ Connects with *Atlantic & Great Western Railway.*

MILES.	STATIONS.		MILES.
38	Little Valley	8	422
31	Cattaraugus	7	429
22	Dayton	9	438
19	Perrysburg	3	441
12	Smith's Mills	7	448
8	Forestville	4	452
0	**DUNKIRK**	8	460

(*Lake Erie.*)

☞ Connects with the *Lake Shore Railroad*, forming a through line of travel to Cleveland, Toledo, Chicago and St. Louis.

To **Chicago,** via Toledo, by this Route, 960 Miles.

ERIE RAILWAY.

Four Express Trains Daily.

BROAD GAUGE, DOUBLE TRACK ROUTE

BETWEEN THE

Atlantic Cities and the Southwest, West and Northwest.

860 Miles without Change of Cars,

Between **New York** and **Rochester, Buffalo, Dunkirk, Salamanca, Corry, Meadville, Cleveland, Dayton, Hamilton** and **Cincinnati.**

☞ *Connects at CINCINNATI with the Broad Gauge OHIO and MISSISSIPPI R. R.*

NEW YORK TO ALBANY, BUFFALO, TOLEDO, ST. LOUIS, &c.,
Via TOLEDO, WABASH AND WESTERN RAILROAD.

Hudson River & New York Central Railroad.

MILES.	STATIONS.		MILES.
737	NEW YORK		0
	30th Street.		
695	Peekskill		42
664	Poughkeepsie*	31	73
622	Hudson	42	115
594	ALBANY	28	143
577	Schenectady	17	160
499	Utica*	78	238
485	Rome	14	252
446	Syracuse	39	291
365	Rochester*	81	373
333	Batavia	32	404
296	BUFFALO	37	441

Lake Shore Railroad.

296	BUFFALO		441
256	Dunkirk*	40	481
239	Westfield	17	498
208	ERIE, Pa	31	529
193	Girard	15	544
167	Ashtabula, Ohio	26	570
142	Painesville	25	595
113	CLEVELAND	29	624
89	Oberlin	24	648
53	Monroeville	36	684
38	Clyde	15	699
0	TOLEDO, Ohio	38	737

To **Detroit,** 65 Miles.

Toledo, Wabash & West. R. R.

MILES.	STATIONS.		MILES.
432	TOLEDO		737
423	Maumee City	9	746
415	Whitehouse	8	754
404	Liberty	11	765
397	NAPOLEON	7	772
382	DEFIANCE	15	787
371	Emerald	11	798
361	Antwerp	10	808
344	New Haven	17	825
338	Fort Wayne	6	831

Junction *Pittsburgh, Fort Wayne and Chicago Railroad.*

323	Roanoke	15	846
314	Huntington	9	855
301	Lagro	13	868
296	WABASH	5	873
282	Peru	14	887
275	Waverly	7	894
266	Logansport	9	903
252	Rockfield	14	917
246	Delphi	6	923
237	Buck Creek	9	932
229	Lafayette	8	940
219	West Point	10	950
208	Attica	11	961
200	West Lebanon	8	969
190	State Line	10	979
182	Danville	8	987
176	Catlin	6	993
169	Fairmount	7	1,000
162	Homer	7	1,007
146	Tolono	16	1,023

Junction *Chicago Division, Illinois Central Railroad.*

135	Norrie	11	1,034
129	Bement	6	1,040
120	Cerro Gordo	9	1,049
109	Decatur	11	1,060

Junction *Illinois Central Railroad.*

* Dining Stations.

ST. LOUIS DIVISION. T. W. & W. R. R.

MILES.	STATIONS.		MILES.
109	**Decatur**.......		1,060
102	Boody.......	7	1,067
90	Stonington......	12	1,079
82	Taylorville......	8	1,087
74	Palmer's......	8	1,095
69	Morrison......	5	1,100
61	Raymond......	8	1,108
49	Litchfield........	12	1,120
36	Staunton........	13	1,133
19	Edwardsville........	17	1,150
1	**East St. Louis**...	18	1,168
0	**ST. LOUIS**.........	1	1,169

☞ Connects with *R. R. & Steamers.*

Toledo, Wabash and Western,
(Continued.)

476	**TOLEDO**..............		0
382	**Fort Wayne**.........		94
326	Peru......................	56	150
310	Logansport..............	16	166
273	**Lafayette**..............	37	203
226	Danville.................	47	250
190	Tolono...................	36	286
153	**Decatur**...............	37	323
128	Mechanicsburg..........	25	348
114	**Springfield**...........	14	362
112	C. & A. Junction.........	2	364
97	Berlin.....................	15	379
91	Alexander..............	6	385
80	**Jacksonville**........	11	396

MILES.	STATIONS.		MILES.
70	Chapin......................	10	406
62	Bluff's.......................	8	414

To **Hannibal**, Mo., 50 Miles.

56	Meredosia....................	6	420
48	Versailles....................	8	428
39	Mt. Sterling.................	9	437
33	Mounds......................	6	443
28	Clayton	5	448

To **Keokuk**, Iowa, 42 Miles.

22	Camp Point.................	6	454
15	Paloma.......................	7	461
9	Cliola........................	6	467
0	**QUINCY**...................	9	476

(Mississippi River.)

☞ Connects with *Hannibal & St. Joseph Railroad.*

Keokuk Branch.

42	Clayton		448
35	C. B. & Q. Junction........	7	455
27	Bowen.......................	8	463
22	Denver	5	468
13	Carthage.....................	9	477
7	Elvaston.....................	6	483
1	Hamilton.....................	6	489
0	**KEOKUK**	1	490

(Mississippi River.)

☞ Connects with *Des Moines Valley Railroad.*

THE TOLEDO, WABASH AND WESTERN RAILROAD,
runs from TOLEDO, Ohio, to
KEOKUK, QUINCY, HANNIBAL and ST. LOUIS,
FORMING A
☞ *Great Route of Travel* ☜
Through Indiana, Illinois, Iowa and Missouri to Kansas and Colorado,
AND FROM THENCE TO
UTAH and CALIFORNIA.

NEW YORK to EASTON, WILLIAMSPORT & ERIE, Pa.

Central New Jersey Railroad.

MILES.	STATIONS.		MILES.
238	**NEW YORK**		0
	Foot of Liberty Street.		
237	**Jersey City**		1
225	ELIZABETH	12	13
214	PLAINFIELD	11	24
202	SOMERVILLE	12	36
192	WHITEHOUSE	10	46
186	CLINTON	6	52
179	JUNCTION	7	59
171	BLOOMSBURY	8	67
164	PHILLIPSBURG	7	74
163	**EASTON**	1	75

Lehigh Valley Railroad.*

MILES.	STATIONS.		MILES.
151	BETHLEHEM	12	87
146	**Allentown**	5	92
142	Catasauqua	4	96
128	Lehigh Gap	14	110
117	MAUCH CHUNK	11	121
110	Penn Haven	7	128

Catawissa Railroad.

MILES.	STATIONS.		MILES.
91	**Quakake**	19	147
88	Summit	3	150
80	Mahonoy	8	158
75	Ringtown	5	163
68	Beaver	7	170
59	Maineville	9	179
52	**Catawissa**	7	186
50	Rupert	2	188
43	Danville	7	195
37	Mooresburg	6	201

MILES.	STATIONS.		MILES.
27	**Milton**	10	211
22	Watsontown	5	216
16	Montgomery	6	222
0	**Williamsport***	16	238

Philadelphia & Erie R. R.

MILES.	STATIONS.		MILES.
248	**Williamsport**		238
242	Susquehanna	6	244
236	Jersey Shore	6	250
223	LOCK HAVEN	13	263
218	Farrandsville	5	268
208	Whetham	10	278
199	North Point	9	287
195	**Renovo***	4	292
183	Keating	12	303
178	Round Island	5	308
168	Driftwood	10	318
155	Cameron	13	331
149	EMPORIUM	6	337
140	Beechwood	9	346
128	ST. MARY'S	12	358
118	Ridgway	10	368
104	Wilcox	14	382
95	KANE*	9	391
79	Sheffield	16	407
66	WARREN	13	420
60	IRVINETON	6	426
54	Pittsfield	6	432
37	**Corry**	17	449
Junc.	Atlantic & Great Western Railway.		
26	Union	11	460
19	Waterford	7	467
7	Belle Valley	12	479
0	**ERIE**	7	486

Lake Superior Line of Steamers run daily from **Buffalo** to **Erie, Cleveland, Detroit, Saut Ste. Marie, Marquette** and **Duluth, Minn.,** forming a *Grand Pleasure Excursion* during the summer months.

* The Lehigh Valley, and the Lehigh and Susquehanna Railroads are competing lines for the business between New York and Williamsport, Pa., and the surrounding country.— The *Lehigh and Susquehanna* connects with the Central New Jersey Railroad at Phillipsburg, and at Tamanend, Pa., with the Catawissa Railroad.

NEW YORK TO ALBANY, DETROIT and CHICAGO, via NEW YORK CENTRAL RAILROAD.

MILES.	STATIONS.		MILES.	MILES.	STATIONS.		MILES.
143	**NEW YORK**..........		0	13	Schodack	6	130
	(Thirtieth Street.)			9	Castleton	4	134
				1	East Albany	8	142
138	Manhattan		5	0	**ALBANY**...............	1	143
136	Fort Washington..........	2	7				
134	Inwood.........................	2	9		(To **Troy**, 6 Miles.)		
133	Spuyten Duyvil............	1	10				
131	Riverdale......................	2	12		*New York Central Railroad.*		
130	Mount St. Vincent........	1	13	304	**ALBANY**...............		143
128	Yonkers......................	2	15	287	**Schenectady**.........17		160
127	Glenwood.....................	1	16	278	Hoffman's	9	169
124	Hastings......................	3	19	271	Amsterdam...................	7	176
122	Dobbs Ferry.................	2	21	265	Tribes Hill....................	6	182
120	Irvington.....................	2	23	260	Fonda	5	187
117	Tarrytown....................	3	26	255	Yost's.........................	5	192
113	Scarborough.................	4	30	252	Spraker's....................	3	195
111	Sing Sing....................	2	32	249	Palatine Bridge............	3	198
108	Croton	3	35	246	Fort Plain	3	201
105	Cruger's	3	38	240	St. Johnsville...........	6	207
104	Montrose.....................	1	39	230	**Little Falls**..........10		217
101	**Peekskill**.............	3	42	223	Herkimer	7	224
97	Fort Montgomery..........	4	46	221	Ilion	2	226
93	Garrison's.....................	4	50	218	Frankfort	3	229
90	Cold Spring.................	3	53	209	**Utica***..................	9	238
88	Cornwall Station...........	2	55	205	Whitesboro'	4	242
84	**Fishkill**	4	59	202	Oriskany.....................	3	245
81	Low Point....................	3	62	195	**Rome**......................	7	252
78	New Hamburg.............	3	65	186	Verona	9	261
74	Milton Ferry...............	4	69	182	**Oneida**...................	4	265
70	**Poughkeepsie***....	4	73	177	Canastota	5	270
64	Hyde Park...................	6	79	173	Canaseraga.................	4	274
60	Staatsburgh.................	4	83	171	Chittenango	2	276
55	Rhinebeck....................	5	88	167	Kirkville	4	280
49	Barrytown...................	6	94	164	Manlius.......................	3	283
45	Tivoli	6	98	156	**Syracuse**................	8	291
39	Germantown.................	6	104	147	Warner's.....................	9	300
32	Catskill Station............	7	111	144	Memphis.....................	3	303
28	**Hudson**	4	115	139	Jordan........................	5	308
24	Stockport....................	4	119	131	Port Byron..................	8	316
21	Coxsackie Station.........	3	122	124	Savannah..........	7	323
19	Stuyvesant	2	124	118	Clyde..........................	6	329

* Dining Stations.

MILES.	STATIONS.		MILES
112	**Lyons**	6	335
105	Newark	7	342
97	Palmyra	8	350
93	Macedon	4	354
85	Fairport	8	362
75	**Rochester***	10	372
65	Spencerport	10	382
63	Adams Basin	2	384
58	Brockport	5	389
54	Holley	4	393
50	Murray	4	397
45	**Albion**	5	402
39	Knowlesville	6	408
35	Medina	4	412
31	Middleport	4	416
26	Gasport	5	421
19	**Lockport**	7	428
9	Sanborn	10	438
0	**Suspension Br'g.**	9	447

To **Niagara Falls**, 2 Miles.

Great Western Railway of Canada.

230	**Suspenston Br'g.**		447
219	St. Catherine's, Can	11	458
187	**Hamilton**	32	490
168	Harrisburg	19	509
158	**Paris**	10	519
139	Woodstock	19	538
111	**London**	28	566
69	Bothwell	42	608
46	Chatham	23	631

MILES.	STATIONS.		MILES.
1	**Windsor**	45	676
0	**DETROIT**	1	677

Michigan Central Railroad.

284	**DETROIT**		677
281	Grand Trunk Junction	3	680
274	Dearborn	7	687
266	WAYNE	8	695
259	Denton's	7	702
254	**Ypsilanti**	5	707
250	Geddes	4	711
246	**Ann Arbor***	4	715
241	Delhi	5	720
237	Dexter	4	724
229	Chelsea	8	732
218	Grass Lake	11	743
215	Leoni	3	746
208	**Jackson**	7	753
197	Parma	11	764
188	Albion	9	773
183	Marengo	5	778
176	**Marshall**	7	785
171	Ceresco	5	790
163	Battle Creek	8	798
149	Galesburg	14	812
140	**Kalamazoo**	9	821
124	Lawton	16	837
116	Decatur	8	845
105	Dowagiac	11	856
93	**Niles***	12	868
82	Dayton	11	879
66	New Buffalo	16	895
56	**Michigan City**	10	905
44	Porter	12	917
35	Lake	9	926
14	Calumet	21	947
0	**CHICAGO**	14	961

CONNECTS WITH

ILLINOIS CENTRAL, CHICAGO, BURLINGTON & QUINCY, CHICAGO, ROCK ISLAND & PACIFIC, CHICAGO & NORTHWESTERN,

And other Railroads diverging from CHICAGO—forming the Great Through Routes of Travel to the **West and Northwest**.

NEW YORK TO PITTSBURGH, INDIANAPOLIS, and ST. LOUIS, Via ALLENTOWN ROUTE.

Central R. R. of New Jersey.

MILES.	STATIONS.		MILES.
430	**NEW YORK**		0
	Foot of Liberty Street.		
429	**Jersey City**		1
427	ELIZABETH	12	13
410	Westfield ...	7	20
406	PLAINFIELD	4	24
399	Bound Brook	7	31
394	SOMERVILLE	5	36
385	WHITEHOUSE	9	45
378	Clinton	7	52
372	JUNCTION	6	58

Junc. Dela., Lack. & Western R. R.

364	Bloomsbury	8	66
356	PHILLIPSBURG	8	74
355	**EASTON*** Pa	1	75

Junction Lehigh Valley Railroad.

343	BETHLEHEM	12	87
338	**Allentown**	5	92
317	Lyons	21	113
302	READING	15	128
274	Lebanon	28	156
248	**HARRISBURG***.26		182

Junc. Northern Central Railroad.

Pennsylvania Central R. R.

220	Newport	28	210
199	MIFFLIN	21	231
151	HUNTINGDON	48	279
116	**Altoona***	35	314
105	GALLITZIN	11	325
78	JOHNSTOWN	27	352
41	LATROBE*	37	389
31	GREENSBURG	10	399
0	**PITTSBURGH**....31		430

Pittsburgh, Fort Wayne and Chicago Railroad.

MILES.	STATIONS.		MILES.
396	**PITTSBURGH**...		430
370	ROCHESTER........	26	456
326	Salem........	44	500
312	**Alliance***	14	514
286	MASSILLON	26	540
272	ORRVILLE	14	554
261	Wooster	11	565
220	MANSFIELD........	41	606
207	**Crestline**.........	13	619

Cleveland, Columbus, Cincinnati & Indianapolis R. R.

203	Galion............	4	623
182	MARION..........	21	644
168	La Rue..........	14	658
142	BELLEFONTAINE..........	26	684
119	Sidney..........	23	707
101	Versailles........	18	725
84	**Union**.......	17	742
54	Muncie.........	30	772
36	ANDERSON........	18	790
21	Fortville..........	15	805
0	**INDIANAPOLIS**.21		826

Ind. and St. Louis R. R.

261	**INDIANAPOLIS.**		826
242	Danville..........	19	845
222	GREENCASTLE........	20	865
189	**Terre Haute**........	33	898
144	CHARLESTON*.........	45	943
133	**Mattoon***	11	954
94	PANA........	39	993
84	NAKOMIS*..........	10	1,003
36	BUNKER HILL........	48	1,051
21	ALTON JUNCTION......	15	1,066
1	**East St. Louis**......	21	1,087
0	**ST. LOUIS**..........	1	1,088

ST. LOUIS to SPRINGFIELD, STATE LINE and FORT SCOTT.

Atlantic & Pacific Railroad.

MILES.	STATIONS.		MILES.
330	**ST. LOUIS**		0
311	Maramec		19
293	**Pacific City***	18	37
288	Catawissa	5	42
286	Calvey	2	44
281	Moselle	5	49
274	St. Clair	7	56
264	Staunton	10	66
259	Sullivan	5	71
252	Bourbon	7	78
247	Leasburg	5	83
239	Cuba	8	91
232	Knobview	7	98
226	St. James	6	104
221	Dillon	5	109
216	**Rolla***	5	114
206	York's	10	124
204	Arlington	2	126
203	Jerome	1	127
192	Dixon	11	138
186	Hancock	6	144
180	Crocker	6	150
174	Woodend	6	156
167	Richland	7	163
159	Stoutville	8	171
152	Sleeper	7	178
145	**Lebanon**	7	185

Junction *Laclede and Fort Scott Rail-road*, 110 Miles.

136	Brush Creek	9	194
128	Conway	8	202
120	Niangua	8	210
113	Marshfield	7	217

MILES.	STATIONS.		MILES.
107	Bunker Hill	6	223
99	Stafford	8	231
89	**Springfield***	10	241
83	Dorchester	6	247
79	Brookline	4	251
69	Plymouth	10	261
64	Logan's	5	266
57	Aurora	7	273
52	Verona	5	278
45	Billings	7	285
39	Pierce City	6	291

Van Buren Branch, 125 Miles.

34	Berwick	5	296
28	Ritchieville	6	302
23	Granby City	5	307
15	**Neosho**	8	315
0	**STATE LINE**	15	330

THE ATLANTIC AND PACIFIC RAILROAD,

now finished to the Kansas State Line, 330 miles, runs for the most part, through a beautiful country, with a fruitful soil and climate as genial as that of Italy. The mineral wealth of this section of Missouri is immense, abounding in iron, lead and copper.

☞ This is the shortest and cheapest Route for Freight and Passengers, to all points in Northern Arkansas, Texas, and the Indian Territory. Stages run from Pierce City to Fort Smith and Fort Gibson. Time from St. Louis, 44 hours.

*Dining Stations.

THE ATLANTIC AND PACIFIC RAILROAD
will be extended through the Indian Territory, along the 35th parallel of latitude.

THE LACLEDE AND FORT SCOTT RAILROAD,
when finished, will form a direct route from St. Louis to Ft. Scott, Kan., 255 miles.

ST. LOUIS TO KANSAS CITY, OTTUMWA AND OMAHA.

North Missouri Railroad.

MILES.	STATIONS.		MILES.
272	**ST. LOUIS**		0
270	Gambles		2
267	Bellefontaine	3	5
265	Jennings	2	7
261	Ferguson	4	11
259	Graham's	2	13
257	Bridgton	2	15
254	Bonfils	3	18
252	Brotherton	2	20
251	**St. Charles**	1	21
247	Elm Point Switch	4	25
242	Dardenne	5	30
238	O'Fallon	4	34
234	Perruque	4	38
232	Gilmore	2	40
229	Wentzville	3	43
223	Millville	6	49
220	Wright's	3	52
214	**Warrenton**	6	58
208	Pendleton	6	64
204	Jonesburg	4	68
199	High Hill	5	73
195	New Florence	4	77
189	**Montgomery***	6	83
182	Wellsville	7	90
177	Martinsburg	5	95
170	Benton City	7	102
163	MEXICO	7	109
158	Thompson	5	114
150	Centralia Junction	8	122
142	Sturgeon	8	130
137	Clark	5	135
132	Renick	5	140
126	**Moberly June**	6	146
119	Huntsville	7	153
112	Clifton	7	160
105	Salisbury	7	167
98	Keytesville	7	174
94	Dalton	4	178
86	**Brunswick**	8	186

MILES.	STATIONS.		MILES.
80	Dewitt	6	192
76	Miami	4	196
70	Wakenda	6	202
63	Carrollton	7	209
54	Norborne	9	218
46	Hardin	8	226
40	R. and L Junction*	6	232

☞ Connects with the *St. Joseph Division.*

35	Camden	5	237
29	Orrick	6	243
17	Missouri City	12	255
12	Liberty Landing	5	260
9	North Missouri Junc	3	263
1	HARLEM	8	271
0	**KANSAS CITY**	1	272

☞ Connects at Kansas City with the *Kansas Pacific*, for all points in Kansas and California; the *Missouri River, Fort Scott and Gulf Railroad*, for Fort Scott, &c.; and the *Leavenworth, Lawrence and Galveston Railroad*, for Humboldt, &c.

NORTHERN DIVISION.

276	**ST. LOUIS**		0
130	**Moberly**		146
124	Cairo	6	152
118	Jacksonville	6	158
112	Woodswitch	6	164
107	**Macon***	5	168

Junction *Hannibal and St. Joseph Railroad.*

95	Atlanta	12	181
86	La Plata	9	190
79	Millard	7	197
72	Kirksville	7	204
64	Sublett's	8	212
61	Green Top	3	215
57	Queen City	4	219

*Dining Stations.

MILES.	STATIONS.		MILES.
49	Glenwood	8	227
41	Coatesville	8	235
34	Moulton	7	242
28	West Grove	6	248
20	Bloomfield	8	256
0	**Ottumwa**	20	276

☞ Connects with the *Des Moines Valley Railroad.*

ST. JOSEPH DIVISION.

MILES.	STATIONS.		MILES.
304	**ST. LOUIS**		0
72	R. and L. Junction		232
67	Richmond	5	247
62	Swanwick	5	242
57	Foote Station	5	247
53	Vibbard	4	251
48	Lawson	5	256
43	Converse	5	261
38	Lathrop	5	266
34	Lyon	4	270
30	Plattsbury	4	274
25	Turner	5	279
21	Gower	4	283
16	Frazier	5	288
12	Agency Ford	4	292
7	Matney	5	297
0	**ST. JOSEPH**	7	304

(*Missouri River.*)

☞ Connects with *Kansas City, St. Joseph and Council Bluffs Railroad.*

Kansas City, St. Joseph and Council Bluffs Railroad.

MILES.	STATIONS.		MILES.
204	**KANSAS CITY**		0
202	Harlem		2
197	Stonington	5	7
194	Parkville	3	10
187	Waldron	7	17
179	E. Leavenworth	8	25
173	Beverly	6	31
163	Iatan	10	41
153	Winthrop, op. Atchis'n	10	51
149	Rushville	4	55
138	Lake Station	11	66
134	Han. & St. Joseph Junc.	4	70
133	**St. Joseph**	1	71
124	Amazonia	9	80
120	Nodaway	4	84
113	Forbes	7	91
105	Forest City	8	99
95	Bigelow	10	109
82	Corning	13	122
69	Phelps	13	135
55	Hamburg	14	149
44	East Nebraska City	11	160
38	Percival	6	166
29	Bartlett	9	175
21	Pacific Junction	8	183
18	Pacific	3	186
4	**Council Bluffs**	14	200
1	Missouri River	3	203
0	**OMAHA**	1	204

NORTH MISSOURI RAILROAD,

The Shortest Line from St. Louis to the

WEST AND NORTH.

Three EXPRESS TRAINS leave St. Louis, Daily, making close connections at OTTUMWA, KANSAS CITY, ST. JOSEPH and COUNCIL BLUFFS.

Pullman's Palace Sleeping Cars on the Night Trains.

48

BOSTON to ALBANY, DETROIT and MILWAUKEE, via GREAT WESTERN RAILWAY OF CANADA.

Boston & Albany Railroad.

MILES.	STATIONS.		MILES.
200	**BOSTON**, Mass.....		0
195	Brighton		5
179	**S. Framingham**.16		21
176	Ashland	3	24
173	Cordaville	3	27
172	Southville	1	28
168	Westboro................	4	32
162	Grafton..................	6	38
156	**WORCESTER**...	6	44
155	Worcester Junction.....	1	45
147	Rochdale.................	8	53
143	Charlton.................	4	57
138	Spencer.................	5	62
133	Brookfield...............	5	67
131	West Brookfield.........	2	69
127	Warren.................	4	73
121	Brimfield	6	79
117	**Palmer**...............	4	83
111	Wilbraham...............	6	89
108	Indian Orchard	3	92
102	**SPRINGFI'LD***	6	98
100	W. Springfield	2	100
92	**Westfield**............	8	108
84	Russell.................	8	116
81	Huntington...............	3	119
74	Chester.................	7	126
69	Middlefield.............	5	131
65	Becket	4	135
62	Washington.............	3	138
57	Hinsdale...............	5	143
54	Dalton	3	146
49	**Pittsfield**............	5	151
46	Shaker Village	3	154
41	.Richmond..............	5	159
38	N. Y. State Line........	3	162
33	Canaan.................	5	167
28	East Chatham...........	5	172
23	**Chatham**............	5	177
19	Chatham Centre.........	4	181
16	Kinderhook..............	3	184
8	Schodack	8	192
1	Greenbush	7	199
0	**ALBANY**............	1	200

New York Central Railroad.

MILES.	STATIONS.		MILES.
304	**ALBANY**, N. Y....		200
287	**Schenectady** 17		217
278	Hoffman's.............	9	226
271	Amsterdam.............	7	233
260	FONDA................	11	244
252	Spraker's................	8	252
249	Palatine Bridge	3	255
246	Fort Plain.............	3	258
240	St. Johnsville.........	6	264
230	**Little Falls**........	10	274
223	Herkimer...............	7	281
221	Ilion.................	2	283
218	Frankfort.............	3	286
209	**UTICA***......	9	295
205	Whitesboro'.............	4	299
202	Oriskany	3	302
195	**Rome**...............	7	309
186	Verona................	9	318
182	**Oneida**.............	4	322
177	Canastota.............	5	327
173	Canaseraga	4	331
171	Chittenango...........	2	333
167	Kirkville.............	4	337
164	Manlius..............	3	340
156	**SYRACUSE**	8	348
147	Warners..............	9	357
139	Jordan...............	8	365
131	Port Byron...........	8	373
124	Savannah	7	380
118	Clyde................	6	386
112	**Lyons**.............	6	392
105	Newark..............	7	399
97	Palmyra.............	8	407
93	Macedon	4	411
85	Fairport.............	8	419
75	**ROCHESTER***..10		429

To **Buffalo**, 69 Miles.

MILES.	STATIONS.		MILES.
66	Spencerport	9	438
63	Adams Basin	3	441
58	Brockport	5	446
54	Holley	4	450
50	Murray	4	454
45	ALBION	5	459
39	Knowlesville	6	465
35	Medina	4	469
31	Middleport	4	473
26	Gasport	5	478
19	**Lockport**	7	485
16	Lockport Junction	3	488
9	Sanborn	7	495
0	**Suspension Br.**	9	504

To **Niagara Falls**, 2 Miles.

Great Western (Canada) R. R.

MILES.	STATIONS.		MILES.
230	**Suspension Br.**		504
221	Thorold, Canada	9	513
219	St. CATHERINE'S	2	515
213	Jordan	6	521
207	Beamsville	6	527
203	Grimsby	4	531
198	Winona	5	536
193	Stoney Creek	5	541
187	**HAMILTON***	6	547

To **Toronto**, 39 Miles.

MILES.	STATIONS.		MILES.
180	Dundas	7	554
175	Copetown	5	559
171	Lynden	4	563
168	HARRISBURG	3	566
158	**Paris**	10	576
	Junc. Buffalo & Goderich R. R.		
151	Princeton	7	583
144	Eastwood	7	590
139	WOODSTOCK	5	595
134	Beachville	5	600
130	Ingersoll	4	604
120	Dorchester	10	614
111	**London***	9	623
101	Komoka	10	633
96	Mt. Brydges	5	638
90	Longwood	6	644
80	Glencoe	10	654
74	Newbury	6	660
69	**Bothwell**	5	665
61	Thamesville	8	673
55	Lewisville	6	679
46	**Chatham**	9	688
32	Baptiste Creek	14	702
27	Stoney Point	5	707
18	Belle River	9	716
1	**Windsor**	17	733
	(Detroit River.)		
0	**DETROIT**, Mich.	1	734

DETROIT to GRAND HAVEN and MILWAUKEE.

Detroit & Milwaukee R. R.

	STATIONS		
274	**DETROIT**		0
270	Grand Trunk Junction		4
248	PONTIAC	22	26
241	Waterford	7	33
227	HOLLY	14	47
	Junc. Flint & P. M. Railroad.		
207	Gaines	20	67
196	**Owosso**	11	78
	Junc. Jackson, Lansing & Saginaw R. R.		
186	Ovid	10	88
176	St. John's	10	98
167	Fowler	9	107
157	Muir	10	117
150	IONIA	7	124
135	Lowell	15	139
116	**Grand Rapids**	19	158
	Junc. Grand Rapids & Indiana R. R.		
107	Berlin	9	167
88	Spring Lake	19	186
87	Ferrysburg	1	187
85	**Grand Haven**	2	189
	(Lake Michigan.)		
0	**MILWAUKEE**	85	274

Connects with *Milwaukee & St. Paul Railway*, and Steamers on *L. Michigan*.

BOSTON to DETROIT CHICAGO AND OMAHA.

Boston and Albany Railroad.

MILES.	STATIONS.		MILES.
734	**BOSTON**		0
690	**Worcester**		44
636	**Springfield**	54	98
583	PITTSFIELD	53	151
534	**ALBANY**	49	200

New York Central Railroad.

MILES.	STATIONS.		MILES.
517	SCHENECTADY	17	217
439	**Utica**	78	295
425	ROME	14	309
387	**Syracuse**	38	347
342	LYONS	45	392
306	**Rochester**	36	428
250	LOCKPORT	56	484
230	**Suspension Br'ge**	20	504

Great Western Railway of Canada.

MILES.	STATIONS.		MILES.
187	**Hamilton**	43	547
158	PARIS	28	576
111	**London**	47	623
46	CHATHAM	65	688
1	WINDSOR	45	733
0	**DETROIT**	1	734

Michigan Central Railroad.

MILES.	STATIONS.		MILES.
284	**DETROIT**, Mich		734
281	Grand Trunk Junc	3	737
274	Dearborn	7	744
270	Inksters	4	748
266	Wayne	4	752
261	Secords	5	757
259	Denton's	2	759
254	**Ypsilanti**	5	764
250	Geddes	4	768
246	**Ann Arbor**	4	772
243	Foster's	3	775
241	Delhi	2	777
239	Scio	2	779
237	Dexter	2	781
229	Chelsea	8	789

MILES.	STATIONS.		MILES.
222	Francisco	7	796
218	Grass Lake	4	800
215	Leoni	3	803
212	Michigan Central	3	806
208	**Jackson**	4	810
203	Trumbull's	5	815
197	Parma	6	821
194	Concord	3	824
192	Bath Mills	2	826
188	Albion	4	830
183	Marengo	5	835
176	**Marshall**	7	842
171	Ceresco	5	847
169	White's	2	849
163	**Battle Creek**	6	855
158	Bedford	5	860
154	Augusta	4	864
149	Galesburg	5	869
144	Comstock	5	874
140	**Kalamazoo**	4	878
135	Ostemo	5	883
128	Mattawan	7	890
124	Lawton	4	894
122	White Oaks	2	896
116	Decatur	6	902
112	Tietsort's	4	906
105	Dowagiac	7	913
99	Pokagon	6	919
93	**Niles**	6	925
87	Buchanan	6	931
82	Dayton	5	936
79	Galien	3	939
75	Avery's	4	943
73	Three Oaks	2	945
66	New Buffalo	7	952
61	Corymbo	5	957
56	**Michigan City**	5	962
50	Furnessville	6	968
44	Porter	6	974
35	**Lake**	9	983
29	Tolleston	6	989
14	Calumet	15	1,004
0	**CHICAGO**	14	1,018

Chicago and Northwestern Railroad.

MILES.	STATIONS.		MILES.
492	**CHICAGO**		1,018
486	Austin	6	1,024
483	Harlem	3	1,027
476	Cottage Hill	7	1,034
472	Lombard	4	1,038
469	Danby	3	1,041
467	Wheaton	2	1,043
464	Winfield	3	1,046
462	**Junction**	2	1,048
456	Geneva	6	1,054
451	La Fox	5	1,059
448	Blackberry	3	1,062
441	Lodi	7	1,069
437	Cortland	4	1,073
434	De Kalb	3	1,076
430	Malta	6	1,082
422	Creston	6	1,088
417	Rochelle	5	1,093
408	Ashton	9	1,102
404	Franklin	4	1,106
399	Nachusa	5	1,111
394	**Dixon**	5	1,116
388	Nelson	6	1,122
382	Sterling	6	1,128
379	Galt	3	1,131
368	Morrison	11	1,142
356	**Fulton**	12	1,154
	(Mississippi River.)		
354	**Clinton**, Iowa	2	1,156

IOWA DIVISION.

MILES.	STATIONS.		MILES.
354	**Clinton**, Iowa		1,156
349	Camanche	5	1,161
344	Low Moor	5	1,166
340	Malone	4	1,170
335	De Witt	5	1,175
323	Calamus	12	1,187

MILES.	STATIONS.		MILES.
319	Wheatland	4	1,191
314	Loudon	5	1,196
307	Clarence	7	1,203
302	Stanwood	5	1,208
290	Lisbon	12	1,220
289	Mt. Vernon	1	1,221
282	Bertram	7	1,228
273	**Cedar Rapids**	9	1,237
264	Fairfax	9	1,246
248	Blairstown	16	1,262
243	Luzerne	5	1,267
238	Belle Plains	5	1,272
232	Chelsea	6	1,278
222	Tama	10	1,288
215	Oxford	7	1,295
212	Legrand	3	1,298
203	Marshall	9	1,307
189	State Center	14	1,321
181	Colo	8	1,329
174	Nevada	7	1,336
162	Ontario	12	1,348
152	**Boone**	10	1,358
140	Ogden	12	1,370
135	Beaver	5	1,375
128	Grand Junction	7	1,382
122	North Jefferson	6	1,388
113	Scranton	9	1,397
104	Glidden	9	1,406
96	Carroll	8	1,414
86	Tip Top	10	1,424
83	West Side	3	1,427
68	**Denison**	15	1,442
59	Crawford	9	1,451
51	Dunlap	8	1,459
41	Woodbine	10	1,469
25	Mo. Valley Junction	16	1,485
10	Crescent	15	1,500
4	**Council Bluffs**	6	1,506
1	Missouri River	3	1,509
0	**OMAHA**, Neb	1	1,510

OMAHA to OGDEN, Utah ....1,032 Miles

OGDEN to SAN FRANCISCO, Cal .... 881 "

Total, BOSTON to SAN FRANCISCO, via Chicago ....3,423 Miles.

OMAHA to CHEYENNE, OGDEN, UTAH & SAN FRANCISCO.

Union Pacific Railroad.

MILES.	STATIONS.		MILES.
1,032	**OMAHA,** Neb.		0
1,022	Gilmore		10
1,017	Papillion	5	15
1,003	Elkhorn	14	29
997	Valley	6	35
985	**Fremont***	12	47
978	Ketchum	7	54
970	North Bend	8	62
956	Schuyler	14	76
948	Richland	8	84
940	COLUMBUS	8	92
933	Jackson	7	99
923	Silver Creek	10	109
911	Clark's	12	121
900	Lone Tree	11	132
890	Chapman's	10	142
878	GRAND ISLAND*	12	154
870	Pawnee	8	162
860	Wood River	10	172
849	Gibbon	11	183
841	KEARNEY	8	191
831	Stevenson	10	201
820	Elm Creek	11	212
811	Overton	9	221
802	Plum Creek	9	230
792	Cayote	10	240
782	Willow Island	10	250
772	Warren	10	260
764	Brady Island	8	268
755	McPherson	9	277
741	NORTH PLATTE*	14	291
733	Nichols	8	299
724	O'Fallon's	9	308
710	Alkali	14	322
700	Roscoe	10	332
690	Ogalalla	10	342
681	Brule	9	351
671	Big Spring	10	361
655	JULESBURG	16	377

MILES.	STATIONS.		MILES.
645	Chappel	10	387
635	Lodge Pole	10	397
624	Colton	11	408
618	SIDNEY*	6	414
609	Brownson	9	423
599	Potter	10	433
590	Bennett	9	442
581	Antelope	9	451
569	Bushnell	12	463
559	Pine Bluff, W. Ter.	10	473
548	Egbert	11	484
536	Hillsdale	12	496
524	Archer	12	508
516	**CHEYENNE**	8	516

To DENVER, 106 Miles.

MILES.	STATIONS.		MILES.
509	Hazard	7	523
501	Otto	8	531
496	Granite Canon	5	536
490	Buford	6	542
483	Sherman, (Summit)	7	549
474	Harney	9	558
468	Red Buttes	6	564
462	Fort Sanders	6	570
459	LARAMIE*	3	573
451	Howell's	8	581
445	Wyoming	6	587
430	Cooper's Lake	15	602
426	Lookout	4	606
409	Rock Creek	17	623
394	Como	15	638
384	Medicine Bow	10	648
376	Carbon	8	656
370	Simpson	6	662
363	Percy	7	669
357	Dana	6	675
352	St. Mary's	5	680
344	Walcott's	8	688
336	Fort Steele	8	696
328	Grenville	8	704

* Dining Stations.

MILES.	STATIONS.	MILES.	MILES.	STATIONS.	MILES.
323	Rawlins*................ 5	709	696	Toano..................... 9	1,217
309	Separation..............14	723	688	Pequop................... 8	1,225
295	Creston..............14	737	676	Independence............12	1,237
280	Wash-a-kie..........15	752	672	Moore's................... 4	1,241
271	Red Desert............. 9	761	668	Cedar.................. 4	1,245
257	Table Rock............ 14	775	662	Wells................. 6	1,251
247	Bitter Creek*........10	785	654	Tulasco................ 8	1,259
238	Black Buttes............ 9	794	642	Deeth.................12	1,271
234	Hallville................. 4	798	625	Halleck................17	1,288
227	Point of Rocks.......... 7	805	615	Osino 10	1,298
215	Salt Wells 12	817	605	Elko*....................10	1,308
201	Rock Springs............14	831	593	Moleen..................12	1,320
187	Green River.............14	845	582	Carlin 11	1,331
174	Bryan.....................13	858	572	Palisade...............10	1,341
156	Granger...............18	876	554	Beowawe..................18	1,359
145	Church Buttes............11	887	544	Shoshone 10	1,369
128	Carter.................17	904	533	Argenta 11	1,380
119	Bridger................. 9	913	516	Battle Mountain.........17	1,397
104	Leroy...................15	928	502	Stone House.............14	1,411
95	Piedmont............... 9	937	490	Iron Point.............12	1,423
77	Aspen....................18	955	478	Golconda...............12	1,435
75	Evanston, Utah 2	957	466	Tule....................12	1,447
66	Wahsatch*............. 9	966	461	Winnemucca* 5	1,452
57	Castle Rock.............. 9	975	450	Rose Creek 11	1,463
41	Echo 16	991	440	Raspberry Creek 10	1,473
25	Weber 16	1,007	433	Mill City................ 7	1,480
13	Devil's Gate..............12	1,019	421	Humboldt* 12	1,492
8	Uintah................. 5	1,024	410	Rye Patch...............11	1,503
0	**OGDEN** 8	1,032	399	Oreana................11	1,514
			388	Lovelock's.............11	1,525
	To Salt Lake City, 37 Miles.		372	Brown's.................16	1,541
			360	White Plains............12	1,553
	Central Pacific Railroad.		345	Hot Springs.............15	1,568
881	**OGDEN**	1,032	334	Desert.................11	1,579
856	Corinne 25	1,057	326	Wadsworth*.......... 8	1,587
820	Promontory.............36	1,093	311	Clark's.................15	1,602
807	Monument 13	1,106	299	Camp..................12	1,614
790	Kelton..................17	1,123	291	Reno................ 8	1,622
759	Terrace 31	1,154	280	Verdi, Cal.........11	1,633
734	Lucin 25	1,179	265	Boca....................15	1,648
725	Tecoma, Nev............ 9	1,188	257	Truckee*.............. 8	1,656
715	Montello..............10	1,198	242	Summit, Sierras..........15	1,671
705	Loray 9	1,208	236	Cascade 6	1,677
			229	Cisco 7	1,684

* Dining Stations.

MILES.	STATIONS.		MILES.	MILES.	STATIONS.		MILES.
220	Emigrant Gap	9	1,693	138	**SACRAMENTO**	8	1,775
215	Blue Canon	5	1,698	112	Galt	26	1,801
206	Alta	9	1,707	91	STOCKTON	21	1,822
204	Dutch Flat	2	1,709	81	Lathrop	10	1,832
201	Gold Run	3	1,712	74	Bantas	7	1,839
191	COLFAX*	10	1,722	69	Ellis	5	1,844
173	Auburn	18	1,740	47	Livermore	22	1,866
168	New Castle	5	1,745	41	Pleasanton	6	1,872
161	Pino	7	1,752	29	Niles	12	1,884
159	Rocklin	2	1,754	6	Oakland	23	1,907
156	Junc. Cal. & Or. R. R.	3	1,757		*(Bay of San Francisco.)*		
146	Arcade	10	1,767	0	**S. FRANCISCO**	6	1,913

THE CENTRAL PACIFIC RAILROAD,

The Last Link in the Great chain of Railroads connecting the

ATLANTIC AND PACIFIC OCEANS.

THE C. P. R. R.

CONNECTS WITH THE

Union Pacific Railroad at Union Junction,

ON THE NORTHERN SHORES OF GREAT SALT LAKE.

FROM THIS POINT TO

SAN FRANCISCO,

THE CENTRAL PACIFIC RAILROAD

Passes over a Route which presents the

Most Varied and Attractive Scenery on the Continent.

The C. P. R. R. is a wonderful achievement of engineering skill and perfection in Railroad construction. The numerous connections of the CENTRAL PACIFIC RAILROAD by Rail, Steamers and Stages, enables the Traveller to reach any point either in

CALIFORNIA, OREGON AND BRITISH AMERICA,

OR ACROSS THE PACIFIC OCEAN TO

JAPAN, CHINA AND INDIA.

5

BOSTON TO ALBANY, BUFFALO, TOLEDO, CHICAGO, DAVENPORT, OMAHA AND SAN FRANCISCO, Via UNION PACIFIC RAILROAD.

Boston and Albany Railroad.

MILES.	STATIONS.		MILES.
200	**BOSTON**		0
179	**S. Framingham**		21
156	**WORCESTER**	23	44

Junc. Norwich and Worcester R. R.

131	**West Brookfield**	25	69
117	**Palmer**	39	83
102	**SPRINGFIELD**	15	98

Junction New Haven, Hartford and Springfield Railroad.

92	**Westfield**	10	108
49	**Pittsfield**	43	151
23	**Chatham**	26	177
0	**ALBANY**	23	200

New York Central Railroad.

298	**ALBANY**		200
281	**Schenectady**	17	217
224	**Little Falls**	57	274
203	**Utica**	21	295
188	**Rome**	14	309
176	**Oneida**	12	321
150	**SYRACUSE**	26	347
105	**Lyons**	45	392
69	**ROCHESTER**	36	428
59	**Chili**	11	439
55	Churchville	4	443

MILES.	STATIONS.		MILES.
52	Bergen	3	446
45	Byron	7	453
37	**Batavia**	8	461
30	Crofts	7	468
25	Corfu	5	473
20	Alden	5	478
17	Wende	3	481
11	Lancaster	6	487
8	Forks	3	490
0	**BUFFALO**	8	498

Lake Shore Railroad.

540	**BUFFALO**		498
530	Hamburgh	10	508
526	Lake View	4	512
519	Angola	7	519
514	Farnham	5	524
511	Irving	3	527
509	Silver Creek	2	529
500	**Dunkirk**	9	538

Connects with *Erie Railway.*

491	Brocton	9	547
483	Westfield	8	555
475	Ripley	8	563
472	State Line	3	566
467	Northeast, Pa	5	571
463	Morehead's	4	575
460	Harbor Creek	3	578
456	Weslevville	4	582
452	**ERIE**	4	586

Connects with *Philadelphia and Erie Railway.*

444	Swanville	8	594
441	Fairview	3	597
437	GIRARD	4	601
432	Springfield	5	606
424	Conneaut	8	614
417	Kingsville	7	621

MILES.	STATIONS.		MILES.	MILES.	STATIONS.		MILES.
411	**Ashtabula**	6	627	226	Wood	7	812
406	Saybrook	5	632	223	Riga	3	815
402	Geneva	4	636	221	Blissfield	2	817
399	Unionville	3	639	217	Palmyra Junction	4	821
396	Madison	3	642	211	**Adrian**	6	827
391	Perry	5	647	206	Dover T't	5	832
386	PAINESVILLE	5	652	200	Clayton	6	838
379	Mentor	7	659	194	Hudson	6	844
375	Willoughby	4	663	187	Pittsford	7	851
371	Wickliffe	4	667	183	Osseo	4	855
366	Euclid	5	672	178	Hillsdale	5	860
357	**CLEVELAND**	9	681	174	Jonesville	4	864
356	Atlantic & Gt. W. Depot	1	682	168	Allen's	6	870
344	Berea	12	694	162	Quincy	9	876
341	Olmsted Falls	3	697	155	**Coldwater**	7	883
336	Ridgeville	5	702	145	Bronson	10	893
331	Elyria	5	707	138	Burr Oak	7	900
323	OBERLIN	8	715	132	Sturgis	6	906
318	Kipton	5	720	127	Side Track	5	911
313	Wakeman	5	725	120	White Pigeon	7	918
308	Townsend	5	730	114	Middlebury	6	924
301	Norwalk	7	737	109	Bristol	5	929
297	**Monroeville**	4	741	101	**Elkhart**	8	937
289	Bellevue	8	749	96	Osceola	5	942
282	**Clyde**	7	756	90	Mishawka	6	948
273	Fremont	9	765	86	South Bend	4	952
267	Lindsey	6	771	74	Terre C'pe	12	964
261	Elmore	6	777	73	N. Carlisle	1	965
257	Genoa	4	781	59	**Laporte**	14	979
252	Millbury	5	786	50	Holmesville	9	988
244	**TOLEDO**	8	794	47	Selkirk's	3	991
				41	Chesterton	6	997
				30	Miller's	11	1,008
				23	Pine	7	1,015
				12	Ainsworth	10	1,026
				6	Englewood	6	1,032
				0	**CHICAGO**	6	1,038

Michigan Southern Railroad.

MILES.	STATIONS.		MILES.
244	**TOLEDO**		794
241	Junction	3	797
233	Sylvania	8	805

CHICAGO to OMAHA, Neb., via Davenport, Iowa, ... 494 Miles.
OMAHA to OGDEN, Utah, via Union Pacific Railroad, ...1,032 "
OGDEN to SAN FRANCISCO, Cal., via Central Pacific Railroad.. 881 "

Total, BOSTON to SAN FRANCISCO, ...3,445 Miles.

BUFFALO to CLEVELAND, TOLEDO AND CHICAGO, Via LAKE SHORE AND MICHIGAN SOUTHERN RAILWAY.

BUFFALO AND ERIE DIVISION.

MILES.	STATIONS.		MILES.
183	**BUFFALO**		0
173	Hamburgh		10
169	Lake View	4	14
162	Angola	7	21
157	Farnham	5	26
154	Irving	3	29
152	Silver Creek	2	31
143	**Dunkirk***	9	40

☞ Connects with the *Erie Railway.*

134	Brocton	9	49
126	WESTFIELD	8	57
118	Ripley	8	65
115	State Line	3	68
110	Northeast	5	73
103	Harbor Creek	7	80
95	**Erie***	8	88

☞ Connects with *Phila. & Erie R. R.*

87	Swanville	8	96
84	Fairview	3	99
80	GIRARD	4	103
75	Springfield	5	108
67	Conneaut	8	116
60	Kingsville	7	123
54	ASHTABULA	6	129
49	Saybrook	5	134
45	Geneva	4	138
42	Unionville	3	141
39	Madison	3	144
34	Perry	5	149
29	PAINESVILLE	5	154
18	Willoughby	11	165
14	Wickliffe	4	169
9	Euclid	5	174
0	**CLEVELAND**	9	183

☞ Connects with *Railroads,* and *Steamers* on Lake Erie.

TOLEDO DIVISION.

113	**CLEVELAND**		183
100	BEREA	13	196

MILES.	STATIONS.		MILES.
87	Elyria	13	209
79	Oberlin	8	217
69	Wakeman	10	227
57	Norwalk	12	239
53	MONROEVILLE	4	243
38	CLYDE	15	258
29	FREMONT	9	267
13	Genoa	16	283
0	**TOLEDO**	13	296

MICHIGAN SOUTHERN DIVISION.

244	**TOLEDO**		296
241	Junction	3	299
233	Sylvania	8	307
223	Riga	10	317
217	Palmyra Junction	6	323
211	**Adrian**	6	329
200	Clayton	11	340
194	Hudson	6	346
187	Pittsford	7	353
183	Osseo	4	357
178	Hillsdale	5	362
174	Jonesville	4	366
162	Quincy	12	378
155	COLD WATER	7	385
145	Bronson	10	395
138	Burr Oak	7	402
132	Sturgis	6	408
120	WHITE PIGEON	12	420
114	Middlebury	6	426
101	**Elkhart**	13	439
96	Osceola	5	444
86	South Bend	10	454
73	North Carlisle	13	467
59	LAPORTE	14	481
50	Holmesville	9	490
41	Chesterton	9	499
30	Miller's	11	510
23	Pine	7	517
12	Ainsworth	11	528
6	Englewood	6	534
0	**CHICAGO**	6	540

Cleveland, Columbus, Cincinnati & Indianapolis R. R.

MILES.	STATIONS.		MILES.
138	**CLEVELAND**		0
	Mahoning Bridge.		
125	Berea		13
122	Olmsted	3	16
119	Columbia	3	19
112	GRAFTON	6	25
108	La Grange	5	30
101	Wellington	7	37
96	Rochester	5	42
90	New London	6	48
83	Greenwich	7	55
77	Shiloh	6	61
71	SHELBY	6	67
67	Sharon Siding	4	71
62	**CRESTLINE***	5	76
58	Galion	4	80
52	Iberia	6	86
45	Gilead	7	93
41	Cardington	4	97
34	Ashley	7	104
30	Eden	4	108
24	**Delaware**	6	114

Springfield Branch, 50 Miles.

20	Berlin	4	118
16	Lewis Centre	4	122
14	Orange	2	124
11	Westerville	3	127
8	Worthington	3	130
0	**COLUMBUS**	8	138

Little Miami Railroad.

120	**COLUMBUS**		138
115	Alton	5	143
105	West Jefferson	10	153
100	Glade Run	5	158
95	LONDON	5	163
89	Florence	6	169
84	South Charleston	5	174

MILES.	STATIONS.		MILES.
79	Selma	5	179
73	Cedarville	6	185
69	Pierce's	4	189
65	**Xenia**	4	193
58	Spring Valley	7	200
56	Claysville	2	202
51	Corwin	5	207
45	Freeport	6	213
41	Fort Ancient	4	217
36	**Morrow**	5	222
31	South Lebanon	5	227
27	Foster's	4	231
23	LOVELAND	4	235
17	Miamiville	6	241
14	Milford	3	244
9	Plainville	5	249
3	Pendleton	6	255
0	**CINCINNATI**	3	258

INDIANAPOLIS DIVISION.

Cleveland, Columbus, Cincinnati & Indianapolis R. R.

282	**CLEVELAND**		0
257	GRAFTON		25
215	SHELBY	42	67
207	**Crestline***	8	75
202	Galion	5	80
195	Side Track	7	87
191	Caledonia	4	91
182	MARION	9	100
175	Gurleys	7	107
172	Cary's	3	110
168	La Rue	4	114
161	Mt. Victory	7	121
158	Ridgeway	3	124
151	Rushsylvania	7	131
148	Harper	3	134
142	BELLEFONTAINE	6	140
133	De Graff	9	149
130	Quincy	3	152
126	Pemberton	4	156

* Dining Stations.

MILES.	STATIONS.		MILES.
120	SIDNEY	6	162
110	Houston	10	172
106	Russia	4	176
102	Versailles	4	180
97	Johnson's Mills	5	185
94	Dallas	3	188
85	**Union***	9	197
81	Harrisville	4	201
75	Winchester	6	207
68	Farmland	7	214
64	Morristown	4	218
60	Selma	4	222
54	MUNCIE	6	228
48	Yorktown	6	234
43	Daleville	5	239
41	Chesterfield	2	241
36	Anderson	5	246
28	Pendleton	8	254
21	Fortville	7	261
16	McCord's	5	266
14	Oakland	2	268
10	Lawrence	4	272
0	**INDIANAPOLIS.**	10	282

NOTE.—This Railway now comprises the *Columbus Division*, 138 miles; the *Springfield Branch*, 50 miles, and the *Indianapolis Division*, 207 miles,— making a total of 395 miles, known as the "BEE LINE."

Indianapolis & St. Louis R. R.

MILES.	STATIONS.		MILES.
262	**INDIANAPOLIS.**		282
250	Avon	12	294
242	Danville	7	301
234	Reno	9	310
223	**Greencastle**	11	321
209	Carbon	14	335
198	Grant	11	346
190	**Terre Haute**	8	354
178	Vermillion	12	366
171	**Paris**	7	373
145	CHARLESTON*	26	399
140	Stockton	5	404
134	**Mattoon***	6	410
122	Windsor	12	422
95	PANA	27	449
83	NOKOMIS*	10	459
67	Hillsboro'	18	477
56	Litchfield	11	488
46	Gillespie	10	498
37	BUNKER HILL	9	507
28	Moro	9	516
22	ALTON JUNCTION	6	522

To **Alton**, 5 Miles.

| 1 | **East St. Louis** | 21 | 543 |
| 0 | **ST. LOUIS** | 1 | 544 |

☞ Connects with the *Atlantic and Pacific*, *Missouri Pacific*, and *North Missouri Railroads*.

THIS IMPORTANT LINE OF TRAVEL

Forms the most Direct Route to

COLUMBUS and CINCINNATI on the SOUTH,

AND TO

INDIANAPOLIS and ST. LOUIS in the SOUTHWEST,

Connecting with RAILROADS running to KANSAS, COLORADO, UTAH and CALIFORNIA.

TOLEDO TO QUINCY, ST. LOUIS AND KEOKUK, Via TOLEDO, WABASH AND WESTERN RAILROAD.

MILES.	STATIONS.		MILES.
476	**TOLEDO**		0
467	Maumee City		9
459	Whitehouse	8	17
448	Liberty	11	28
441	NAPOLEON	7	35
426	DEFIANCE	15	50
415	Emerald	11	61
405	Antwerp	10	71
388	New Haven	17	88
382	**Fort Wayne**	6	94

☞ Connects with *Pittsburgh, Fort Wayne and Chicago Railroad.*

367	Roanoke	15	109
358	Huntington	9	118
345	Lagro	13	131
340	WABASH	5	136
326	PERU	14	150
319	Waverly	7	157
310	LOGANSPORT	9	166
296	Rockfield	14	180
290	Delphi	6	186
281	Buck Creek	9	195
273	**Lafayette**	8	203
263	West Point	10	213
252	Attica	11	224
244	West Lebanon	8	232
234	State Line	10	242
226	DANVILLE	8	250
220	Catlin	6	256
213	Fairmount	7	263
206	Homer	7	270
190	TOLONO	16	286

Junction *Illinois Central Railroad.*

179	Norrie	11	297
173	Bement	6	303
164	Cerro Gordo	9	312
153	**Decatur***	11	323

ST. LOUIS DIVISION.

MILES.	STATIONS.		MILES.
109	**Decatur**		323
102	Boody	7	330
90	Stonington	12	342
82	Taylorville	8	350
74	Palmer's	8	358
69	Morrison	5	363
61	Raymond	8	371
49	Litchfield	12	383
42	Drummond	7	390
36	Staunton	6	396
19	Edwardsville	17	413
1	**East St. Louis**	18	431
0	**ST. LOUIS**	1	432

153	**Decatur**		323
128	Mechanicsburg	25	348
114	**Springfield**	14	362
112	C. and A. Junction	2	364
97	Berlin	15	379
91	Alexander	6	385
80	JACKSONVILLE	11	396
70	Chapin	10	406
62	BLUFF'S	8	414

☞ Connects with *Hannibal and Naples Branch*, 50 Miles.

56	MEREDOSIA	6	420
48	Versailles	8	428
39	Mt. Sterling	9	437
33	Mounds	6	443
28	CLAYTON	5	448

☞ Connects with *Keokuk Branch,* 42 Miles in length.

22	Camp Point	6	454
15	Paloma	7	461
9	Cliola	6	467
0	**QUINCY**	9	476

(*Mississippi River.*)

☞ Connects at Quincy and Hannibal, with *Han. & St. Joseph R. R.*

HANNIBAL AND QUINCY TO ST. JOSEPH AND KANSAS CITY, Via HANNIBAL AND ST. JOSEPH RAILROAD.

MILES.	STATIONS.		MILES.	MILES.	STATIONS.		MILES.
206	**QUINCY**		0	29	Osborn	6	177
204	West Quincy		2	21	Stewartsville	8	185
198	North River	6	8	12	Easton	9	194
191	PALMYRA JUNCTION*	7	15	6	Saxton	6	200
				0	**ST. JOSEPH**	6	206
206	**HANNIBAL**		0		(*Missouri River.*)		
196	Barkley		10				
191	PALMYRA Junction	5	15				

Connects at St. Joseph with all the Railroads running *South, North* and *West*,—running to *Missouri, Kansas, Indian Territory, Nebraska, Colorado, Wyoming, Utah, Nevada* and *California*.

MILES.	STATIONS.		MILES.	MILES.	STATIONS.		MILES.
191	PALMYRA Junction*			55	CAMERON Junction		171
176	Monroe	15	30	45	Turney	10	181
169	Hunnewell	7	37	39	LATHROP	6	187
164	Lakenan	5	42	32	Holt	7	194
159	Shelbina	5	47	25	Kearney	7	201
147	Clarence	12	59	20	Robertson	5	206
142	Round Grove	5	64	15	Liberty	5	211
139	Carbon	3	.67	7	Arnold	8	219
136	**Macon**	3	70	1	HARLEM	6	225
	Junction *North Missouri Railroad.*			0	**KANSAS CITY**	1	226

Connects with *Kansas Pacific Railroad,* and with *Kansas City, St. Joseph and Council Bluffs Railroad.*

MILES.	STATIONS.		MILES.
131	Bevier	5	75
127	Callao	4	79
120	New Cambria	7	86
112	Bucklin	8	94
106	St. Catherine	6	100
102	BROOKFIELD*	4	104
97	Laclede	5	109
90	Meadville	7	116
85	Wheeling	5	121
76	Chillicothe	9	130
71	Utica	5	135
66	Mooresville	5	140
61	Breckenridge	5	145
50	Hamilton	11	156
43	Kidder	7	163
35	CAMERON Junction*	8	171

THREE FAST EXPRESS TRAINS,

Crossing the Mississippi at Quincy, and the Missouri at Kansas City, on Iron Bridges,—running PALACE DAY COACHES, and PULLMAN'S SLEEPING PALACES from Chicago and Quincy to St. Joseph, Kansas City and Omaha—without change of Cars.

* Dining Stations.

CHICAGO to ST. LOUIS, Via CHICAGO, ALTON & ST. LOUIS R. R.

MILES.	STATIONS.		MILES.	MILES.	STATIONS.		MILES.
281	**CHICAGO**............		0	43	Shipman.....................	4	238
278	Bridgeport....................		3	38	Miles...........................	5	243
276	Brighton Course..........	2	5	36	Brighton	2	245
269	Summit.......................	7	12	30	Godfrey	6	251
263	Willow Springs............	6	18	24	**Alton**	6	257
256	Lemont.......................	7	25	20	Milton	4	261
249	Lockport.....................	7	32	17	Edwardsville Junction...	3	264
243	**Joliet**....................	6	38	12	Mitchell....	5	269
235	Elwood.......................	8	46	7	Kinder	5	274
232	Hampton.....................	3	49	5	Venice	2	276
228	Wilmington.................	4	53	1	**East St. Louis**.......	4	280
224	Braidwood	4	57	0	**ST. LOUIS**	1	281
220	Braceville...................	4	61				
215	Gardner.......................	5	66		**JACKSONVILLE DIVISION.**		
212	Grundy.......................	3	69		**CHICAGO**.............		0
207	Dwight	5	74	180	**Bloomington**........		126
199	Odell...........................	8	82	174	Covel.......................	6	132
194	Cayuga........................	5	87	168	Stanford....................	6	138
189	Pontiac.......................	5	92	157	Hopedale...................	11	149
178	Chenoa 11		103	149	Delavan	8	157
170	Lexington.....................	8	111	144	San Jose....................	5	162
163	Towanda......................	7	118	135	Mason City................	9	171
157	Normal.......................	6	124	127	Greenview	8	179
155	**Bloomington**	2	126	119	Petersburg	8	187
148	Shirley.......................	7	133	112	Tallula	7	194
140	McLean......................	8	141	106	Ashland	6	200
135	Atlanta.......................	5	146	91	**Jacksonville** 15		215
131	Lawn Dale..................	4	150	80	Murrayville................11		226
124	Lincoln......................	7	157	74	Manchester.................	6	232
117	Broadwell	7	164	70	Roodhouse.................	4	236
113	Elkhart	4	168	66	Whitehall	4	240
108	Williamsville..............	5	173	57	Carrollton	9	249
103	Sherman......................	5	178	49	Kane........................	8	257
96	**SPRINGFIELD**..	7	185	44	Jerseyville	5	262
94	Toledo, W. & W. Junc...	2	187	38	Delhi........................	6	268
87	Chatham......................	7	194	29	Godfrey.....................	9	277
81	Auburn.......................	6	200	23	Alton......................	6	283
75	Virden........................	6	206	0	**East St. Louis**.......23		306
71	Girard........................	4	210				
62	Anderson....................	9	219				
58	Carlinville...............	4	223				
52	Macoupin....................	6	229				
47	Plainview...................	5	234				

☞ Connects with the *Atlantic and Pacific, Missouri Pacific, North Missouri* and *Iron Mountain Railroads;* also, with Steamboats of the Memphis and St. Louis Packet Company

63

CHICAGO to QUINCY AND ST. JOSEPH, Mo.

Chicago, Burlington and Quincy Railway.

MILES.	STATIONS.		MILES.
263	**CHICAGO**		0
251	Riverside		12
245	Hinsdale	6	18
240	Downer's Grove	5	23
234	Naperville	6	29
225	AURORA	9	38
220	Oswego	5	43
217	Bristol	3	46
210	Plano	7	53
206	Sandwich	4	57
203	Somonauk	3	60
197	Leland	6	66
190	Earl	7	73
184	Meriden	6	79
179	**Mendota***	5	84

Crossing *Illinois Central Railroad.*

MILES.	STATIONS.		MILES.
171	Arlington	8	92
164	Malden	7	99
158	Princeton	6	105
150	Chicago, R. I., & P. Junc.	8	113
146	Buda	4	117
139	Neponset	7	124
131	Kewanee	8	132
123	GALVA	8	140
116	Altona	7	147
112	Oneida	4	151
107	Wataga	5	156
100	**Galesburg***	7	163

BURLINGTON DIVISION, 44 Miles.

90	Abingdon	10	173
84	St. Augustine	6	179
80	Avon	4	183
77	Prairie City	3	186
71	Bushnell	6	192
67	Bardolph	4	196
59	MACOMB	8	204

MILES.	STATIONS.		MILES.
53	Colchester	6	210
51	Tennessee	2	212
45	Colmar	6	218
40	PLYMOUTH	5	223
36	Augusta	4	227
29	La Prairie	7	234
27	Toledo, W. & W. Junc.	2	236
21	Camp Point	6	242
16	Coatsburg	5	247
13	Paloma	3	250
11	Fowler	2	252
9	Cliola	2	254
0	**QUINCY***	9	263

(*Mississippi River.*)

Hannibal & St. Joseph R. R.

206	**QUINCY**		263
191	**Palmyra,** Mo	15	278
176	Monroe	15	293
169	Hunnewell	7	300
159	Shelbina	10	310
147	Clarence	12	322
139	Carbon	8	330
136	**Macon***	3	333
131	Bevier	5	338
127	Callao	4	342
120	New Cambria	7	349
112	Bucklin	8	357
106	St. Catherine	6	363
102	BROOKFIELD*	4	367
97	Laclede	5	372
90	Meadville	7	379
85	Wheeling	5	384
76	CHILLICOTHE	9	393
71	Utica	5	398
61	Breckenridge	10	408
50	Hamilton	11	419
43	Kidder	7	426
35	CAMERON*	8	434

* Dining Stations.

MILES.	CAMERON and KANSAS CITY BRANCH. STATIONS.	MILES.
55	Cameron Junction	434
39	Lathrop	16 450
15	Liberty	24 474
1	HARLEM	14 488
0	**KANSAS CITY**	1 489

Junction *Kansas & Pacific Railroad.*

MILES.	STATIONS.		MILES.
35	Cameron Junction		434
29	**Osborn**	6	440
21	Stewartsville	8	448
12	Easton	9	457
6	Saxton	6	463
0	**ST. JOSEPH**	6	469

☞ Connects with *Kansas City, St. Joseph and Council Bluffs Railroad.*

CHIGAGO to BURLINGTON AND OMAHA.

C., B. & Q., and Bur. & Missouri Railroad.

503	**CHICAGO**		0
419	MENDOTA*		84
340	**Galesburg***	79	163
331	Cameron	9	172
324	MONMOUTH	7	179
318	Young America	6	185
311	Biggsville	7	192
306	Sagetown	5	197
297	Carthage Junction	9	206

(Mississippi River.)

| 296 | **BURLINGTON,** I. | 1 | 207 |

Bur. & Missouri River R. R.

296	**BURLINGTON**		207
287	Middletown	9	216
283	Danville	4	220
277	New London	6	226
268	Mt. Pleasant	9	235
261	Rome	7	242
254	Glendale	7	249
246	Fairfield	8	257
241	Whitfield	5	262
234	Batavia	7	269
227	Agency City	7	276
221	**Ottumwa**	6	282

Junction *North Missouri Railroad.*

213	Chillicothe	8	290
205	Frederic	8	298
196	ALBIA	9	307

188	Tyrone	8	315
182	Melrose	6	321
174	Russell	8	329
166	Chariton	8	337
158	Lucas	8	345
150	Woodburn	8	453
140	OSCEOLA	10	363
130	Murray	10	373
124	Thayer	6	379
116	Afton	8	387
106	CRESTON	10	397
101	Cromwell	5	402
92	Prescott	9	411
85	Corning	7	418
81	Brookville	4	422
76	Nodaway	5	427
71	Villisca	5	432
63	Stanton	8	440
55	RED OAK	8	448

Connects with *Nebraska City Branch.*

50	Hawthorn	5	453
46	Emerson	4	457
35	Milton	11	468
30	Loudon	5	473
25	Glenwood	5	478
21	**Pacific Junction.**	4	482

To PLATTSMOUTH, 4 Miles.

19	Pacific City	2	484
11	Trader's Point	8	492
5	**Council Bluffs**	6	498
2	Missouri River	3	501
0	**OMAHA**	2	503

CHICAGO to CAIRO & ST. LOUIS, Via ILLINOIS CENTRAL R. R.

CHICAGO DIVISION.

MILES.	STATIONS.		MILES.
365	**CHICAGO**............		0
359	Hyde Park...................		6
351	CALUMET...................	8	14
342	Thornton..................	9	23
337	MATTESON.................	5	28
336	Richton.	1	29
331	Monee....................	5	34
325	Peotone...................	6	40
319	Manteno...................	6	46
310	Kankakee..................	9	55
301	Chebanse.................	9	64
296	Clifton...................	5	69
288	Danforth..................	8	77
284	GILMAN	4	81
281	Onarga...................	3	84
278	Spring Creek..............	3	87
273	Bulkley..................	5	92
267	Loda..................	6	98
263	Paxton...................	4	102
257	Pera..................	6	108
252	Rantoul..................	5	113
247	Thomasboro'	5	118
238	CHAMPAIGN*.............	9	127
233	Savoy....................	5	132
228	TOLONO..................	5	137
224	Pesotum.................	4	141
216	Tuscola	8	149
208	Okaw..................	8	157
202	Milton..................	6	163
193	MATTOON.................	9	172
186	Ætna..................	7	179
181	Neoga	5	184
175	Sigel	6	190
166	**Effingham***..........	9	199
99	**Effingham**		199
95	Funkhouser...............	4	203
82	St. Elmo...................13		216
76	Brownstown.................	6	222
68	**Vandalia***	8	230

Crossing *Main Line Illinois Cen. R. R.*

MILES.	STATIONS.		MILES.
64	Hagarstown................	4	234
50	Greenville 14		248
40	Pocahontas...................10		258
36	Oakdale....................	4	262
31	Highland.................	5	267
18	Troy....................13		280
12	Collinsville.................	6	286
1	**East St. Louis** 11		297
0	**ST. LOUIS**.............	1	298
160	Watson..................	6	205
154	Mason................	6	211
151	EDGEWOOD.................	3	214
147	Laclede..................	4	218
143	Farina................	4	222
137	Kinmundy..................	6	228
132	Alma	5	233
127	Tonti..................	5	238
121	ODIN..................	6	244
115	Central City.............	6	250
113	**Centralia***	2	252
107	Irvington.................	6	258
100	Ashley.................	7	265
92	Dubois..................	8	273
86	Tamaroa.................	6	279
79	St. John's.................	7	286
77	**Du Quoin**.............	2	288
70	Elkville.................	7	295
64	De Soto.................	6	301
58	CARBONDALE.............	6	307
50	Makanda.................	8	315
43	Cobden.................	7	322
37	Jonesboro'	6	328
28	Dongola	9	337
25	Wetaug..................	3	340
21	Ullin..................	4	344
17	Pulaski.................	4	348
13	Villa Ridge..............	4	352
9	Mounds..	4	356
0	**CAIRO**.................	9	365

☞ Connects with Steamers on the Ohio and Mississippi Rivers.

5

CAIRO to DUBUQUE, Iowa, Via ILLINOIS CENTRAL RAILROAD, Connecting with STEAMERS on the OHIO and MISSISSIPPI RIVER.

MILES.	STATIONS.	MILES.	MILES.	STATIONS.	MILES.
456	**CAIRO**	0	190	El Paso......17	266
419	Jonesboro'	37		Junction *Toledo, Peoria & Warsaw Railroad.*	
399	Carbondale......20	57	168	Wenona......22	288
380	**Du Quoin**......19	76	147	La Salle......21	309
	Junction *Bellville & Illinois Southern Railroad.*			Junction *Chicago, Rock Island & Pacific Railroad.*	
358	Ashley......22	98	131	**Mendota**......16	325
343	**Centralia***......15	113		Junction *Chicago, Burlington and Quincy Railroad.*	
	Junction *Chicago Branch Illinois Central Railroad.*		115	Amboy......16	341
337	**Sandoval**...... 6	119	103	Dixon......12	353
	Junc. *Ohio and Mississippi Railroad.*			Junction *Chicago and Northwestern Railroad.*	
313	**Vandalia***......24	143	90	Polo......13	366
	Crossing *St. Louis, Vandalia & Indianapolis Railroad.*		67	**Freeport***......23	389
284	Pana...... 29	172		Junction *Chicago and Northwestern Railroad.*	
	Junction *Indianapolis & St. Louis Railroad.*		54	Lena......13	402
261	Macon......23	195	43	Warren......11	413
251	**Decatur**......10	205		Junction *Warren & Mineral Point Railroad.*	
	Junction *Toledo, Wabash & Western Railroad.*		29	Scales Mound......14	427
230	Clinton......21	226	17	Galena......12	439
207	**Bloomington***......23	249	1	Dunleith......16	455
	Junction *Indianapolis, Bloomington & Western Railroad.*		0	**DUBUQUE**...... 1	456

The Main Line of the **Illinois Central Railroad** connects at **Dubuque** with the Iowa Division, extending to Sioux City, 325 Miles; and with Steamers, running on the Upper Mississippi, to Prairie du Chien, La Crosse, Winona and St. Paul.

CHICAGO to DUBUQUE AND SIOUX CITY, Iowa.

Chicago & Northwestern R. R.

MILES.	STATIONS.		MILES.
188	**CHICAGO**		0
182	Austin		6
179	Harlem	3	9
178	Cottage Hill	1	10
172	Lombard	6	16
165	Danby	7	23
163	Wheaton	2	25
160	Winfield	3	28
158	JUNCTION	2	30
152	Wayne	6	36
149	Clintonville	3	39
146	ELGIN	3	42
138	Gilberts'	6	50
133	Huntley	5	55
125	Union	8	63
122	Marengo	3	66
116	Garden Prairie	6	72
110	Belvidere	6	78
104	Cherry Valley	6	84
95	**Rockford**	9	93
88	Winnebago	7	100
81	Pecatonica	7	107
74	Ridot	7	114
67	**Freeport**	7	121

Illinois Central Railroad.

MILES.	STATIONS.		MILES.
67	**Freeport**		121
59	Eleroy	8	129
54	Lena	5	134
47	Nora	7	141
43	WARREN	4	145
37	Apple River	6	151
29	Scales Mound	8	159
24	Council Hill	5	164
17	GALENA	7	171
8	Menominee	9	180
1	DUNLEITH	7	187

(*Mississippi River.*)

| 0 | **Dubuque** | 1 | 188 |

IOWA DIVISION.

MILES.	STATIONS.		MILES.
325	**DUBUQUE**		188
315	Julien	10	198
310	Peosta	5	203
302	Farley	8	211
295	Dyersville	7	218
288	Earlville	7	225
284	Delaware	4	229
278	Manchester	6	235
271	Masonville	7	242
264	Winthrop	7	249
255	Independence	9	258
247	Jesup	8	266
239	Raymond	8	274
232	WATERLOO	7	281
227	Junc. C. F. & Minn. Div.	5	286
226	CEDAR FALLS	1	287
216	New Hartford	10	297
208	Parkersburg	8	305
203	Aplington	5	310
193	Arckley	10	320
183	IOWA FALLS	10	330
176	Alden	7	337
168	Williams	8	345
163	Blairsburg	5	350
153	Webster City	10	360
145	Duncombe	8	368
134	**Fort Dodge**	11	379
116	Manson	18	397
108	Pomeroy	8	405
99	Marvin	9	414
91	Newell	8	422
81	Storm Lake	10	432
75	Alta	6	438
68	Aurelia	7	445
60	Cherokee	8	453
53	Hazard	7	460
43	Marcus	10	470
35	Remsen	8	478
25	Le Mars	10	488
0	**SIOUX CITY**	25	513

(*Missouri River.*)

CHICAGO to MADISON, Wis., PRAIRIE DU CHIEN, and ST. PAUL.

Chicago & Northwestern R. R.

WISCONSIN DIVISION.

MILES.	STATIONS.		MILES.
138	**CHICAGO**		0
126	Canfield		12
121	Des Plaines	5	17
116	Dunton	5	22
112	Palatine	4	26
106	Barrington	6	32
95	CRYSTAL LAKE	11	43
92	Ridgefield	3	46
87	Woodstock	5	51
75	HARVARD JUNCTION*	12	63
60	Caledonia	15	78
54	Roscoe	6	84
47	**Beloit**	7	91
40	Afton	7	98
34	Hanover	6	104
31	Footville	3	107
27	Magnolia	4	111
22	Evansville	5	116
10	Oregon	12	128
0	**MADISON**	10	138

Milwaukee & St. Paul R. R.

MILES.	STATIONS.		MILES.
313	**MADISON**		138
307	Middleton	6	144
299	Cross Plains	8	152
294	Black Earth	5	157
291	Mazomanie	3	160
284	Arena	7	167
277	Spring Green	7	174
270	Lone Rock	7	181
264	Avoca	6	187
258	MUSCODA	6	193
243	Boscobel	15	208
233	Wauzeka	10	218
226	Wright's Ferry	7	225

MILES.	STATIONS.		MILES.
223	Bridgeport	3	228
215	**Prairie du Chien**	8	236
	(Mississippi River.)		
215	**N. McGregor**		236
209	Giard	6	242
200	Monona	9	251
189	Postville	11	262
178	Ossian	11	273
172	Calmer	6	279
162	Ridgeway	10	289
153	CRESCO	9	298
142	Lime Springs	11	309
137	Chester	5	314
130	Le Roy	7	321
119	Adams	11	332
104	**Austin**	15	347
101	RAMSEY	3	350
98	Lansing	3	353
89	Blooming Prairie	9	262
80	Aurora	9	371
71	**Owatonna**	9	380
	Junction *Winona & St. Peter R. R.*		
65	Medford	6	386
56	FARIBAULT	9	395
45	Dundas	11	406
42	Northfield	3	409
36	Castle Rock	6	415
29	Farmington	7	422
22	Rosemount	7	429
9	St. Paul Junction	13	442
8	MENDOTA	1	443
5	Minne-ha-ha	3	446
0	**Minneapolis**	5	451
	ST. PAUL		448

☞ Connects with the *St. Paul and Pacific Railroad*, and *Lake Superior and Mississippi Railroad*. •

MILWAUKEE TO PRAIRIE DU CHIEN AND ST. PAUL.

Milwaukee and St. Paul R. R.

PRAIRIE DU CHIEN DIVISION.

MILES.	STATIONS.		MILES.
194	**MILWAUKEE**.....		0
189	Wauwatosa...................		5
184	Elm Grove............	5	10
180	Brookfield Junction......	4	14

☞ Connects with *La Crosse Div.*

177	Forest House.............	3	17
173	Waukesha..............	4	21
166	Genesee	7	28
163	North Prairie.....	3	31
152	Palmyra	11	42
143	WHITEWATER.............	9	51
138	Lima.......	5	56
132	MILTON.	6	62

☞ Connects with *Monroe Br. R. R.*

| 130 | Milton Junction............ | 2 | 64 |

Junction *Chicago and N. W. R. R.*

123	Edgerton.....	7	71
114	Stoughton	9	80
105	McFarland.	9	89
98	**MADISON**.............	7	96

☞ Connects with *Madison Division, Chicago and N. W. Railroad.*

92	Middleton..................	6	102
84	Cross Plains..............	8	110
79	Black Earth..............	5	115
76	Mazomanie.............	3	118
69	Arena	7	125
62	Spring Green............	7	132
55	Lone Rock	7	139
49	Avoca	6	145
43	MUSCODA.............	6	151
28	Boscobel....................	15	166
18	Wauzeka.................	10	176
11	Wright's Ferry............	7	183
8	Bridgeport	3	186

(*Mississippi River.*)

| 0 | **Prairie du Chien.** | 8 | 194 |

IOWA AND MINNESOTA DIVISION.

MILES.	STATIONS.		MILES.
212	**North McGregor**..		194
206	Giard...................	6	200
197	Monona....................	9	209
193	Luana....................	4	213
186	Postville...............	7	220
180	Castalia.................	6	226
175	Ossian.....................	5	231
169	Calmer.....................	6	237
166	Conover.	3	240
159	Ridgeway....................	7	247
150	CRESCO	9	256
139	Lime Springs..............	11	267
134	Chester	5	272
127	Le Roy....................	7	279
116	Adams...............	11	290
101	**Austin**...................15		305
98	RAMSEY	3	308

Junction *Southern Minnesota R. R.*

95	Lansing.	3	311
86	Blooming Prairie.........	9	320
77	Aurora...................	9	329
68	**Owatonna**.............	9	338

Junction *Winona and St. Peter R. R.*

62	Medford....................	6	344
53	FARIBAULT.............	9	353
42	Dundas.....................	11	364
39	Northfield................	3	367
33	Castle Rock	6	373
26	FARMINGTON...............	7	380
19	Rosemount...................	7	387
6	St. Paul Junction........13		400

	MENDOTA..	1	401
	Minne-ha-ha..............	3	404
	Minneapolis.........	5	409

| 0 | **ST. PAUL**............. | 6 | 406 |

☞ Connects with *St. Paul and Pacific,* and *Lake Superior and Mississippi Railroads.*

CINCINNATI TO INDIANAPOLIS AND CHICAGO.

Indianapolis, Cincinnati and Lafayette Railroad.

MILES.	STATIONS.		MILES.
179	**CINCINNATI**		0
176	Sedamsville		3
174	South Side	2	5
171	Trautman's	3	8
168	Delhi	3	11
164	NORTH BEND	4	15
163	Cleves	1	16
161	Valley Junction	2	18
159	Elizabethtown	2	20
154	**Lawrenceburg**	5	25
153	Newtown	1	26
146	Guilford	7	33
145	Hansell's	1	34
139	Harman's	6	40
137	Weisburg	2	42
136	Vanwedden's	1	43
128	MORRIS*	8	51
125	Batesville	3	54
119	New Point	6	60
115	McCoy's	4	64
111	GREENSBURG	4	68
105	Adam's	6	74
101	St. Paul	4	78
98	Waldron	3	81
95	Prescott	3	84
91	**Shelbyville**	4	88

Junction *Columbus Branch Railroad.*

84	FAIRLAND	7	95
80	London	4	99
79	Brookfield	1	100
77	Acton	2	102
73	Gallaudet	4	106
64	**INDIANAPOLIS**	9	115

☞ Connects with all the Railroads running from Indianapolis,—East, West, North and South.

MILES.	STATIONS.		MILES
54	AUGUSTA	10	125
49	Zionville	5	130
43	Whitestown	6	136
40	Holmes	3	139
36	LEBANON	4	143
31	Hazelrigg	5	148
26	Thorntown	5	153
21	Colfax	5	158
12	Stockwell	9	167
8	Culver's	4	171
1	Junction	7	178
0	**Lafayette**	1	179

Louisville, New Albany and Chicago Railroad.

NORTHERN DIVISION.

146	**Lafayette**		179
140	Battle Ground	6	185
133	Brookston	7	192
129	Chalmers	4	196
123	Reynolds	6	202
115	Bradford	8	210
107	Francisville	8	218
100	Medaryville	7	225
92	San Pierre	8	233
87	Kankakee	5	238
82	La Crosse	5	243
76	WANATAH	6	249
73	Haskell's	3	252
68	Westville	5	257
64	La Croix	4	261
63	Beatty's	1	262
56	**Michigan City**	7	269

☞ Connects with *Michigan Central Railroad.*

35	LAKE	21	290
14	Calumet	21	311
0	**CHICAGO**	14	325

PORTLAND, Me., TO MONTREAL, QUEBEC, TORONTO
AND DETROIT, Mich.

	Grand Trunk Railway.				MILES.	STATIONS.	MILES.
MILES.	STATIONS.	MILES.			54	Acton...............12	243
297	**PORTLAND**........	0			42	Britannia Mills............12	255
292	Falmouth..................	5			35	St. HYACINTHE......... 7	262
286	Yarmouth................ 6	11			22	St. Hilaire................13	275
285	Yarmouth Junction...... 1	12			15	St. Bruno............... 7	282
275	New Gloucester...........10	22			10	St. Hubert............... 5	287
270	Danville Junction......... 5	27			7	St. Lambert............... 3	290
256	Oxford...................14	41			0	**MONTREAL**........ 7	297
250	SOUTH PARIS.............. 6	47				(*St. Lawrence River.*)	
242	West Paris................ 8	55			333	**MONTREAL**........	297
232	Locke's Mills..............10	65			319	Pointe Claire............14	311
227	Bethel.................. 5	70			312	St. Anne's................. 7	318
217	Gilead...................10	80				(*Ottawa River.*)	
211	Shelburne................ 6	86			309	Vaudreuil................ 3	321
206	GORHAM.................. 5	91			296	Coteau Landing...........13	334
199	Berlin Falls............... 7	98			279	Lancaster................17	351
194	Milan.................. 5	103			266	CORNWALL.............13	364
175	Northumberland...........19	122			256	Dickinson's Landing.....10	374
167	Stratford................ 8	130			241	Morrisburg 15	389
155	Wenlock................12	142			234	Matilda............... 7	396
148	**Island Pond***........ 7	149			229	Edwardsburg............... 5	401
137	Norton Pond............11	160			221	**Prescott**.............. 8	409
122	Coaticooke, Can...........15	175				Junc. *St. Lawrence and Ottawa R. R.*	
114	Compton 8	183			213	Maitland................ 8	417
104	Lennoxville...............10	193			208	BROCKVILLE............... 5	422
101	SHERBROOKE.............. 3	196				Junc. *Brockville and Ottawa R. R.*	
86	Windsor 15	211			195	Malorytown..............13	435
76	RICHMOND...............10	221			178	Gananoque............17	452
					161	**Kingston**............17	469
97	RICHMOND..............	221			146	Ernestown...............15	484
85	Danville 12	233			136	Napanee...............11	495
72	Warwick...............13	246			120	Shannonville 15	510
65	ARTHABASKA............. 7	253			113	BELLEVILLE............... 7	517
56	Stanford 9	262			101	Trenton 12	529
50	Somerset.............. 6	268			92	Brighton............... 9	538
42	Becancour.............. 8	276			84	Colborne............... 8	546
21	Black River...........21	297			77	Grafton............... 7	553
1	**Point Levi**..........20	317			69	COBOURG.............. 8	561
0	**QUEBEC**.............. 1	318			63	Port Hope............... 6	567
					47	Newcastle...............16	583
76	RICHMOND..............	221					
66	New Durham...........10	231					

MILES.	STATIONS.		MILES.	MILES.	STATIONS.		MILES.
43	Bowmanville....................	4	587	134	St. Mary's...................	10	728
34	Oshawa.........................	9	596	124	Granton.....................	10	738
30	Port Whitby..............	4	600	118	Lucan.......................	6	774
21	Frenchman's Bay.........	9	609	112	Ailsa Craig.................	6	750
17	Port Union..................	4	613	104	Park Hill...................	8	758
11	Scarboro.....................	6	619	95	Widder......................	9	767
0	**TORONTO**...........	11	630	86	Forrest......................	9	776
				77	Camlachie..................	9	785
				64	**Sarnia**...................	13	798

Junction *Northern Railway* and *Hamilton Branch Railroad.*

Connects with Steamers on *St. Clair River* and *Lake Huron.*

MILES.	STATIONS.		MILES.	MILES.	STATIONS.		MILES.
232	**TORONTO**...........		630	62	**Port Huron,** Mich.	2	800
224	Weston.......................	8	638	41	Ridgeway...................	21	821
217	Malton......................	7	645	35	New Baltimore...........	6	827
211	Brampton...................	6	651	25	Mount Clemens...........	10	837
203	Georgetown	8	659	8	Milwaukee Junction......	17	854
197	Acton West.................	6	665	3	Detroit Junction...........	5	859
191	Rockwood...................	6	671	0	**DETROIT**...........	3	862
184	Guelph......................	7	678				
174	Breslau.......................	10	688				
170	Berlin........................	4	692				
163	Petersburgh.................	7	699				
157	Hamburgh..................	6	705				
150	Shakespeare................	7	712				
144	**Stratford**...............	6	718				

June. *Buffalo and Goderich Division.*

Connects with *Detroit and Milwaukee, Michigan Central,* and *Michigan Southern Railroad;* also with Steamers for *Chicago* and *Lake Superior.*

BUFFALO TO GODERICH, Canada.

MILES.	STATIONS.		MILES.	MILES.	STATIONS.		MILES.
160	**BUFFALO**...........		0	63	Bright.......................	5	97
158	Fort Erie.....................		2	53	Tavistock....................	10	107
151	Bertie	7	9	45	**Stratford**..............	8	115
141	Port Colborne..........	10	19		Crossing *Grand Trunk Railway.*		
128	Feeder......................	13	32	32	Mitchell		128
122	Dunnville..................	6	38	27	Carron Brook..............		133
114	Canfield....................	8	46	12	Clinton......................		147
101	Caledonia..................	13	59	0	**GODERICH**.........		160
84	Brantford.................	17	76				
76	**Paris**.....................	8	84		Connects with Steamers running on *Lake Huron.*		
68	Drumbo.....................	8	92				

ST. LOUIS TO ST. PAUL AND ST. ANTHONY FALLS,
Via MISSISSIPPI RIVER.

MILES.	LANDINGS, &C.		MILES.
460	**ST. LOUIS**		0
454	Venice, Ill.		6
448	Madison, Ill	6	12
440	Mouth Missouri River...	8	20
435	**Alton,** Ill	5	25
426	Portage des Sioux	9	34
417	Grafton, Ill	9	43
415	Mouth Illinois River	2	45
410	Milan, Ill	5	50
395	Cap au Gris, Mo	15	65
383	Sterling, "	12	77
378	Falmouth, "	5	82
374	Hamburg, Ill	4	86
358	CLARKVILLE, Mo	16	102
346	LOUISIANA "	12	114
324	Saverton "	22	136
316	**Hannibal** "	8	144

Junction *Han. & St. Joseph R. R.*

| 306 | Marion, Mo | 10 | 154 |
| 296 | **Quincy,** Ill | 10 | 164 |

Junction *Chicago, Burlington and Quincy Railroad,* and *Toledo, Wabash and Western Railroad.*

284	Langrange, Mo	12	176
274	CANTON, "	10	186
254	Alexandria, "	20	206
252	WARSAW, Ill	2	208
248	**Keokuk,** Iowa	4	212

Junc. *Des Moines Valley Railroad.*

| | HAMILTON, Ill | | 212 |

Junction *Toledo, W. and W. R. R.*

242	Sandusky, Iowa	6	218
236	Montrose, "	6	224
234	NAUVOO CITY, Ill	2	226

MILES.	LANDINGS, &C.		MILES.
226	**Fort Madison,** Ia..	8	231
220	Pontoosuc, Ill	6	240
218	Dallas City, "	2	242
205	**Burlington,** Iowa	13	255

Junction *Burlington & Missouri River Railroad.*

190	OQUAWKA, Ill	15	270
178	Keithsburg, "	12	282
172	NEW BOSTON, Ill	6	288
162	Port Louisa, Iowa	10	298
144	**Muscatine** "	18	316
135	Fairport, "	9	325
124	Buffalo, Ill	11	336
118	Rockingham, Iowa	6	342
113	**Rock Island,** Ill	5	347

Crossing *Chicago, Rock Island and Pacific Railroad.*

113	**Davenport,** Iowa		347
110	MOLINE, Ill	3	350
95	Le Claire, Iowa	15	365
	Port Byron, Ill		365
89	Princeton, Iowa	6	371
	Cordova, Ill		371
79	Camanche, Iowa	10	381
76	Albany, Ill	3	384
70	**Clinton,** Iowa	6	390

Cross. *Chicago, & Northwestern R. R.*

68	FULTON, Ill	2	392
	LYONS, Iowa		392
48	Sabula "	20	412
44	SAVANNA, Ill	4	416
20	Bellevue, Iowa	24	440
	Dunleith. Ill		
0	**DUBUQUE.** Iowa	20	460

Junction *Illinois Central Railroad.*

MILES.	LANDINGS, &C.	MILES.	MILES.	LANDINGS, &C.	MILES.
373	**DUBUQUE,** Iowa...	460	125	WABASHA, Minn..........10	708
358	Potisi, Wis..................15	475	119	Reed's Landing, Minn... 6	714
343	Buena Vista, Iowa.......15	490	117	Foot Lake Pepin......... 2	716
339	Cassville, Wis.................4	494	111	North Pepin, Wis....... 6	722
329	GUTTENBURG, Iowa......10	504	105	**Lake City,** Minn....... 6	728
317	Clayton, " 12	516	98	Maiden Rock, Wis........ 7	735
306	**McGregor,** Iowa......11	527	94	Frontenac, Minn.......... 4	739
			89	Head Lake Pepin......... 5	744
	Crossing *Milwaukee & St. Paul R. R.*		77	RED WING, Minn.........12	756
303	**Prairie du Chien.** 3	530	49	PRESCOTT, Wis............28	784
289	Lynxville, Wis............14	544		Mouth St. Croix River.	
273	LANSING, Iowa............16	560			
267	De Soto, Wis............. 6	566	48	Point Douglass, Minn... 1	785
257	Victory, " 10	576	45	**Hastings,** " ... 3	788
247	Bad Ax City..............10	586		Junction *Hastings and Dakota R. R.*	
231	BROWNSVILLE, Minn....16	602	39	Ninninger, Minn.......... 6	794
219	**La Crosse,** Wis......12	614	13	**ST. PAUL**..............26	820
	Junc. *Milwaukee & La Crosse R. R.*		8	MENDOTA................... 5	825
217	La Crescent, Minn........ 2	616	7	Fort Snelling............. 1	826
201	Richmond, " 16	632	5	Falls of Minne-ha-ha..... 2	828
196	Trempeleau, Wis......... 5	637	0	**MINNEAPOLIS**... 5	833
179	**Winona,** Minn........17	654			

Junction *Winona & St. Peter's R. R.*

MILES.	LANDINGS, &C.	MILES.
167	FOUNTAIN CITY, Wis....12	666
153	Mount Vernon, Minn....14	680
149	MINNEISKA " 4	684
135	Alma, Wis.......... 14	698

Falls of St. Anthony.

☞ The *Lake Superior and Mississippi Railroad* runs from St. Paul to Duluth, Minn., 155 Miles; and the *St. Paul and Pacific Railroad* runs to the Red River of the North, to connect with the *Northern Pacific Railroad.*

A Daily Line of Steamers, of a large class, run from St. Louis to Dubuque and St. Paul, affording a most delightful Summer Excursion.

RAILROADS IN THE UNITED STATES AND CANADA,

FINISHED AND IN PROGRESS OF CONSTRUCTION.

NAME.	FROM	TO	MILES.
ADIRONDACK, N. Y.	Saratoga Springs	North River	60
ALABAMA AND CHATTANOOGA	Chattanooga, Tenn	Green Pond	169
Southern Division*	Meridian, Miss	Black Warrior	67
Albany and Susquehanna.	Albany, N. Y.	Binghamton	142
Alexandria and Fredericksburg*	Alexandria, Va	Fredericksburg	40
Alexandria and Washington	Alexandria, Va	Washington	7
Alleghany Valley	Oil City, Pa	Pittsburgh	131
Androscoggin	Brunswick, Me	Farmington	63
Arkansas Central*	Helena, Ark	Little Rock	100
Ashuelot	Keene, N. H	South Vernon	23
Atchison, Topeka and Santa Fé*	Atchison, Kan	Emporia	61
Atlanta and Richmond*	Atlanta, Geo	Charlotte, N. C	250
Atlanta and West Point.	Atlanta, Geo	West Point	87
Atlantic and Great Western	Salamanca, N. Y	Cincinnati, O	446
" " " "	Meadville, Pa	Cleveland, O	112
ATLANTIC AND GULF	Savannah, Geo	Bainbridge	236
Florida Branch	Lawton, "	Quincy, Fla	156
Atlantic and North Carolina	Goldsboro, N. C	Morehead City	95
ATLANTIC AND PACIFIC	St. Louis, Mo	State Line	330
Van Buren Branch*	Pierce City "	Van Buren, Ark	125
Augusta and Savannah	Augusta, Geo	Millen	58
Avon, Genesee and Mt. Morris	Avon, N. Y	Mt. Morris	16
BALTIMORE AND OHIO	Baltimore, Md	Wheeling, W. Va	379
Washington Branch	Relay House	Washington, D. C.	31
Annapolis Branch	Annapolis Junction	Annapolis	21
Frederick Branch	Monocacy Station	Frederick	3
Metropolitan Branch*	Point of Rocks, Md	Washington, D. C.	
Washington County	Hagerstown, Md	Hagerstown Junc.	25
Winchester and Potomac	Harper's Ferry	Strasburg, Va	51
Connellsville Branch	Cumberland, Md	Pittsburgh, Pa	150
Parkersburg Branch	Grafton, W. Va	Parkersburg	104
Central Ohio Division	Bellaire, Ohio	Columbus	137
Lake Erie Division	Newark, "	Sandusky	116
Baltimore and Potomac*	Baltimore, Md	Potomac River	72
Bangor and Piscataquis	Oldtown, Me	Dover	40
Barclay and Coal Company	Towanda, Pa	Barclay	16
Baring and Lewy's Island	Baring, Me	Lewy's Island	17
Baton Rouge and Opelousas	Baton Rouge, La	Lombard	28
Belfast and Moosehead	Belfast, Me	Burnham	33
Belvidere Delaware	Trenton, N. J	Manunka Chunk	68
Bennington and Rutland	Rutland, Vt	Chat. 4 Cor'ns	114

* Unfinished Railroads.

NAME.	FROM	TO	MILES.
Blossburg and Corning	Corning, N. Y	Fall Brook	48
Blue Ridge	Anderson, S. C...:	Walhalla	33
BOSTON AND ALBANY	Boston, Mass	Albany, N. Y	200
Brookline Branch	Boston, "	Brookline	4
Newton Branch	West Newton	Newton	3
Saxonville Branch	Natick	Saxonville	5
Milford Branch	Framingham	Milford	12
Millbury Branch	Grafton	Millbury	4
Grand Junction	Brighton	East Boston	9
Boston, Concord and Montreal	Concord, N. H	Littleton	113
Boston, Clinton and Fitchburg	South Framingham	Fitchburgh	37
BOSTON, HARTFORD AND ERIE	Boston, Mass	South Bridge	70
Woonsocket Division	Boston, "	Woonsocket, R. I	38
Norwich and Worcester Division	New London, Conn	Worcester	73
Western Division	Moore's Mills, Conn	Fishkill L'g, N. Y.	
BOSTON AND LOWELL	Boston	Nashua, N. H	40
Woburn Branch	"	Woburn Cen	10
Lowell and Lawrence	Lowell	Lawrence	13
Stoneham Branch	Boston	Stoneham	12
Stony Brook	Nashua	Wilton	15
Salem and Lowell	Lowell	Salem	24
BOSTON AND PROVIDENCE	Boston, Mass	Providence, R. I	44
Dedham Branch	" "	Dedham	10
Stoughton	" "	Stoughton	18
Mill Village Branch	Dedham	Mill Village	
BOSTON AND MAINE	Boston	Portland, Me	111
Reading Branch	Boston	South Reading	
Medford Branch	Boston	Medford	5
Great Falls Branch	Rollingsford, N. H	Great Falls	3
Brooklyn, Bath and Coney Island	Brooklyn, N. Y	Coney Island	8
Brockville and Ottawa	Brockville, Can	Sand Point	75
Perth Branch	Smith's Falls	Perth	10
Brunswick and Albany	Brunswick, Geo	Willicoochie	100
Buffalo and Washington	Buffalo, N. Y	East Aurora	17
Buffalo, Corry and Pittsburgh	Brocton, "	Corry, Pa	43
Buffalo, Bayou, Brazos and Col*	Harrisburg, Texas	Austin	200
BURLINGTON AND MISSOURI RIVER	Burlington, Iowa	Omaha, Neb	296
" " " "	Plattsmouth	Lincoln, Neb	55
Nebraska City Branch	Red Oak, Iowa	East Nebraska	50
Burlington, Cedar Rapids and Minn.	Burlington, Iowa	Mankato, Minn	330
Burlingtown and Keokuk, Iowa	" "	Keokuk	43
Cairo and Fulton*	Cairo	Fulton, Ark	
Calais and Baring	Calais, Me	Baring	6
California and Oregon	Sacramento	Tehama, Cal	122
California Pacific	Vallejo, Cal	Sacramento	69
Marysville Branch	Davis Junction	Marysville	43

* Unfinished Railroads.

NAME.	FROM	TO	MILES.
CAMDEN AND AMBOY	South Amboy	Camden, N. J	62
" " "	New Brunswick	Trenton	26
Trenton Branch	Trenton, N. J	Bordentown	6
Burlington and Mount Holly	Burlington, N. J	Mt. Holly	7
Pemberton and Heightstown	Camden	Heightstown	50
Vincentown Branch	Vincentown	Mount Holly	3
Freehold and Jamesburg	Monmouth Junction	Farmingdale	
Camden and Atlantic	Cooper's Point	Atlantic, N. J	61
Canada Central	Ottawa	Carleton Place	29
Cape Cod	Middleboro, Mass	Orleans	94
Cape May and Millville	Millville	Cape May	44
Carrollton and Oneida	Carrollton	Oneida	12½
Catasauqua and Fogellsville	Catasauqua, Pa	Alburtis	
Catawissa, Pa	Williamsport	Tamaqua	99
Central Georgia	Savannah	Macon	190
Milledgeville and Eatonton Br	Gordon	Eatonton	28
Central Iowa*	Mason City	Mo. State Line	240
Central of New Jersey	New York	Harrisburg, Pa	182
South Branch	Somerville	Flemington	
Central Ohio	Bellaire, Ohio	Columbus	137
Central Branch Union Pacific	Atchison, Kan	Waterville	100
CENTRAL PACIFIC	Ogden, Utah	San Francisco	881
Alameda Branch	San Francisco	Haywards	
Oakland Branch	Oakland, Cal	Brooklyn	
San Jose Branch	San Francisco	San Jose	47
Visalia Branch	Lathrop, Cal	Modesto	20
Central Texas*			
Charleston and Savannah	Charleston, S. C	Coosawatchie	62
Charlotte, Columbia and Augusta	Charlotte, N. C	Augusta, Geo	195
Cheraw and Darlington	Cheraw, S. C	Florence	
CHESAPEAKE AND OHIO	Richmond, Va	White Sulphur Sps	227
Cheshire	Fitchburg, Mass	Bellows Falls	64
Chester Valley	Bridgeport, Pa	Downingtown	22
CHICAGO AND ALTON	Chicago	East St. Louis	280
Jacksonville Division	Bloomington	Monticello, Junc	151
CHICAGO, BURLINGTON AND QUINCY	Chicago, Ill	Quincy	263
Burlington Branch	Galesburg	Burlington	43
Peoria "	"	Peoria	53
Rushville "	Buda	Rushville	110
Batavia and Galena	Aurora	Galena Junction	
Galva and New Boston	Galva	New Boston	51
Chicago, Cincinnati and Louisville	Laporte, Ind	Peru	73
Chicago, Danville and Vincennes	Chicago, Ill	Momence	53
Chicago and Michigan Lake Shore	New Buffalo, Mich	Kal. & S. H. Junc.	61
CHICAGO AND NORTHWESTERN	Chicago, "	Green Bay, Wis	242
Milwaukee Division	"	Milwaukee	84
Peninsula Division	Escanaba, Mich	Negaunee	63
Madison Division	Chicago	Madison, Wis	138

NAME.	FROM	TO	MILES.
Kenosha Division	Kenosha	Rockford	72
Fox River Valley	Elgin	Richmond	33
Galena Division	Chicago	Freeport	121
" "	Junction	Clinton, Iowa	138
Iowa Division, (East)	Clinton	Boone, "	202
" " (West)	Boone	Missouri River	151
CHICAGO, ROCK ISLAND AND PACIFIC	Chicago, Ill	Rock Island	182
Iowa Division, (East)	Davenport, Iowa	Mitchelville	158
" " (West)	Mitchelville	Missouri River	153
Peoria Branch	Bureau, Ill	Peoria	47
Oskalossa Branch	Wilton, Iowa	Washington	49
Chicago and St. Paul*	St. Paul	Winona, Minn	105
Chicago and South Western*	Davenport, Iowa	Leavenworth	
Cinn., Cumber'd Gap and Charleston	Morristown, Tenn	Wolf Creek	40
CINN., SANDUSKY AND CLEVELAND	Sandusky, Ohio	Cincinnati	215
Findlay Branch	Carey	Findlay	16
London "	Springfield	London	20
CINCINNATI, HAMILTON AND DAYTON			
Dayton and Michigan	Cincinnati, Ohio	Detroit, Mich	267
Cincinnati and Indianapolis	" "	Indianapolis	124
Junction Railway	Connersville	Muncey	43
Cincinnati, Richmond and Chicago	Hamilton, Ohio	Chicago	294
Cincinnati and Muskingum Valley	Cincinnati	Zanesville	168
CLEVELAND, COLUMBUS, CINCINNATI AND			
INDIANAPOLIS	Cleveland, Ohio	Columbus	138
Indianapolis Division	Crestline	Indianapolis	207
Springfield Branch	Columbus	Springfield	50
Cleveland and Pittsburgh	Cleveland, Ohio	Pittsburgh, Pa	150
Tuscarawas Branch	Bayard	New Philadelphia	32
Cleveland, Mt. Vernon and Delaware	Cleveland, Ohio	Millersburg	87
Cobourg and Peterboro, Canada	Cobourg	Peterboro	29
Colebrookdale, Pa	Pottstown	Boyerstown	8½
Colorado Central	Denver, Col	Golden City	16
Columbus and Hocking Valley	Columbus, Ohio	Nelsonville	62
Concord, Claremont and Contoocook	Concord, N. H	Bradford	27
Contoocook River Branch	Contoocook	Hillsboro Bridge	15
Concord, N. H	Nashua	Concord	35
Concord and Portsmouth	Concord, N. H	Portsmouth	59
Connecticut River	Springfield, Mass	Brattleboro, Vt	60
Chicopee Falls Branch	" "	Chicopee Falls	5½
Connecticut and Passumpsic Rivers	North Derby, Vt	White River Junc.	110
Cooperstown and Susquehanna	Junction	Cooperstown, N. Y.	16
Cumberland and Pennsylvania	Cumberland	Piedmont	34
Cumberland Valley	Harrisburg, Pa	Hagerstown, Md	74
Danbury and Norwalk	Norwalk, Conn	Danbury	23
Danville, Urbana and Pekin	Danville, Ill	Pekin	117
Dayton and Union	Dayton, Ohio	Union	47
Dayton, Xenia and Western	Xenia, "	Richmond	57

NAME.	FROM	TO	MILES.
Delaware	Wilmington	Crisfield†	135
Smyrna Branch	Clayton	Smyrna	1½
Delaware and Hudson	Scranton, Pa	Carbondale	17
DELAWARE, LACKAWANNA & WESTERN	New York	Great Bend	196
Lackawanna and Bloomsburg Div.	Scranton, Pa	Northumberland	80
Cayuga Division	Oswego, N. Y	Ithaca	33
Denver Pacific	Denver, Col	Cheyenne	106
Denver and Rio Grande*	Denver, "	Colorado City	80
Denver and Santa Fé*	Denver, "	Santa Fé	430
Des Moines Valley	Keokuk, Iowa	Grand Junction	211
Detroit and Milwaukee	Detroit, Mich	Grand Haven	189
Dexter and Newport	Dexter, Me	Newport	14
Dorchester and Delaware	Cambridge	Seaford, Md	33
Dover and Winnipissiogee	Dover, N. H	Alton Bay	28
Dubuque and Southwestern	Dubuque, Iowa	Cedar Rapids	79
DUBUQUE AND SIOUX CITY	Dubuque, "	Sioux City	325
East Pennsylvania	Allentown	Reading	36
East Tennessee and Georgia	Chattanooga, Tenn	Knoxville	110
Dalton Branch	Cleveland	Dalton	
East Tennessee and Virginia	Knoxville, Tenn	Bristol, Va	130
EASTERN	Boston, Mass	Portsmouth, N. H.	56
Marblehead Branch	Salem	Marblehead	4
Lawrence Branch	Salem	Lawrence	21
Saugus Branch	South Malden	Lynn	6
South Reading Branch	Salem	Lynnfield	
Gloucester Branch	Beverly	Rockport	20
Amesbury Branch	Salisbury	Amesbury	5
Eastern Kentucky	Hunnewell	Riverton	13
Eastern Shore	Delmar, Del	Crisfield	38
Edgefield and Kentucky	Nashville	Guthrie	47
ERIE, New York	New York	Dunkirk	460
Buffalo Division	Elmira	Buffalo	142
Rochester Division	Corning	Rochester	94
Northwestern Division	Hornellsville	Buffalo	91
Mahoning Division	Cleveland	Youngstown	65
Newburgh Branch	Greenwood	Newburgh	19
Newark Branch	Paterson	Newark	11
Warwick Branch	Greycourt	Warwick	10
Montgomery Branch	Goshen	Guilford	23
Unionville Branch	Middletown	Unionville	14
Honesdale Branch	Lackawaxen	Honesdale	25
Bradford Branch	Carrollton	Gilesville	26
Erie and Pittsburgh	Erie, Pa	Pittsburgh	148
European and North American, Can.	St. John, New B	P'nt du Chene‡	108
Western Division	St. John, "	Maine State Line	88
European and North American*	Bangor, Me	Mattawamkeag	58

† Connects with Steamers for Charlottetown and Quebec.
‡ Connects with Steamers running to Norfolk Va.

NAME.	FROM	TO	MILES.
Evansville and Crawfordsville	Evansville, Ind	Rockville	132
Evansville, Henderson and Nashv'le.	Evansville, "	Madisonville	51
" " "	Guthrie, Ken	Hopkinsville	26
Evansville, Terre Haute and Chicago.	Terre Haute, Ind	Dansville, Ill	55
Fairhaven, Mass	New Bedford	Hyannis	
FITCHBURG, Mass	Boston	Fitchburg	50
Watertown Branch	Boston	Waltham	10½
Marlboro' Branch	South Acton	Marlboro'	13
Peterboro' and Shirley	Groton Junction	Mason Village	23
Fitchburg and Worcester	Fitchburg, Mass	Worcester	26
Flemington	Flemington, N. J	Lambertville	12
Flint and Pere Marquette*	Holly, Mich	Averill's	77
Bay City Branch	East Saginaw	Bay City	13
Florida	Fernandina	Florida Keys	154
Florida, Atlantic and Gulf	Junction	Jacksonville	138
Flushing and North Side	Hunter's Point, L. I.	Bayside	
Fort Wayne, Jackson and Saginaw	Fort Wayne	Jackson	100
Fort Wayne, Muncie and Cincinnati.	Connersville	Fort Wayne	109
Galveston, Houston and Henderson	Galveston, Texas	Houston	50
GEORGIA	Augusta	Atlanta	171
Athens Branch	Union Point	Athens	40
Augusta and Milledgeville	Camak	Milledgeville	
Washington Branch	Barnett	Washington	18
Grand Rapids and Indiana*	Fort Wayne	Paris, Mich	202
Grand River Valley	Jackson, Mich	Hastings	62
GRAND TRUNK, Canada	Montreal	Portland, Me	297
Quebec Division	Richmond	Point Levi	96
Riviere du Loup Branch	Point Levi	Riviere du Loup	125
Arthabaska Branch	Arthabaska	Three Rivers	35
Montreal and Champlain	Montreal	Rouses P't, N. Y	49
Montreal, Lachine & Province Line.	Montreal	Province Line	40
Montreal to Toronto	Montreal	Toronto	333
Toronto to Sarnia	Toronto	Point Edward	168
Sarnia to Detroit	Fort Gratiot, Mich	Detroit	73
Buffalo to Goderich	Buffalo, N. Y	Goderich, Can	160
GREAT WESTERN, Canada	Suspension Bridge	Detroit, Mich	230
Erie and Niagara Line	Fort Erie, Can	Niagara	31
Toronto Branch	Hamilton, "	Toronto	39
Guelph Branch	Harrisonburg	Guelph	28
Sarnia Branch	London	Sarnia	61
Petrolia Branch	Petrolia	Wyoming	6
GREENVILLE AND COLUMBIA	Greenville, S. C	Columbia	144
Abbeville Branch	Cokesbury	Abbeville	12
Anderson Branch	Belton	Andersonville	9
HANNIBAL AND ST. JOSEPH	Hannibal, Mo	St. Joseph	206
Quincy Branch	Quincy	Palmyra, Mo	15
Kansas City Branch	Cameron	Kansas City	55
Hannibal and Naples	Bluffs, Ill	Hannibal	50

NAME.	FROM	TO	MILES.
Hannibal and Moberly	Hannibal, Mo	Moberly	70
Hanover Branch and Gettysburg	Hanover Junction	Gettysburg, Pa	30
Hartford, Providence & Waterbury	Providence, R. I	Waterbury	123
Hastings and Dakota*	Hastings, Minn	Lakeville	30
Hempfield	Wheeling, Va	Washington, Pa	35
Housatonic	Bridgeport, Conn	Pittsfield, Mass	110
State Line Branch	Van Deusenville	N. Y. State Line	15
Houston-Tap and Brazoria	Houston, Tex	Columbia	50
Houston and Texas Central	Houston, "	Calvert	130
Hudson River	New York	Troy	150
Hudson and Boston	Hudson, N. Y	Chatham	17
Hunnewell	Greenupsburgh	Cannell Mines	14
Huntingdon and Broad Top	Huntingdon	Mt. Dallas	44
Broad Top City Branch	Saxton	Dudley	
Illinois Central	Dunleith	Cairo	456
Chicago Branch	Chicago	Centralia	253
Iowa Division	Dubuque, Iowa	Sioux City	326
Cedar Falls and Minnesota	Cedar Falls, Iowa	Mona	75
Indianapolis, Bloomington & Western	Indianapolis	Peoria, Ill	212
Indianapolis, Cinn. and Lafayette	Cincinnati	Lafayette	179
Martinsville Division	Fairfield	Martinsville	
White Water Valley Division	Cincinnati	Hagerstown	88
Indianapolis and Vincennes	Indianapolis, Ind	Vincennes	116
Indianapolis, Peru and Chicago	Indianapolis, "	Peru	75
Indianapolis and St. Louis	Indianapolis, "	St. Louis	262
Ionia and Lansing	Ionia, Mich	Lansing	37
Iowa Falls and Sioux City	Iowa Falls		
Iron, Ohio	Ironton	Centre	13
Jamestown and Franklin	Jamestown	Oil City	50
Jackson, Lansing and Saginaw	Jackson, Mich	Wenona	116
Jeffersonville, Mad. & Indianapolis	Jeffersonville	Indianapolis	108
Madison Branch	Columbus	Madison	45
Jeffersonville and New Albany	Jeffersonville, Ind	New Albany	
Junction and Breakwater	Lewes, Del	Harrington	40
Kalamazoo and Grand Rapids	Kalamazoo, Mich	Grand Rapids	58
Kalamazoo and South Haven	Kalamazoo, "	South Haven	
Kansas City, St. Joseph & C. Bluffs	Kansas City, Mo	Council Bluffs	200
Kansas and Neosho Valley*			
Kansas City & Santa Fé Division	Kansas City	Ottawa, Kan	53
Kansas Pacific	Kansas "	Dener, Col	638
Leavenworth Branch	Junction	Leavenworth	31
Kentucky Central	Covington	Nicholasville	112
Kentucky Improvement	Greenupsburgh	Coal Mines	15
Keokuk, Iowa City and Minnesota	Keokuk		
Keokuk and St. Paul	Keokuk	Burlington	44
King's Mountain	Chester, S. C	Yorkville	22
Kingston and Rocky Hill, N. J	Monmouth Junction	Rocky Hill	
Knoxville and Charleston	Knoxville, Tenn	Maryville	16

NAME.	FROM	TO	MILES.
Knoxville and Kentucky..................	Knoxville..............		
LAKE SHORE AND MICHIGAN SOUTHERN.			
Buffalo and Erie Division..............	Buffalo, N. Y...........	Cleveland, O.........	183
Toledo Division..............	Cleveland	Toledo	113
Michigan Southern Division........	Toledo	Chicago.....	243
Detroit Division........	Toledo	Detroit, Mich........	64
Monroe Branch........	Monroe........	Adrian.................	32
Jackson Branch............	Adrian........	Jackson.................	45
Kalamazoo Division...................	White Pigeon............	Grand Rapids.......	
Lake Erie and Louisville................	Fremont, Ohio..........	Findlay..............	37
LAKE SUPERIOR AND MISSISSIPPI........	Duluth, Minn...........	St. Paul.............	155
Minneapolis Branch....................	White Bear Lake.......	Minneapolis........	14
Stillwater Branch....................	" " "	Stillwater............	13
Laurel Fork and Sand Hill..............	Volcano, W. Va.........	Laurel Junction...	
Leavenworth, Lawrence & Galveston.	Lawrence, Kan.........	Thayer.................	94
Lebanon Valley, Pa...................	Reading......	Harrisburg..........	54
Lehigh and Susquehanna..............	Green Ridge.............	Easton, Pa...........	120
Lehigh Valley & Penn. & N. Y. Canal.	Easton, Pa..............	Waverly Junction.	206
Mahonoy and Hazleton Branches..	Easton, "	Mt. Carmel..........	100
Lexington and Arlington.....	Boston, Mass...........	Lexington...........	11
Lexington and Big Sandy..............	Bellefont, Ky...........	Buena Vista.......	10
Little Miami, Ohio...................	Columbus	Cincinnati..........	120
Little Rock and Fort Smith*..........	Little Rock, Ark.......	Fort Smith..........	160
Little Schuylkill...................	Port Clinton, Pa........	Tamaqua..........	20
London and Port Stanley..	London, Can...........	Port Stanley........	24
Long Branch and Sea Shore..........	Sandy Hook, N. J......	Long Branch........	11
Long Island, N. Y...................	Hunter's Point..........	Greenport	94
Sag Harbor Branch........	Manor, L. I.............	Sag Harbor..........	35
Louisville, Cincinnati and Lexington.	Louisville, Ky.........	Covington............	107
Lexington Branch...................	Junction	Lexington	66
LOUISVILLE, N. ALBANY AND CHICAGO...	New Albany, Ind......	Mich. City, Ind.....	288
Louisville, New Albany & St. Louis*.	Louisville................	St. Louis..............	250
LOUISVILLE AND NASHVILLE..............	Louisville, Ky..........	Nashville	185
Bardstown Branch...................	Bardstown Junction...	Bardstown..........	17
Knoxville Branch........	Bardstown "	..Mt. Vernon.......	107
Richmond Branch...................	Richmond "	..Richmond...........	34
Macon and Brunswick................	Macon, Geo.............	Hawkinsville........	50
Macon and Western..................	Macon, "	Atlanta	103
Mahanoy and Little Schuylkill........	Herndon, Pa.............	Tamaqua.............	62
Maine Central......	Portland	Bangor..............	138
Manchester and Lawrence............	Manchester, N. H......	Lawrence	20
Manchester and North Weare..........	Manchester, "	North Weare........	19
MARIETTA AND CINCINNATI...............	Cincinnati, O............	Marietta.............	199
Hillsboro' Branch...................	Blanchester	Hillsboro'...........	
Portsmouth Branch...................	Hamden.	Portsmouth..........	
Marquette and Ontonagon..............	Marquette, Mich.......	Champion............	32
Maryland and Delaware..............	Clayton, Del............	Hillsboro'...........	
Massawippi Valley....................	North Derby, Vt........	Lenoxville, Can....	

NAME.	FROM	TO	MILES.
Mauch Chunk and Summit Hill	Mt. Pisgah, Pa	Summit Hill	9
McGregor and Missouri River	McGregor, Iowa	Mason City	130
McMinville and Manchester	McMinville, Tenn	Tullahoma	34
MEMPHIS AND LOUISVILLE	Louisville, Ky	Memphis, Tenn	377
Memphis and Little Rock	Huntersville, Ark	Duvall's Bluff	40
Memphis, El Paso and Pacific*	Memphis	San Diego, Cal	
MEMPHIS AND CHARLESTOWN	Memphis, Tenn	Chattanooga	309
Florence Branch	Tuscumbia	South Florence	
MICHIGAN CENTRAL	Detroit, Mich	Chicago, Ill	284
Middleburgh and Schoharie	Middleburgh, N. Y	Central Bridge	
Middleboro' and Taunton	Middleboro', Mass	Taunton	10½
Mill Creek and Mt. Carbon	Pottsville, Pa	Trackville	
Millstone and New Brunswick	Millstone, N. J	New Brunswick	
MILWAUKEE AND ST. PAUL	Milwaukee, Wis	Prairie du Chien	194
Iowa and Minnesota Division	N. McGregor, Iowa	St. Paul, Minn	212
La Crosse Division	Milwaukee, Wis	La Crosse	195
Northern Division	Milwaukee "	Portage City	96
" "	Watertown	Sun Prairie	26
" "	Horicon	Winneconne	58
Madison Line	Junction	Madison	42
Monroe Line	Milton Junction	Monroe	43
Mine Hill and Schuylkill Haven	Schuylkill Haven	Trevorton	28
Mineral Point	Warren, Ill	Mineral Point, Wis.	32
MISSISSIPPI CENTRAL	Humboldt, Tenn	Canton, Miss	253
Mississippi, Gainesville & Tuscaloosa	Gainesville, Ala	Gainesville Junc	22
Mississippi and Tennessee	Memphis, Tenn	Grenada	100
Missouri, Kansas and Texas*	Junction City	Chetopa	178
Missouri River, Fort Scott and Gulf*	Kansas City	Fontana	55
Missouri Valley	Harlem, Mo	Savannah	84
Mobile and Girard	Columbus, Ga	Troy	84
MOBILE AND OHIO†	Mobile, Ala	Columbus, Ky	472
Columbus Branch	Artesia	Columbus, Miss.	13
Mobile and Montgomery	Montgomery, Ala	Mobile	186
Montclair, N. J	Jersey City	Greenwood Lake	
Montgomery and Decatur	Montgomery		
Montgomery and West Point	Montgomery	West Point	88
Columbus Branch	Opelika	Columbus, Ga	28
Montgomery and Eufala	Montgomery	Mitchell's	
MORRIS AND ESSEX	New York	Easton, Pa	85
Boonton Branch	Denville, N. J	Boonton	6
Chester, "	Dover, "	Chester	13
Sussex, "	Waterloo "	Newton	11
Mountain Link & Schuylkill Valley	Pottsville, Pa	Tamaqua	17½
NASHVILLE AND CHATTANOOGA	Nashville, Tenn	Chattanooga	151
Shelbyville Branch	Wartrace	Shelbyville	
Nashville and Decatur	Nashville	Decatur	122
Nashville and Northwestern	"	Hickman	170

† Connects by Steamer with Cairo, Ill., 20 Miles.

NAME.	FROM	TO	MILES.
Naugatuck, Conn.	Bridgeport.	Winsted	61
Newark and Bloomfield.	Newark.	Montclaire	5
Newark and New York.	"	New York	9
New Brunswick and Canada.	St. Andrew's, N. B.	Richmond	89
St. Stephen's Branch.	Watt's Junction.	St. Stephens	19
New Bedford & Taunton & Branch.	New Bedford.	Providence.	55
Newburyport, Mass.	Boston	Newburyport.	40
New Haven, Hartford, & Springfield.	New Haven, Conn.	Springfield, Mass..	62
Middletown Branch.	Berlin.	Middletown	10
N. Haven, N. London & Stonington.	New Haven, Conn.	Providence.	112
N. Haven, Middleton & Willim'ntic.	"	" Willimantic.	52
New Haven and Northampton.	"	" Williamsburg.	84
Collinsville Branch.	Farmington.	Collinsville.	8
New Jersey	New York.	New Brunswick.	32
New Jersey Midland*.	Weehawken, N. J.	N. York State L.	68
New Jersey Southern.	Sandy Hook.	Philadelphia	89
Long Branch.	Junction.	Long Branch.	5
Tom's River Branch.	Junction.	Tom's River.	8
New Lisbon, Ohio.	Leetonia.	New Lisbon	11
New London and Northern.	New London.	Grout's Corner.	100
New Orleans and Carrollton.	New Orleans.	Carrollton.	
New Orleans, Jackson and G. North.	New Orleans.	Canton, Miss.	206
New Orleans, Mobile & Chattanooga.	New Orleans.	Mobile.	140
N. Orleans, Opelousas & Gt. Western†.	Algiers, La.	Brashear.	80
New Orleans and Ohio.	Paducah, Ky.	Union City.	62
New York and New Haven.	New York.	New Haven.	76
New York and Harlem.	"	Rutland, Vt.	241
NEW YORK CENTRAL.	Albany.	Buffalo.	296
" "	Rochester.	Suspension Bridge.	76
" "	Troy.	Schenectady.	21
Athens Branch.	Schenectady.	Athens.	
Auburn Branch.	Syracuse.	Rochester.	104
Rochester and Charlotte Branch.	Rochester.	Charlotte.	6
Canandaigua, Batavia & Tonawa'a.	Canandaigua.	Towanda.	86
Batavia and Attica.	Batavia.	Attica.	12
Buffalo, Niagara Falls & Lewiston.	Buffalo.	Lewiston.	28
NEW YORK AND OSWEGO MIDLAND*.	Oswego, N. Y.	N. Jersey State L.	215
Auburn Branch*.	Auburn "	Norwich.	65
New Berlin Branch.	New Berlin "	Guilford.	22
Delhi Branch.	Delhi "	Walton.	15
Ellenville Branch.	Ellenville "	Summitville.	8
Montclair Branch*.	Greenwood Lake.	Jersey City.	40
Moristown Branch.	Montclair, N. J.	Morristown.	13
Niles and New Lisbon.	Niles, Mich.	New Lisbon.	33
Norfolk and Petersburg.	Norfolk, Va.	Petersburg.	81
North Carolina.	Goldsboro.	Charlotte.	223
North Easton, S. C.	Charleston.	Florence.	102

† Connects at Brashear, La., with Morgan's Line of Steamships for Galveston, Texas, 240 Miles.

NAME.	FROM	TO	MILES.
North Louisiana and Texas*	Delta, La	Monroe	72
North Missouri			
Eastern and Western Divisions	St. Louis, Mo	Kansas City	272
Northern Division	Moberly Junction	Ottumwa	130
Columbia Branch	Centralia	Columbia	22
North Pennsylvania	Philadelphia	Bethlehem	55
Northern Pacific*	Duluth, Minn	Puget Sound	1,775
Portland Branch*	Mississouri River	Portland, Or	1,100
Puget Sound Branch*	Portland	Puget Sound	145
Northern, Canada	Toronto	Collingwood	94
Northern New Jersey	New York	Piermont	24
Northern Central			
Baltimore and Susquehanna Div	Baltimore, Md	Sunbury, Pa	138
Elmira Division	Sunbury	Elmira, N. Y	218
Canandaigua Division	Elmira, N. Y	Rochester, N. Y	98
Shamokin Division	Sunbury	Mount Carmel	28
Wrightsville Branch	York, Pa	Wrightsville	14
Northern New Hampshire	Concord	Wells River Junc.	69
Bristol Branch	Franklin	Bristol	15
Norwich and Worcester	Norwich	Worcester	73
Nova Scotia, Canada	Halifax	Pictou	113
Windsor Branch	"	Windsor	45
Ogdensburg and Lake Champlain	Ogdensburg, N. Y	Rouse's Point	118
Ohio and Mississippi	Cincinnati, Ohio	St. Louis, Mo	340
Louisville Branch	North Vernon	Jeffersonville	53
Oil City and Pithole	Oleopolis, Pa	Pithole	7
Oil Creek and Alleghany River	Irvineton	Corry	95
Old Colony and Newport	Boston, Mass	Newport, R. I	67
Middleboro and Myrick's	Middleboro	Myrick's	
Plymouth and South Braintree	South Braintree	Plymouth	26
Dorchester and Milton	Dorchester	Milton	8
Abington and Bridgewater	Abington	Bridgewater	7
Omaha and Southwestern	Omaha, Neb	Lincoln	67
Orange, Alexandria & Manassas	Washington, D. C	Lynchburgh, Va	178
Manassas Branch	Manassas	Harrisburg	85
Warrenton Branch	Warrenton Junction	Warrenton	
Oregon and California*			
Oswego and Rome	Oswego, N. Y	Rome	71
Oswego and Syracuse	" "	Syracuse	35
Pacific, Missouri	St. Louis	Atchison, Kan	330
Boonville Branch	Tipton	Boonville	25
Paducah and Gulf	Paducah, Ken	Troy	63
Peninsula	Climax, Mich	Lansing	55
Pennsylvania & New York Canal	Waverly	Tonawanda	20
Pennsylvania Central	Philadelphia	Pittsburgh	354
Columbia Branch	Intersection	Rohrerstown	30
York Branch	Columbia	York, Pa	13
Mifflin and Centre County Branch	Penn. Railro'd Depot	Milroy	13

NAME.	FROM	TO	MILES
Ebensburg and Cresson Branch	Cresson	Ebensburgh	11
Butler Branch	Intersection	Butler	21
Indiana Branch	Blairsville Inter	Indiana	19
Hollidaysburg and Newry Branch	Altoona	Newry	11
Waynesburg Branch	Downington	Waynesboro	18
Bald Eagle Division	Tyrone	Lock Haven	55
Clearfield Division	"	Clearfield	38
Western Pennsylvania Branch	Blairsville Inter	Alleghany City	64
Pensacola and Louisville	Pensacola, Fla	Junction	44
Peoria, Pekin and Jacksonville	Peoria, Ill	Jacksonville	83
Perkiomen, Pa	Perkiomen	Skippack	10
Perth Amboy and Woodbridge	Junction, N. J	Perth Amboy	
Petersburg and Weldon	Petersburg, Va	Weldon	63
Gaston Branch	Hickford	Gaston	
Philadelphia and Baltimore Central	Philadelphia	Port Deposit	57
PHILADELPHIA AND ERIE	"	Erie	288
Phila., Germantown & Norristown	"	Norristown	17
Philadelphia and Reading	"	Pottsville	93
Philadelphia and Trenton	"	Trenton	28
Phila., Wilmington and Baltimore	"	Baltimore	98
PITTSBURGH, CINCINNATI & ST. LOUIS	Pitsburgh, Pa	Columbus, O	193
" " " "	Columbus	Indianapolis	188
" " " "	Indianapolis	St. Louis	162
Pittsburgh and Connellsville	Pittsburgh	Cumberland, Md.	150
PITTSBURGH, FORT WAYNE & CHICAGO	"	Chicago	468
Pittsfield and North Adams	Pittsfield, Mass	North Adams	20
Plattsburgh and Montreal	Plattsburgh, N. Y	Montreal, Can	63
Ponchartrain	New Orleans	Lake Ponchartr'n.	
Port Hope, Lindsay and Beaverton	Port Hope, Can	Lindsay	34
Port Hope and Peterboro	" "	Peterboro	31
Port Huron and Milwaukee*	Port Huron, Mich		
Portland and Kennebec	Portland, Me	Skowhegan	100
Bath Branch	Brunswick	Bath	9
Portland and Ogdensburg	Portland, Me	Fryeburg	48
Portland and Oxford Central	Sumner	Mechanics' Falls	
Portland and Rochester	Portland	Alfred	
Portland, Saco and Portsmouth	"	Portsmouth	52
Portsmouth, Great Falls & Conway	Portsmouth, N. H	Union	26
Providence and Worcester	Providence, R. I	Worcester, Me	43
Providence, Warren and Bristol	"	Bristol	14
Raleigh and Gaston	Raleigh, N. C	Weldon	97
Reading and Columbia	Reading, Pa	Columbia	46
RENSSELAER AND SARATOGA	Troy, N. Y	Rutland, Vt	95
Albany Division	Albany	Junction	12
Schenectady Division	Schenectady	Ballston Spa	22
Glens Falls Branch	Fort Edward	Glens Falls	5
Richmond, Danville and Piedmont	Richmond, Va	Greensboro	189
Richmond, Fredericksburg & Poto'c.	" "	Washington	130

NAME.	FROM	TO	MILES.
Richmond and Petersburg	Richmond, Va.	Petersburg	23
Richmond and York River	"	" West Point	38
Roanoke Valley, Va	Valley Junction	Clarksville	22
Rock Island and Peoria	Rock Island, Ill	Coal Valley	11
Rockford, Rock Island & St. Louis*	St. Louis,	Sterling, Ill.	294
Rockville	Rockville, Cinn	Vernon	5
Rome	Rome, Geo.	Kingston	20
Rome, Watertown and Ogdensburg	Rome, N. Y.	Ogdensburg	142
Potsdam Branch	De Kalb Junction	Potsdam	25
Rondout and Oswego*	Rondout, N. Y	Oswego.	
Rutland, Burli'n & Vermont Valley	Brattleboro, Vt.	Burlington	144
Sandusky, Mansfield and Newark	Sandusky, Ohio	Newark	116
Schoharie Valley	Schoharie	Middleburg.	
Schuylkill and Susquehanna	Pottsville, Pa.	Harrisburg	59
Seaboard and Roanoke	Portsmouth, Va	Weldon	80
Selma and Meridian	Selma, Ala.	Meridian	107
Selma, Marion and Memphis*	" "		
Selma, Rome and Dalton	" "	Kingston	217
Sheboygan and Fond du Lac	Sheboygan	Fond du Lac	45
Sioux City and Pacific	Missouri Valley	Sioux City, Iowa	76
Fremont Division	" "	Fremont	38
South and North Alabama	Montgomery	Calera	63
SOUTH CAROLINA	Charleston	Columbia	137
Aiken Branch	Aiken, S. C	Augusta, Geo	75
Camden Branch	Camden	Columbia	63
South Shore, Mass.	Boston	Cohasset	21
South Side, Long Island	Brooklyn, N. Y.	Patchogue	54
Far Rockaway Branch	Valley Stream	Far Rockaway	6
South Side, Virginia	Petersburg	Lynchburg	123
Southern Central	Auburn, N. Y.	Oswego	68
Southern Minnesota	La Crosse	Wells	148
Southern Pacific	Shreveport, La.	Hallsville	56
Southern Pacific*	San Francisco, Cal.	Colorado River	
SOUTHERN TRANS-CONTINENTAL*	Memphis.	El Paso	
South Western Georgia	Macon	Eufaula	143
" "	"	Columbus	100
Spartansburg and Union	Spartansburg	Alston	68
Springfield and Illinois	Springfield	Pana	43
Staten Island	Vanderbilt Land	Tottenville	13
Stanstead, Shefford and Chambly	St. John, Canada	Waterloo	43
Sterling Mountain	Sterling Junction	Lakeville	
Stonington and Providence	Providence	New London	62
St. Joseph Valley, Mich.	Kalamazoo	White Pigeon	36
St. Joseph and Council Bluffs	St. Joseph, Mo.	Omaha, Neb	132
St. Joseph and Denver*	" "		
St. Lawrence and Ottawa	Prescott, Can	Ottawa	54
St. Louis and Southeastern	East St. Louis	Mt. Vernon, Ill	76
St. Louis and St. Joseph	North Lexington	St. Joseph	76

NAME.	FROM	TO	MILES.
St. Louis, Alton and Terre Haute	Indianapolis, Ind	St. Louis	263
Belleville Branch	East St. Louis	Du Quoin	71
St. Louis and Iron Mountain	St. Louis, Mo	Belmont	195
St. Louis, Vandalia and Terre Haute	East St. Louis	Indianapolis	238
St. Louis and Southeastern	" "	Shawneetown	139
St. Paul and Chicago	St. Paul	Winona, Minn	101
ST. PAUL AND PACIFIC*	"	Benton	135
Branch Line	St. Anthony	Sauk Rapids	68
St. Paul and Sioux City*	St. Paul	St. James	121
Sunbury and Lewistown	Sunbury, Pa		
Sycamore and Cortland	Sycamore	Cortland	
Syracuse, Binghampton & New York	Syracuse	Binghampton	80
TALLAHASSEE AND GEORGIA	Quincy, Fla	Jacksonville	189
St. Mark's Branch	Tallahassee	St. Marks	21
Tennessee and Pacific	Nashville	Lebanon	31
Terre Haute and Indianapolis	Indianapolis	Terre Haute	73
TOLEDO, PEORIA AND WARSAW	State Line	Warsaw	277
TOLEDO, WABASH AND WESTERN	Toledo, Ohio	Quincy, Ill	476
St. Louis Division	Decatur, Ill	St. Louis	109
Keokuk Branch	Clayton, "	Keokuk, Iowa	42
Troy and Boston	Troy, N. Y	North Adams	48
Troy and Bennington	Hoosick Junction	State Line	
UNION PACIFIC	Omaha, Neb	Ogden, Utah	1,032
Central Branch	Atchison, Kan	Waterville	100
Southern Branch	Junction City, Kan	Burlington	89
Utah Central	Ogden, Utah	Salt Lake City	40
Utica, Chenango and Susquehanna	Utica	Norwich	54
Utica and Black River	"	Lowville, N. Y	59
VERMONT CENTRAL	Bellows Falls, Vt	Rouse's Point	184
Vermont and Massachusetts	Fitchburg	Hoosac Tunnel	86
" " "	Grout's Corner	Brattleboro, Vt	21
Vicksburg and Meridian	Vicksburg, Miss	Meridian	140
VIRGINIA AND TENNESSEE	Lynchburg, Va	Bristol, Tenn	204
Washington, Alexandria & Georget'n	Washington	Alexandria	7
Washington and Ohio	Alexandria, Va	Hamilton	44
Welland, Canada	Port Dalhousie	Port Colborne	
Westchester and Philadelphia	West Philadelphia	Westchester	27
Westchester, Pa	West Chester Inter	"	
Western	West Point, Geo	Montgomery	88
Western and Atlantic	Atlanta, Geo	Chattanooga	138
Western, North Carolina	Salisbury	Old Fort	115
WESTERN UNION	Racine, Wis	Rock Island, Ill	197
West New Jersey	Camden	Bridgeton	37
" " "	Glassboro	Millville	22
" " "	Elmer	Salem	17
WESTERN PACIFIC	San Francisco, Cal	Sacramento	138
Western Maryland	Relay	York Road	44
West Wisconsin	Tomah, Wis	Eau Claire	88

NAME.	FROM	TO	MILES.
Whitehall and Plattsburgh	Plattsburgh, N. Y	Ausable River	20
Wicomico and Pocomoke	Berlin, N. C	Salisbury	23
Wilmington, Charlotte & Rutherford.	Wilmington, N. C	Sand Hill	110
Wilmington and Manchester	" "	Kingsville	171
Wilmington and Reading	Wilmington, Del	Reading, Pa	73
Wilmington and Weldon	Wilmington, N. C	Weldon	162
Windsor and Annapolis	Windsor, N. S	Annapolis	84
Winona and St. Peter	Winona, Minn	St. Peter	140
Worcester and Nashua	Worcester, Mass	Nashua, N. H	46

TONNAGE OF THE UNITED STATES—1870.

BY

STATES AND TERRITORIES.

ATLANTIC AND GULF COASTS.

STATES, &C.	TONNAGE.
Maine	389,388
New Hampshire, (*Portsmouth*)	12,967
Massachusetts, (*Boston, 342,358*)	534,642
Rhode Island	45,003
Connecticut	84,338
New York, (*City*)	1,136,628
Sag Harbor	10,940
New Jersey	88,209
Pennsylvania, (*Philadelphia*)	212,624
Delaware	18,857
Maryland, (*Baltimore, 114,939*)	132,217
District of Columbia, (*Georgetown*)	27,002
Virginia	29,434
North Carolina	15,153
South Carolina	15,545
Georgia	29,247
Florida	17,296
Alabama, (*Mobile*)	27,428
Mississippi, (*Pearl River*)	1,274
Louisiana	59,450
Texas	18,755
Total	**2,905,798**

PACIFIC COAST.

California, (*San Francisco*)	148,776
Oregon	10,971
Washington Territory, (*Puget Sound*).	24,827
Total	**184,574**

Total, Atlantic and Pacific Coasts—Sea-going Vessels	3,090,372

NORTHERN LAKES.

STATES, &C.	TONNAGE.
Vermont, (*Burlington*)	5,797
New York, (*Buffalo, 143,888*)	312,745
Pennsylvania, (*Erie*)	4,924
Ohio, (*Cleveland, 56,885*)	84,136
Michigan, (*Detroit, 71,458*)	109,860
Illinois. (*Chicago*)	104,314
Wisconsin, (*Milwaukee*)	39,590
Total	**661,366**

WESTERN RIVERS.

Louisiana, (*New Orleans*)	46,658
Mississippi	1,316
Tennessee	11,398
Kentucky	18,646
Missouri, (*St. Louis*)	104,700
Iowa	4,825
Minnesota, (*St. Paul*)	18,316
Illinois	23,713
Indiana	5,148
Ohio, (*Cincinnati*)	61,618
West Virginia	12,369
Pennsylvania, (*Pittsburgh*)	84,194
Total	**392,902**

RECAPITULATION.

Atlantic and Gulf Coasts	2,905,798
Pacific Coasts	184,574
Northern Lakes	661,366
Western Rivers	392,901
Grand Total	**4,144,639**

VARIATION OF TIME
IN
CROSSING THE CONTINENT.

NOON	AT	WASHINGTON, D. C.	NOON	AT	WASHINGTON, D. C.
1 37	P. M. at	St. John, N. F.	11 36	A. M. at	Columbus, O.
12 54	"	Halifax, N. S.	11 36	"	Detroit, Mich.
12 44	"	St. John's, N. B.	11 30	"	Cincinnati, Ohio.
12 27	"	Portland, Me.	11 30	"	Lansing, Mich.
12 25	"	Portsmouth, N. H.	11 30	"	Atlanta, Ga.
12 24	"	Boston, Mass.	11 29	"	Frankfort, Ky.
12 23	"	Newport, R. I.	11 26	"	Louisville, "
12 23	"	Quebec, Can.	11 24	"	Indianapolis, Ind.
12 22	"	Concord, N. H.	11 23	"	Montgomery, Ala.
12 16	"	New Haven, Conn.	11 21	"	Nashville, Tenn.
12 14	"	Montreal, Can.	11 17	"	Chicago, Ill.
12 13	"	Albany, N. Y.	11 16	"	Mobile, Ala.
12 12	"	NEW YORK.	11 16	"	Milwaukee, Wis.
12 09	"	Trenton, N. J.	11 12	"	Cairo, Ill.
12 07	"	Philadelphia.	11 10	"	Madison, Wis.
12 06	"	Wilmington, Del.	11 08	"	New Orleans.
12 05	"	OTTAWA, Can.	11 07	"	Memphis, Tenn.
12 03	"	Norfolk, Va.	11 07	"	St. Louis, Mo.
12 02	"	Baltimore, Md.	11 05	"	Dubuque, Iowa.
12 00	Noon at	Harrisburg, Pa	11 05	"	Vicksburg, Miss.
12 00	"	Elmira, N. Y.	10 59	"	Little Rock, Ark.
12 00	"	Kingston, Can.	10 56	"	St. Paul, Minn.
11 58	A. M. at	Richmond, Va.	10 53	"	Des Moines, Iowa.
11 58	"	Wilmington, Del.	10 49	"	Galveston, Texas.
11 52	"	Buffalo, N. Y.	10 49	"	Leavenworth, Kan.
11 50	"	Toronto, Can.	10 44	"	Omaha, Neb.
11 50	"	Panama, N. G.	10 43	"	Vera Cruz.
11 50	"	Raleigh, N. C.	10 32	"	Mexico.
11 48	"	Pittsburgh, Pa.	10 08	"	Denver, Col.
11 48	"	Charleston, S. C.	10 04	"	Santa Fé, N. M.
11 45	"	Wheeling, W. Va.	9 40	"	Salt Lake City, U.
11 44	"	Columbia, S. C.	9 02	"	Sacramento, Cal.
11 44	"	Savannah, Ga.	8 58	"	San Francisco.
11 42	"	St. Augustine, Fla.	8 56	"	Portland, Or.
11 41	"	Cleveland, O.	8 44	"	Vancouver's Island.
11 38	"	Havana, Cuba.	7 28	"	Sitka, Alaska.

☞ Making a difference of 6 h. 9 min. in the Sun's rising on crossing the Continent.

COMMENCEMENT OF RAILROADS

IN THE

UNITED STATES.

IT is now forty years since the completion of the first Railroad in the United States, several being projected as early as 1828. To the late HENRY S. TANNER, author of a "Description of Canals and Railroads in the United States," published in 1840, we are indebted for most of the following reliable information.

The BALTIMORE AND OHIO RAILROAD, the first important line undertaken, was incorporated on the 28th of February, 1827, by the Legislature of Maryland. The work was commenced on the 4th of July, 1828, and fourteen miles opened for traffic in 1830; in 1831 it was extended to Frederick, 62 miles, and in 1832, to the Point of Rocks, 68 miles, being soon thereafter opened to Harper's Ferry, 81 miles from Baltimore. Until 1831 it was operated by horse power.

The PENNSYLVANIA RAILROAD, authorized by Act of the Legislature, passed March, 1828, was commenced as a State work. It was divided into two divisions, and known as PHILADELPHIA and COLUMBIA RAILROAD, 81 miles in length, and the ALLEGHANY PORTAGE RAILROAD, 36 miles, running from Hollidaysburg to Johnstown, across the Alleghany Mountains. The latter road had several inclined plains, with stationary engines to facilitate the transportation of freight and passengers, connecting at each termini with the *Pennsylvania Canal* running

between Philadelphia and Pittsburgh. In September, 1832, twenty miles of single track was ready for use on the Eastern Division, and in April, 1834, the entire route, from Philadelphia to Columbia, was opened for travel. Total cost of the Philadelphia and Columbia Railroad, $3,754,577.

The ALLEGHANY PORTAGE RAILROAD, which was considered a great achievement in engineering, attained an altitude of 2,490 ft. above the Atlantic Ocean. It had one tunnel 900 feet in length. This important work was commenced early in 1831, and finished in March, 1834.

The MOHAWK AND HUDSON, running from Albany to Schenectady, 17 miles, was commenced in August, 1830, and completed in 1832, being the first railroad finished to completion in the United States; at each termini was an inclined plane with stationary engines.

The SARATOGA AND SCHENECTADY RAILROAD was commenced in 1831, and opened July, 1832. Length, 21 miles.

The SOUTH CAROLINA RAILROAD was commenced in 1830, and 62 miles of it finished in 1832. In 1834 it was completed to Hamburg, opposite Augusta, Georgia, 136 miles; at the time of its completion it was the longest railroad in the world, being the first upon which a locomotive engine of American manufacture was used.

The NEW YORK AND HARLEM RAILROAD was commenced in 1831, and a portion of it within the City of New York opened the latter part of the same year.

The PHILADELPHIA, GERMANTOWN AND NORRISTOWN RAILROAD, 6 miles, to Germantown, was opened in 1832. In December a locomotive was put on this road, built by M. W. Baldwin of Philadelphia. The following Advertisement was issued, dated December 13, 1832, and inserted in a Philadelphia paper:—

Notice.—The engine with a train of cars, will be run daily, (commencing this day,) when the weather is fair. When the weather is not fair, the horses will draw the cars. Passengers are requested to be punctual at the hours of starting. Points of starting are at Green and Ninth streets, and from the Main street, the centre of Germantown, near Wunder's Hotel. Whole cars may be taken. Tickets, 25 cents.

The CAMDEN AND AMBOY RAILROAD was commenced in 1831, and 14 miles, extending from Bordentown to Hightstown, was completed in 1832. It was finished from Camden to South Amboy, 62 miles, in 1834, there connecting with Steamers running to the City of New York.

The NEW JERSEY RALROAD was commenced in 1832, and completed to New Brunswick, 31 miles, in 1834.

The PHILADELPHIA AND TRENTON RAILROAD, 28 miles, was completed in 1833.

The NEW CASTLE AND FRENCHTOWN RAILROAD, connecting the Chesapeake and Delaware Bays, was completed in 1832.

The WASHINGTON BRANCH of the Baltimore and Ohio Railroad, 31 miles in length, was opened in 1835.

The RICHMOND, FREDERICKSBURG AND POTOMAC RAILROAD was opened from Richmond to Fredericksburg, Va., in 1837; and, in 1838, the RICHMOND AND PETERSBURG RAILROAD was completed.

The PHILADELPHIA, WILMINGTON AND BALTIMORE RAILROAD, 98 miles, was opened its whole length in 1838, —with other roads forming a through line of Railroad from New York to Washington.

The WILMINGTON AND WELDON RAILROAD, 162 miles in length, was opened in 1840; and, in 1843, the PETERSBURG AND ROANOKE RAILROAD was finished, forming a continuous line of Railroad from the Potomac, at Acquia Creek, to Wilmington, N.C., and by Steamer to Washington, D. C.

The WESTERN RAILROAD of Massachusetts, now known as the *Boston and Albany Railroad*, 200 miles in length, was opened from Boston to Albany, N. Y. in 1841. The BOSTON AND WORCESTER RAILROAD formed a part of this line of travel, extending from Boston to Worcester, 45 miles.

In 1842 the important lines of Railroad, under different names, extending from Albany to Buffalo, 298 miles, was completed, afterwards being consolidated under the name of the NEW YORK CENTRAL RAILROAD. The completion of this great work, affording a through line of Railroad from Boston to Buffalo, was an event of great magnitude in the Railway history of the country.

The PHILADELPHIA AND READING RAILROAD, extending from Philadelphia to the Schuylkill coal fields, was opened in 1842, being soon followed by other Railroads throughout the coal region of Pennsylvania.

At this time (1842) there was about 4,000 miles of Railroad finished in the United States; after that period the growth gradually increased for the next eight years; in 1850 there being nearly 10,000 miles of Railroad completed. In 1860 there was about 20,000 miles completed. For four years the increase was small, owing to the breaking out of the rebellion, but since its close, in 1865, the increase has been very rapid, there being in 1871 upwards of 54,000 miles finished and in operation.

RAILROAD STATISTICS.—1871.

THE Annual figures in regard to Railway construction throughout the United States have been made up, and show a total of 54,435 miles constructed in 1870. The average cost per mile of new road was $40,000.

The following Table shows the distribution of mileage and cost of Railroads in the several States and Territories:—

STATES & TERRITORIES.	LENGTH IN MILES. TOTAL.	OPEN.	COST OF ROAD & EQUIPMENT.
Maine	972	810	$26,241,901
New Hampshire	987	735	28,647,935
Vermont	658	618	34,488,594
Massachusetts	1,739	1,478	77,496,830
Rhode Island	136	136	4,805,996
Connecticut	978	729	34,976,834
	5,470	4,506	$199,658,090
New York	5,453	3,892	$234,049,545
New Jersey	1,241	1,092	74,525,196
Pennsylvania	6,313	5,056	296,739,037
Delaware and Maryland	1,429	885	44,782,459
West Virginia	712	375	30,493,739
	15,078	11,300	$680,589,976
Virginia	2,253	1,466	$53,386,858
North Carolina	1,574	1,178	33,164,298
South Carolina	1,438	1,138	32,863,588
Georgia	2,314	1,933	44,322,919
Florida	607	440	11,781,919
	8,186	6,155	$174,519,582
Alabama	2,120	1,396	$46,598,605
Mississippi	1,118	978	33,208,839
Louisiana	945	478	19,523,798
Texas	4,071	656	22,050,000
Arkansas	1,054	286	8,798,000
Tennessee	2,016	1,490	51,528,745
Kentucky	1,375	907	35,640,699
	12,699	6,201	$217,348,686

STATES & TERRITORIES.	LENGTH IN MILES. TOTAL.	OPEN.	COST OF ROAD & EQUIPMENT.
Ohio	4,801	3,608	$192,538,214
Michigan	2,903	1,733	75,817,748
Indiana	4,865	3,278	135,957,186
Illinois	8,813	5,423	237,553,000
Wisconsin	3,142	1,475	59,833,881
	24,614	15,547	$701,700,029
Missouri	4,573	2,140	$106,663,464
Kansas	3,698	1,501	56,723,700
Colorado	1,268	368	17,400,000
Iowa	4,472	2,550	111,978,000
Nebraska	1,205	588	39,300,000
Wyoming Ter	492	492	46,700,000
Minnesota	2,654	972	34,720,000
Dakota Territory	700		300,000
Montana and Idaho Territories	600		
	19,662	8,611	$413,785,164
California	3,294	997	$70,624,582
Nevada	1,493	593	60,000,000
Utah Territory	404	364	49,000,000
Oregon	2,648	159	6,100,000
Washington Ter	420		
	8,529	2,113	$185,724,582

RECAPITULATION.

	LENGTH IN MILES. TOTAL.	OPEN.	COST OF ROAD & EQUIPMENT.
N. England States	5,470	4,506	$199,658,090
Middle States	15,079	11,300	680,589,976
S. Eastern States	8,186	6,156	174,519,582
Gulf & S. W. States	12,699	6,201	217,348,686
Interior E. of Mississippi	24,614	15,547	701,700,029
Interior W. of Mississippi	19,663	8,612	413,785,164
Pacific States	8,259	2,113	185,724,582
Grand Total	93,970	54,435	$2,573,526,109

RAILWAY SYSTEM OF THE UNITED STATES—1871.

THE GREAT TRUNK RAILWAYS of the United States and Canada, with their Connections, which are made subservient to foreign commerce, flowing from Europe on the East and Asia on the West, diverge from the principal Atlantic ports lying within the Temperate Zone, and extend across the Continent to the Pacific Ocean. Other important Lines of Railway run from North to South, forming altogether a complete net-work system of Railroads, extending from the Atlantic to the Pacific Ocean.

Baltimore, Norfolk, Philadelphia, New York, Boston and Portland, are the principal sea-ports from which the above Great Lines of commerce diverge and run Westward. East of the Alleghany Mountains there are now finished *five* principal Trunk Railways, connecting with other Lines of Railroad running to the Mississippi River and the Great Lakes.

THE **Baltimore and Ohio Railroad**, with its Branches, forms the first Great Line that is finished—running from tide-waters at Baltimore and Washington to the Ohio River—there connecting with Railroads traversing the Valley of the Mississippi and the basin of the Great Lakes. In addition to its terminus at Wheeling, West Virginia, 379 miles west of Baltimore, it has a Branch running to Parkersburg, West Virginia, and another from Cumberland, Maryland to Pittsburgh, Pennsylvania, running over the Alleghany Mountains,—thus making three important connections with western Railroad Lines running to the

Mississippi River, there connecting with the Great Lines of Travel running through Kansas and Nebraska to the Pacific Ocean.

THE **Pennsylvania Central Railroad** forms the second Great Line crossing the Alleghany Mountains, uniting at Pittsburgh, 354 miles from Philadelphia, with the *Pittsburgh, Fort Wayne and Chicago Railroad, Pittsburgh, Cincinnati & St. Louis R. R.*, and all the Trunk Lines of Railways in the Valley of the Mississippi, and those extending westward across the Continent. This Road connects with the *Northern Central Railway*, starting from Baltimore, and with the "Allentown Line," leaving New York by the *Central New Jersey Railroad*,—both uniting at Harrisburg, Pennsylvania,—thus forming three Great Lines of Travel from the sea-board, in addition to its connection with the *Philadelphia and Erie Railroad*,—which forms, in part, an important Line of Travel from Philadelphia and New York to Erie, Pennsylvania,—there connecting with Steamers running to the different ports on Lake Erie and the Upper Lakes.

THE **Erie Railway,** with its Branches, is the third Trunk Line, forming a Through Route of Travel from the sea-board to the basin of the Great Lakes and the Valley of the Mississippi. It starts from Jersey City, opposite New York, and runs through the State of New Jersey and Southern New York to Dunkirk, on Lake Erie, 460 miles, while Branches diverge to Rochester, Buffalo, Niagara Falls, &c. The continuation of this Great Line of Travel, via the *Atlantic and Great Western Railway*, being under one control, forms a speedy mode of conveyance from New York to Cleveland and Cincinnati, Ohio,—connecting with other Railroads running to Chicago, St. Louis, &c.

THE **New York and Oswego Midland Railroad**, now approaching completion, will form another Through Line of Travel from the City of New York to the Great Lakes, having a double terminus,—one at Oswego, on Lake Ontario, and another at Buffalo, on Lake Erie,—forming the shortest route to the basin of the Great Lakes and the Valley of the St. Lawrence River.

THE **Hudson River & New York Central Railroad**, in connection with the BOSTON AND ALBANY RAILROAD is the fourth Trunk Line extending from the sea-board; forming in part a Through Route of Travel from the Atlantic to the Pacific Ocean. This important Railroad Route, starting from New York, passes up the Valley of the Hudson to Albany, and from thence through Western New York to Buffalo and Niagara Falls, there connecting with the *Lake Shore Railroad*, and with the *Great Western Railway of Canada*, making close connections with Lines of Railroad running to Chicago, St. Louis, &c. The Great Line of Travel from Boston, westward, unites at Albany with the *New York Central Railroad*, and other Railroads crossing the State of New York, extending to the Lakes and Canada.

THE **Grand Trunk Railway** of Canada, forming the fifth Trunk Line, controls the Line of Travel running from Portland, Maine to the Canada Line. It extends to Quebec on the Lower St. Lawrence, on the North, and to Montreal, Toronto and Detroit, Michigan, on the West, connecting with all the Main Lines of Travel running to Chicago, Cincinnati, St. Louis, &c. This important Railway, with its Branches, is the great artery that furnishes Canada with a speedy mode of conveyance from the Atlantic and Gulf of St. Lawrence to the Great Lakes and Valley of the Mississippi,—thus forming an international thoroughfare, passing through a deeply interesting section of the Country.

The sixth Trunk Line, approaching completion, is the **Chesapeake and Ohio Railroad**, running from Richmond, Virginia, across the Alleghany Mountains to the Ohio River, there connecting with Railroads running through the Valley of the Mississippi, forming a short Line of Travel from Norfolk, on the sea-board, to Cincinnati, Louisville, Memphis and St. Louis, and from thence to the Pacific Ocean.

The Great Trunk Railways running West of the Mississippi, and crossing the Rocky Mountains, are the UNION PACIFIC RAILROAD and the CENTRAL PACIFIC RAILROAD, forming a combined line of 1,914 miles of Road, extending from Omaha to San Francisco. For further description, see page 100.

The KANSAS PACIFIC, and the DENVER PACIFIC RAILROADS, 744 miles in length, unite with the above Great Line at Cheyenne, Wyoming Territory, thus affording, in part, two Routes of Travel across the Continent, making close connections with all the Great Lines of Travel in the Valley of the Mississippi.

THE CENTRAL PACIFIC RAILROAD which extends from San Francisco to Ogden, Utah, 881 miles, with its Branches, now has 1,025 miles of Road in operation, and 500 miles in course of construction,—covering nearly the whole Railroad system of the Pacific States.

THE CALIFORNIA AND OREGON RAILWAY is finished from the Junction of the Central Pacific to Chico, California, 96 miles, and will extend North to the Oregon State Line, there to unite with the *Oregon and California Railroad*, to extend further North to the Columbia River.

On the completion of the SOUTHERN PACIFIC RAILROAD, running from a point west of the Mississippi River and extending through the States of Arkansas, Texas, Arizona and California to the Pacific Ocean, there will be formed a great channel of commerce that will benefit all the Southern States and Territories.

THE NORTHERN PACIFIC RAILROAD, now in progress of construction, when finished, will form the *third* Great Line of Travel crossing the Rocky Mountains, extending from Lake Superior and the Mississippi River to the Columbia River and Puget Sound. For further description, see page 105.

Toledo, Wabash and Western Railroad.

—This important Railroad starting at Toledo, Ohio, crosses the States of Indiana and Illinois and reaches out to Iowa and Missouri,—forming the most direct Route from Lake Erie to the Mississippi River, and from there to the Pacific Ocean. The Main Line runs from Toledo to Quincy, Ill., a distance of 476 miles.

The completion of the *Decatur and St. Louis Branch* of the above Railway, now enables this Company to run their own trains direct from Toledo to St. Louis, a distance of 432 miles; and in connection with the Lake Shore Railroad and the New York Central Railroad, forms a direct Through Route from Boston and New York to St. Louis, &c.

The *Toledo, Wabash and Western Railroad* now has four important termini on the Mississippi, — Quincy, Hannibal, St. Louis and Keokuk. The new Bridge across the River at Keokuk affords direct uninterrupted connection, via the *Des Moines Valley Railroad*, with the Iowa System of Railroads, and thence to Omaha and the West. The termini at Quincy and Hannibal furnishes a direct Route to Kansas and Colorado; and the South terminus, at St. Louis, facilitates for competing with other Eastern Lines for the travel and trade of the great business centre of the Mississippi,—forming in connection with Lake Erie and the St. Lawrence River a direct communication with the European ports.

Chicago, Burlington and Quincy Railroad.

—This important Railway runs from Chicago in a southwesterly direction to the Mississippi River, having a double termini,—one at Burlington, Iowa, and another at Quincy, Illinois. At the former terminus it connects with the *Burlington and Missouri River Railroad*, and at the latter with the *Hannibal and St. Joseph Railroad*,—thus furnishing two great Routes of Travel from Chicago to the Missouri River; there connecting with the great Through Routes of Travel to Colorado, Utah, California, &c.

The Main Line extends from Chicago to Quincy, 263 miles; the *Burlington Branch*, from Galesburg to Burlington, Iowa, 43 miles; the *Peoria Branch*, from Galesburg to Peoria, Ill., 53 miles; the *Rushville Branch*, from Buda to Rushville, 110 miles; the *New Boston Branch*, from Galva to New Boston, 51 miles; the *Carthage Branch*, from Burlington to Mendon, Ill., 57 miles; the *Keokuk Branch*, from Burlington to Keokuk, Iowa, 43 miles; connecting with the Des Moines Valley Railroad.

At Burlington and Quincy there are iron bridges over the Mississippi River, which enable Through Trains to run, without change of cars, from Chicago to Council Bluffs, Iowa, over the *Burlington and Missouri River Railroad*, and to Kansas City, St. Joseph, &c., over the *Hannibal and St. Joseph Railroad*.

Burlington and Missouri River Railroad.

—This Road running from the Mississippi River to the Missouri River, opposite Omaha, Nebraska, forms the third Great Line of Travel running across the State of Iowa, connecting with the *Union Pacific Railroad*, forming a Through Line of Travel to Colorado, Utah and California.

The *Nebraska City Branch*, 50 miles in length, terminates on the Missouri River, opposite Nebraska City; and the *Nebraska Division* extends from Plattsmouth to Lincoln, Neb., 55 miles. This Line will be extended to Fort Kearny, situated on the north bank of the Platte River, making a short connection with the *Union Pacific Railroad*. In connection with the *Chicago, Burlington and Quincy Railroad* it will form a direct Line of Travel from Chicago to San Francisco.

Chicago and Northwestern Railway.

—This Great Railway, with its Branches, leaves Chicago by three Lines of Railroad, running West, Northwest and North—passing through the States of Illinois, Iowa and Wisconsin.

Lines of Railroad owned and operated by this Company, are as follows:—

GALENA DIVISION.—Chicago to Clinton, Iowa, 138 miles; Junction, 30 miles west of Chicago to Freeport, Ill., 91 miles; Elgin, 42 miles Northwest of Chicago to Richmond, Ill., 33 miles.

IOWA DIVISION.—Clinton to Missouri River, opposite Omaha, 354 miles.

WISCONSIN DIVISION.—Chicago to Fort Howard, Wis., 242 Miles; Rockford, Ill. to Kenosha, Wis., 72 miles.

MADISON DIVISION.—Belvidere, Ill. to Madison, Wis., 68 miles.

MILWAUKEE DIVISION.—Chicago to Milwaukee, Wis., 85 miles.

PENINSULA DIVISION.—Escanaba to Negaunee, Mich., 68 miles, forming a Through Line of Travel to Lake Superior.

The *Winona and St. Peter Railroad*, 126 miles in length, running from Winona to St. Peter, Minn., is owned and operated by the above Company, forming a Through Line of Travel to Minneapolis and St. Paul. Total length of Road, owned and operated, about 1,300 miles.

☞ The Trains on this Road connect with STEAMERS on the Mississippi River on the West, and with Green Bay and Lake Superior on the North.

Chicago, Rock Island and Pacific Railroad.

—This great Line of Travel forming in part a direct Through Line of Railroad from the Atlantic to the Pacific Ocean, runs westwardly from Chicago to Rock Island, Ill., there crossing the Mississippi River, by a substantial bridge, to Davenport, Iowa. From Davenport this Road is extended, westward, across the State of Iowa to the Missouri River, opposite Omaha, Neb., 494 miles from Chicago, there connecting with the *Union Pacific Railroad*,—thus forming a direct Through Railroad Route from Chicago to San Francisco,—a total distance of 2,408 miles.

The *Peoria Branch Railroad* runs from Bureau to Peoria, Ill., 46 miles. The *Southwestern Branch*, finished from Wilton to Ashland, Iowa, 94 miles, when completed will extend to Leavenworth, Kansas, crossing the State of Iowa and the Northwestern part of Missouri, thus forming another Line of Travel from Chicago to the Missouri River, connecting with all the Great Lines of Travel running through Kansas to Denver, Santa Fé, &c.

Pacific Railroad (OF MISSOURI.)

—This Road runs from St. Louis, westward, to Kansas City and the State Line, 284 miles, connecting with the *Kansas Pacific Railroad;* then northward to Leavenworth and Atchison, Kansas, 46 miles further. It is an old, well built, and well managed Railroad, offering both safety and comfort to the travelling public. Being on a medium parallel of latitude, (the 39th south of the Missouri River,) and forming a principal connecting link between the East and extreme West, great numbers are constantly passing over it, and the amount of passenger business done by this Road is much greater than by any other Railway of the same length west of the Mississippi.

Through the Main Line of this Railroad, its Branches to Boonville and Lexington, and its connections in Western Missouri and Kansas, immense quantities of produce flow into the St. Louis market from Missouri, Kansas and Colorado; and merchandise of great value is sent out from the same market to supply the wants of two or three millions of people.

"It may be interesting to the traveller to know that the average speed on most of the Railroads of Missouri does not exceed twenty miles to the hour. If he is travelling on an express or mail train west of the Mississippi, he can approximate very closely to the time by dividing the distance in miles by twenty; the result will show the hours very nearly."

North Missouri Railroad.

—This Road extends from St. Louis to Kansas City on the west, 272 miles, and to Ottumwa, Iowa, on the north, 132 miles from Moberly Junction, connecting with the *Des Moines Valley Railroad*. At Centralia, 121 miles North of St. Louis, commences the *Boone County and Jefferson City Railroad*, extending to Columbia, 22 miles. At R. and L. Junction on the Western Division, the *St. Louis and St. Joseph Railroad* intersects the Main Line, being operated by this Company.

This important Line of Travel runs through a rich section of country, and connects with the *Kansas Pacific Railroad* at Kansas City and with the *Kansas City, St. Joseph and Council Bluffs Railroad*, at Harlem, one mile east of Kansas City, and at St. Joseph, 70 miles north of Kansas City, running to opposite Omaha, Neb.; another Branch Railroad is being constructed from Brunswick, Mo. direct to Omaha, 188 miles. When completed, this Road in connection with others, will afford a direct communication with Western Iowa, Nebraska, and Dakota, thereby sucuring a portion of the growing trade of the upper Missouri River to St. Louis. The whole number of miles of Railroad under the management of this Company is over five hundred.

Atlantic and Pacific Railroad, (formerly SOUTH PACIFIC.)—

This important Road, running from St. Louis across the State of Missouri, was commenced several years since, but suffered from a multitude of delays during its early organization. It is now completed to the Missouri State Line, 330 miles from St. Louis, and has become one of the great thoroughfares of the Southwest. The Line of the Road is for the most part, through a beautiful section of country, with a fruitful soil, and climate as genial as that of Italy.

The Company have a charter for a Road from Springfield, Mo. to San Francisco, crossing the Continent near the 35th parallel, which is considered by many as the shortest and most desirable as to grade, running through a fertile country rich in agricultural or mineral productions its entire length, and free from all climatic obstructions—hence in many important respects the most desirable of any Route built or projected. It will run through the Indian Territory, New Mexico, Arizona and California to the Pacific Coast.

A Branch Road is being built to extend from Pierce City, Mo. to Van Buren, Arkansas; a distance of 125 miles.

The Land Grant at the disposal of this Company is very large and valuable.

Kansas Pacific Railroad.

—Copied from "TRACY'S GUIDE TO THE GREAT WEST." This important Road, 638 miles in length, traverses the entire State of Kansas from east to west, a distance of 420 miles, and pushes on into Colorado, until it reaches Denver, and there assuming the name of *Denver Pacific*, goes on a hundred and six miles to Cheyenne, Wyoming, connecting with the *Union Pacific Railroad*, thus forming a Through Line of Travel from Missouri and Kansas to Colorado, California, &c.

No other agency has done so much towards making Kansas what she is as the above Railroad. The present business over the Road is enormous. The cattle business alone is very great, and constantly increasing. Kansas is rapidly becoming the great source of cattle supply for the east. Along the whole Line, towns are constantly springing up, and soon become thriving seats of trade. The Kansas Pacific has put its immense land grant into market, on the most favourable terms.

Perhaps in the near future, the great Kansas Pacific Railway may be the chief thoroughfare across the Continent. Already the Rocky Mountains are within its iron grasp, and should it decide to branch at Kit Carson, and sweep along the 35th parallel, its locomotives will soon be whistling a welcome to the Pacific Coast,—even now, with its present connection by Denver and Cheyenne, with the Union Pacific, a great share of the travel and traffic across the Continent, will undoubtedly take this Route. Passing through the beautiful valley, and over the rich prairies of Kansas, with the newly opened farms on every side, that portion of the trip is made delightful, and as the western border of the State is approached, exciting, by the vast herds of Buffalo and Antelope thronging along the track. After leaving Kansas, the Railroad passes almost due west through Colorado to Denver, skirting the edges of the noted Pine Ridges. Along its path through Colorado immense coal fields exists, some of the veins being fourteen feet in thickness.

KANSAS CITY, the western terminus of the *Missouri Pacific and North Missouri Railroad* from St. Louis, and the *Hannibal and St. Joseph Railroad* connecting with Chicago and Toledo, is the point where trains are made up every day for the long Route to San Francisco, via Denver and Cheyenne. But the Kansas Pacific has another terminus at LEAVENWORTH CITY, one of the largest and most prosperous and beautiful cities in Kansas. This Road connects with the Main Line at Lawrence, another important station, where the *Leavenworth, Lawrence and Galveston Railroad* unites with the former.

"The KANSAS PACIFIC RAILROAD was formerly opened to the travel and business of the country on the 1st of September, 1870. The time from Kansas City to Denver is thirty-six hours. Tourists and pleasure-seekers will find this a preferable Route, as they will have an opportunity to see the rich and productive Valleys of the Kansas and Smoky Hill Rivers, and the grand mountain scenery between Denver and Cheyenne."

Running Southward from Denver, the DENVER AND RIO GRANDE RAILWAY is being built to connect this system of Roads with the arable and grazing Valleys of Southern Colorado, and the great mineral deposits of the tributaries of the Arkansas, the Pecos, and the Rio Grande. This Road, at a distance of 80 miles from Denver, reaches, at the foot of Pikes Peak, the celebrated Soda Springs of the "Boiling River," which are already largely resorted to for their medicinal virtues. Here the mineral and grazing districts of the South Park have their outlet.

Passing southward, 130 miles from Denver, it touches the town of Pueblo with 1500 inhabitants, and then Cañon City with its rich coal mines; thence into the Rio Grande Valley through the vast possessions of the United States Freehold Land and Emigration Company, which are being settled by General Burnside and friends, and near the rich Maxwell Land Co.'s property,—one gold mine of which is netting $120,000 per year to its proprietors.

Passing through Santa Fé with some 6,000 people, and Albuquerque with about 4,000 inhabitants, it will be extended through the line of towns along the Rio Grande, between rich silver, gold and copper districts to the Mexican line, and the celebrated silver districts of Chihuahua.

Union Pacific Railroad.

—The completion of the *Union Pacific Railroad*, extending from Omaha, Nebraska, to Ogden, Utah, a distance of 1,032 miles, and the *Central Pacific Railroad*, 881 miles in length, forming a Through Line of Travel across the Continent, was a bright event that will forever be remembered with delight by the American public. From Ocean to Ocean the most direct Route passes through thirteen States and Territories of the Union, this being the main artery of the System of Railroads in the United States, from which extend

Branches reaching every part of our extended country.

The construction of the Road was commenced in December, 1863; but no considerable amount of work was done till the commencement of 1865, owing to the difficulties that arose in the location of the Line. In 1865 over 100 miles were graded and bridged, and rails laid upon 40 miles. In 1866, 265 miles of Road were completed; in 1867, 245 miles; in 1868, 350 miles. The Road was completed to a junction with the Central Pacific Railroad of California on the 10th of May, 1869, which event was duly celebrated by the united Companies at Promontory, Utah. The last tie was made of laurel wood, finely inlaid with gold and silver, while the spikes were composed of precious metals and iron.

The Route for the eastern portion of the Line, starting from Omaha, is up the Valley of the Platte, which has a course nearly due east from the base of the Rocky Mountains. Till these are reached, this Valley presents, probably, the most favorable Line ever adopted for such a work for an equal distance. It is not only nearly straight, but its slope is very nearly uniform towards the Missouri River, at the rate of about 10 feet to the mile. The soil on the greater part of the Line forms an admirable road bed, while but few bridges are required until the North Platte is reached.

The base of the mountains is assumed to be at Cheyenne, Wyoming Territory, 516 miles from the Missouri River. This point is elevated 6,040 feet above the sea, and 5,074 feet above Omaha. From Cheyenne to the summit of the mountains at Sherman, which is elevated 8,242 feet above the sea, the distance is 32 miles. The grades for reaching this summit do not exceed 80 feet to the mile. The elevation of the vast plain from which the Rocky Mountains rise is so great that these summits, when they are reached, present no obstacles so formidable as those offered by the Alleghany ranges to several Lines of Railroads which cross them before descending into the Valley of the Mississippi.

After crossing the *Eastern Crest* of the mountains, the Line traverses an elevated plateau for about 400 miles to the *Western Crest* of the mountains, which forms the eastern *rim* of the Salt Lake Basin, and which has an elevation of 7,500 feet above the sea. Upon this elevated table is a succession of extensive plains, which present great facilities for the construction of the Road. From Ogden, westward, runs the *Central Pacific Railroad*.

St. Paul and Sioux City Railroad.—This Road runs southwest from St. Paul, through the Minnesota Valley to Mankato, and Sioux City on the Missouri River, a distance of 276 miles, where it connects with the *Sioux City and Columbus Branch* of the Union Pacific Railroad, now being constructed. When finished, this Line of Road in connection with the *Lake Superior and Mississippi Railroad*, will form a Railroad Route 100 miles shorter to Duluth, on Lake Superior, than to Chicago, on Lake Michigan. This is one of the most important Lines of Railroad that crosses the fertile State of Minnesota on account of its relations with the Union Pacific Railroad and Lake Superior. Shipments can be made, via Lake, River and Canal transportation, by this Route, to Canada and all the northern sea-ports of the United States.

Lake Superior and Mississippi Railroad.—The Line of the *Lake Superior and Mississippi Railroad* runs from St. Paul, the head of navigation on the Mississippi River, to the city of Duluth, at the head of Lake Superior, a distance of 155 miles, with branches to Minneapolis and Stillwater. Duluth is at the extreme west end of the Lake System of the Continent, the terminal point of twelve hundred miles of continuous lake navigation from the Atlantic coast, midway to the heart of the Continent, and on the completion of the *Northern Pacific Railroad*, westward, will be within four days of the Pacific coast by rail, and within twenty days by rail and water of the ports of China and Japan; and the territory between the lakes and the Pacific Ocean will soon be covered by an active and energetic population, engaged in agriculture, mining, and manufactures, whose products and supplies will come and go, by way of the Lakes, to and from the markets of the East and of Europe.

The *Lake Superior and Mississippi Railroad* connects at St. Paul, its southern terminus, with the trade of the Mississippi and Minnesota Rivers, and with all the long Lines of Railroads now pushing rapidly westward to people and develop the entire region from Lake Superior to the Pacific Ocean; which, within the limits of the State of Minnesota, at the close of the year 1870, foot up 1,086 miles in operation, and 1,163 miles in progress of construction,—of which 457 miles will be completed by the close of the year 1871; besides 1,500 miles projected, which will no doubt be constructed as demanded by the development of the State.

As is well understood, the course of trade is by way of the shortest and cheapest Route to market, and as the principal portion of the trade of the territory west of the Mississippi River must go, either to Lake Michigan or Lake Superior, it only remains to show what portions of country are nearer to each, to indicate the area tributary and belonging to these respective Routes.

The distance by Rail from St. Paul to Chicago, is 440 miles; Duluth 155 miles; and all Southwestern Minnesota and Northwestern Iowa will reach lake navigation at the port of Duluth by shorter Railroad transit than by the head of Lake Michigan, as is true also of a vast region extending to the Pacific Ocean.

This circumstance will control the course of trade, since the commerce of Lakes Michigan and Superior, when eastward bound, meets in Lake Huron; the navigation of the lakes being limited by the simultaneous departure of ice from the St. Mary's River and the Straits of Mackinaw. Even San Francisco and all the points of the Union Pacific Railroad are nearer Lake Superior at the harbor of Duluth, than to Lake Michigan at Chicago.

The distance from San Francisco to Chicago, via Union Pacific Railroad, is 2,400 miles; to Duluth by the Sioux City and Lake Superior and Mississippi Railroads, connecting with the above Road, is 2,300 miles, making a distance in favor of the Minnesota port of 100 Miles.

The rapidity with which the vast region tributary to the Lake Superior and Mississippi Railroad, and to Lake Superior, will be settled and developed may be illustrated by the progress and development of the State of Minnesota. This State was admitted into the Union in 1858, was unconnected with the east by Railways until the past **three** years, but is now taking a prominent position as a producing State among the old States of the Union. This progress will appear from the following statements compiled in the Department of State, and repeated in the messages of Governor Marshall:—

	1866.	1867.	1868.	1869.
No. of acres under cultiva'n.	895,412	1,092,593	1,337,170	1,660,090
No. of acres in Wheat	547,521	683,784	359,316	1,000,000
In Corn	88,183	100,618	129,909	175,000
In Oats	187,023	162,722	212,064	274,300
In Potatoes	18,297	17,647	24,474	25,500
Prod. of W., bu.	7,921,442	10,014,828	15,331,022	18,500,000
Corn, bu.	2,056,717	3,216,010	4,849,936	6,125,000
Oats, bu.	4,372,477	5,620,395	7,831,528	11,816,000
Potatoes, bu.	1,351,096	1,736,053	2,592,636	2,475,000

These results, advancing in this large ratio, may be taken as legitimately illustrating the future progress in settlement and production of the country further west and northwest; as the development of the same follows the construction of the Lines of Railway now projected and being constructed over this region.

The opening of the Lake Superior and Mississippi Railroad having its terminus located at the extreme top of the Lake System, and the construction of the Northern Pacific Railroad from the same lake terminus, westward, assures the transportation of emigrants from Europe by this shortest, cheapest, and most healthy Route to Duluth as the great distributing point for the entire Northwest. These emigrants following the Lines of the Railroads stretching out to the Pacific, cannot be diverted to points not tributary to Lake Superior, but must add from year to year to the vast and increasing product flowing and to flow by that channel to the eastern markets; and the time is not far distant when 20,000,000 of people will occupy the territory tributary to Lake Superior,—a large portion

of whose products and wants must be transported by this Route.

To sum up the whole matter:—Here is a territory, comprising portions of Wisconsin, Minnesota, Iowa and Dakota, rapidly increasing in population, —the present grain products of which are not less than 60,000,000 bushels,—a large percentage of which must go over the Line of the Lake Superior and Mississippi Railroad, and all of which will eventually go by the chain of the Great Lakes to the markets of the East and of Europe.

In estimating the value of the Lake Superior Route, the following facts should be carefully noted:—

First: The time of propellers or sailing vessels from Duluth to Lake Erie ports, is frequently less from two to three days than from Chicago or Milwaukee to the same points. The movement of boats against the winds, across Lake Michigan, makes this difference in time in favor of the boats that follow the currents to the head of Lake Superior.

Second: The same rates on produce are got from Duluth to points above named as from Chicago to Milwaukee, while as thus by the Lake Superior Route the Rail distance from St. Paul, or average point of production, being some 300 miles less, the through rate is necessarily considerably lower than the Route via Lake Michigan.

These facts entirely settle the question of transportation, and makes prominent the superior advantages possessed by the lands of this Company over those situated further westward, as the value of land depends not so much on the quality of the soil as on the facilities and cheapness with which the various products can be transported to market.

THE LAND GRANT of the Company comprises nearly 1,700,000 acres of land, portions of which are covered with Pine and other valuable timber, and interspersed with prairie and natural meadows or grazing lands, and many contain deposits of valuable minerals; while at numerous points there is abundance of water-power for manufacturing purposes.

The Pine lands will prove a source of large revenue to the Road, not only from receipts from stumpage, but from the transportation of manufacturer's lumber and supplies, and from the travel necessarily arising from the location of the mills engaged in the business. Liberal inducements are offered by the Company to parties desiring to engage in the lumber business on the Line of the Road, and every facility will be afforded to make the business both permanent and profitable.

The hard wood and prairie lands of the Company are equal to any in the northwest for the production of wheat, rye, oats and other grains, and all kinds of vegetables yield large crops, throughout this entire region.

The meadow lands are for stock raising the most valuable in the State, and require but a small amount of drainage to render them of permanent value. These meadows produce from 2 to 3½ tons per acre of the most nutritious grasses, on which cattle will thrive during the entire winter without grain; while from numerous lakes and running streams abundance of the purest water can be obtained.

These advantages, with the abundance of of timber from which strong, warm and substantial buildings can be erected, at a cost little exceeding the cutting and hauling of the timber, and the cheapness with which cattle and horses can be transported by Rail to Duluth, and by vessel to all points along the Lake, with the development of the entire region traversed by the Road, as shown by the influx of population now rapidly covering the entire grant, and particularly of the manufacturing sites along its Line, ensure such demand for stock of all kinds as cannot fail to make the business of stock-raising among the most profitable in the State.

The farming and grazing lands of the Company are sold in tracts of 40 acres and upwards, for cash or on long credit, at prices ranging from $2.50 to $8.00 per acre. A liberal reduction being made for entire cash payment.

For instance:—80 acres is sold on long time at $5.00 per acre, making $400; the payments would be as follows:—

		PRINCIPAL.	INTEREST.	AMOUNT.
1st Year	....	$22.00	$26.46	$48.46
2nd	"	54.00	22.68	76.68
3rd	"	54.00	18.90	72.90
4th	"	54.00	15.12	69.12
5th	"	54.00	11.34	65.34
6th	"	54.00	7.56	61.56
7th	"	54.00	3.78	57.78
8th	"	54.00		54.00

The purchaser having the privilege to pay up in full at any time he desires, thereby saving the payment of interest.

Any other information will be furnished on application in person or by letter.   Apply to

FRANK H. CLARK,
President and Land Com.
ST. PAUL, Minnesota.

St. Paul and Pacific Railroad, consolidated with the NORTHERN PACIFIC RAILROAD, November 25, 1870, consists of two divisions,—the Main Line, or First Division extends from St. Paul to Breckinridge, Minnesota, 216 miles, with the right to extend the Line from Breckinridge, on the Red River of the North, to the boundary line between the United States and British America.

The Second Division extends from St. Paul to Watab, Minnesota, a distance of 80 miles, and will extend northwesterly on the west side of the Mississippi River, connecting with the Main Line of the Northern Pacific Railroad west of Crow Wing, and extend on to the British border at Pembina, on the Red River, to the 49th parallel of latitude,—thus securing the carrying trade of British America.

The purchased Lines have liberal land grants through the richest parts of Minnesota, which accrue to the Northern Pacific Railroad Company, and the completion of all the Lines will give the Northern Pacific Company nearly nine hundred miles of Road in the State.

Northern Pacific Railroad.—The Act of Congress donating lands for this Road, prescribes that it shall be laid north of the 45th parallel of north latitude. Its termini are at DULUTH, Minnesota, at the head of Lake Superior, and a point, not yet designated, on Puget Sound, with a Branch Road terminating at PORTLAND, Oregon. The charter, as amended, authorizes the Company to construct a Branch Road, starting from "some convenient point" on the Trunk Line, across the Rocky Mountains, to Portland, and a Branch from Portland, northward, to the terminus on Puget Sound. These two Branch Roads are given (by amended charter) the same proportionate land grant as the Main Line, namely, 25,600 acres, per lineal mile of Road, through the Territories, and 12,800 acres, per lineal mile, through the organized States. The Main Branch Road will leave the Trunk Line somewhere near the junction of the Yellow Stone and Missouri Rivers, following up the valley of the former stream, through Deer Lodge Pass, and then down the Snake and Columbia Rivers to Portland, Oregon.

Estimated length of Main Line, connecting the navigation of the Great Lakes with the commerce of the Pacific Ocean, 1,775 miles; probable length of Trunk Line and Branches, 2,300 miles. The total amount of land to which the Northern Pacific Railroad is entitled, by its grant, is about *sixty million acres*, almost entirely fertile, with a salubrious climate, being capable of sustaining a dense population. The Winter months are comparatively mild, with but a small fall of snow, while the Summer months are warm and favorable for the growth of the cereals, grasses, and vegetables of almost every variety.

"The lands are within the parallels of latitude which in Europe and Asia embrace the most enlightened, creative, conquering and progressive populations. They lie within the climatic conditions of the isothermal lines of mean annual temperature, (50° to 52° Fahr.,) which mark on the Pacific Coast in latitude 47° north the mildness of the climate of the Chesapeake Bay, on the Atlantic side in latitude 38°, and which give to the region of this Railroad between the Red River of the North and the Pacific a

milder atmosphere, (at the same altitude) than is to be found anywhere
else at the same distance from the
Equator, except upon the western
coast of Europe."

By the purchase of the St. Paul and
Pacific Railroad, the Northern Pacific
Railroad controls the entire Railroad
traffic in the "New Northwest," and
connects with the Railways of Wisconsin and Illinois, as well with the navigable waters of the Mississippi River
and Lake Superior.

The work was begun in July, 1870,
on the eastern portion of the Line, and
the money provided, by the sale to
stockholders of some six millions of

the Company's bonds, to build and
equip the Road from Lake Superior
across Minnesota to the Red River of
the North, 232 miles. The grading
on this division is now well advanced,
the iron is being rapidly laid; several
thousand men are at work on the Line,
and about the first of August next this
important section of the Road will be
in full operation. In the meantime
orders have been sent to the Pacific
coast for the commencement of the work
on the western end in early Spring of
1871, and thereafter the work will be
pushed, both eastward and westward,
with as much speed as may be consistent with solidity and a wise economy.

TABLE OF DISTANCES AND ELEVATIONS,

NORTHERN PACIFIC RAILROAD,

PASSING THROUGH MINNESOTA, DAKOTA, MONTANA, IDAHO, OREGON AND WASHINGTON TER.

STATIONS.	MILES.	ALT. FT.
Du Luth, Minn.........	0	600
(*Lake Superior.*)		
Main Divide................	32	1,158
(Between L. S. & Miss. R.)		
Mississippi River...........	111	1,152
Hauteur des Terres.........	177	1,479
Red River of the North..	232	985
Dakota River...............	335	1,410
Plateau du Coteau.........	365	2,400
Missouri River.............	485	1,800
Yellow Stone River.......	675	2,100
Big Horn River............	825	2,250
Point Judith Mountains..	935	3,495
Missouri River 1,025		3,050
Cadott's Pass* 1,115		6,167
Flathead River...............1,225		2,410
Pend d'Oreille Lake.......1,355		2,020
Spokane River...............1,405		1,720

STATIONS.	MILES.	ALT. FT.
WALLA WALLA............		
Columbia River.............1,555		330
Snoqualmie Pass............1,694		3,030
Puget Sound.........1,775		00

The Distance from New York City
to Puget Sound, by the navigation of
the Erie Canal and Great Lakes, and
the *Northern Pacific Railroad*, is 3,285
miles, being about the same distance
as the most direct Route from New
York to San Francisco, via the *Union
Pacific Railroad.*

The distance from Puget Sound to
the mouth of the Amoor River, is
about 4,000 miles; to Hakodadi, Japan,
direct, 4,400 miles; and to Shanghai,
China, 5,716 miles.

* Deer Lodge Pass, 4,950 feet.

Projected Railroad FROM CHEYENNE TO HELENA, Montana.— The UNION PACIFIC RAILROAD and the DENVER PACIFIC RAILROAD, uniting at Cheyenne, Wyoming Territory, has induced the inhabitants of this new territory to look toward the north with the view of constructing an important Line of Railroad, the extreme northern terminus being Helena, Montana.

"The object is primarily to develop a wonderfully rich section of unoccupied country, and afterwards to give Cheyenne a connection with the Northern Pacific Railroad, rapidly stretching away from Duluth on the East and creeping out from Olympia at the West. The project exhibits the enterprise and wisdom of the inhabitants of Cheyenne, who, in this instance, find their greatest good in assisting to develop the country tributary to them. This Indian named town is directly connected with St. Louis by the Kansas Pacific and Denver Pacific Railroads. The Montana Railroad scheme which is now agitating its citizens, promises abundantly, and there is no reason, apparently, why the anticipations of its projectors should not be fulfilled. The proposed Route from Cheyenne—and here our readers are requested to consult their atlases—would extend up the Valley of the Crow Creek to the base of the Black Hills, then turning northward pass along the parallel Valley that seems designed by nature for a Railroad to the Chug Valley; thence down this Valley to some point near its junction with the Big Laramie, thence across the plains to the Valley of the North Platte, and up that stream to the Red Buttes. From this point it will not be difficult, it is claimed, to find an easy Route across the eastern base of the Big Horn Mountains, when it will pass through some of the most fertile and attractive Valleys of the West. The Line should then skirt the base of the mountains and extend to some point on the Yellowstone near the mouth of the Big Horn River. The principal obstacles are here passed, and the connection with the Main Branch of the Northern Pacific will be determined without difficulty.

Such a Road, we are informed, would open up to settlement a vast extent of country similar in many respects to the best portions of Colorado, and a section containing hundreds of thousands of acres of unclaimed land of the greatest fertility. The climate is so mild, and the season so delightful, that ready credence is given to the statement of the resident Indians, who affirm that the Great Spirit gave them this tract, the best and richest of his possessions, because they are a favored people. Cattle need no other shelter in Winter than the deep valleys afford. Iron and copper and magnetic ores abound in the mountains, and undiscovered minerals enrich the earth. Colonization schemes will be employed to rapidly populate the region, and hasten the development of its wealth."

Southern Pacific Railroad. — This projected Railroad, chartered by the State of Texas, July 27, 1870, to "*Incorporate the* SOUTHERN TRASCONTINENTAL RAILROAD COMPANY," with a capital of $30,000,000, will commence at the eastern boundary of Texas, and extend westward to *El Paso*, on the Rio Grande, with a privilege to construct Branch Roads, connecting with the great Railroads terminating on the sea-board. The Company is also authorised to purchase the rights, franchises and property of the Memphis and El Paso Pacific Railroad Company, and of any other Company, incorporated by any other State, or by the United States or any Territory, so that it may have a complete and continuous connection from the Atlantic to the Pacific Ocean.

"All the other Pacific Lines are in the hands of Northern and Western men, and are operated almost exclusively in the interest of the North and West. But here is one entirely Southern, extending, by its amended charter, from Memphis, Tennessee, to Little Rock, Arkansas; thence to Jefferson, Texas, and thence along the Route above designated to the town and bay of San Diego. The *Transcontinental Company* is already organized under a State charter, granted by the Legislature of Texas, and will soon begin practical operations through that partially undeveloped empire Commonwealth. The Texas Branch is about 800 miles in length. The Company's franchise over this enormous distance is wholly distinct from that of Congress, though additional or precedent thereto. It is impossible to over-estimate or even to describe the advantages of this Transcontinental Railroad, politically, commercially, and financially. Traversing the moderate zone, where winter is almost unknown, it will open up what many claim to be the richest region of our country, and what all concede to be the most magnificent cotton field in the world. Its wealth in minerals and agriculture; its neighborhood to Mexico, soon to be revolutionized by the arts of peace; its easier and short access to the two Oceans, will speedily arouse a universal interest in its behalf."

RAILROAD COMPANIES,

HAVING OFFICES IN THE CITY OF NEW YORK.

Allentown Line, 254 Broadway.

Atlantic and Great Western. Ticket Office, 241 Broadway.

Baltimore and Ohio, Freight and Ticket Office, 229 Broadway. C. W. Perveil, Gen. Agent, N. Y.

Burlington and Missouri River, Ticket Office, 8 Astor House.

Camden and Amboy, Pier 1, N. R., and foot of Cortlandt St. Office, 111 Liberty Street. Hoyt Sanford, Agent, N. Y.

Central, (of New Jersey,) 119 Liberty St. H. P. Baldwin, Gen. Passenger Agent. ☞ Passengers leave from foot of Liberty St.

Central Pacific, 54 William St. C. P. Huntington, Vice President.

Chicago and Alton, 12 Wall St.

Chicago, Burlington and Quincy, Freight and Ticket Office, 8 Astor House. R. G. Hoyt, Agent.

Chicago and Northwestern, Office, 52 Wall St.

Chicago, Rock Island and Pacific, 13 William St. John F. Tracy, President; John T. Sanford, General Agent. Ticket Office, 257 Broadway.

Cleveland, Columbus, Cincinnati and Indianapolis, 241 Broadway. John J. Hollister, Agent.

Columbus, Chicago and Indiana, 57 Broadway. B. E. Smith, President.

Delaware, Lackawanna and Western, 26 Exchange Place. Samuel Sloan, President.

Detroit and Milwaukee, Ticket Office, 349 Broadway. C. E. Noble, General Agent.

Erie Railway, Ticket Office, 241 Broadway, and foot of Chambers St. Wm. R. Barr, General Passenger Agent. Passengers leave from foot of Chambers St. and foot of 23rd St.

Flushing and North Side, foot of James Slip, E. R., or 34th St.

Grand Trunk, (Canada) Ticket Office, 175 Broadway. E. P. Beach, General Agent.

Great Southern Mail Route, Ticket Office, 229 Broadway. J. B. Yates, General Agent.

Great Western, (Canada) Ticket Office, 349 Broadway. C. E. Noble, General Agent.

Hudson River, West 30th St., cor. Tenth Avenue. C. Vanderbilt, President; C. H. Kendrick, General Ticket Agent. Ticket Office, 413 Broadway.

Illinois Central, 31 Nassau St., & 9 Astor House. John J. Sproull, General Agent.

Lake Shore and Michigan Southern, Ticket Office, 247 Broadway. H. C. Barr, Agent.

Long Island, Depot, James Slip, E. R. O. Charlick, President.

Michigan Central, Ticket Office, 349 Broadway. Charles E. Noble, General Agent.

Milwaukee and St. Paul, Office, 25 William St. Ticket Office, 319 Broadway. Joseph W. Prince, General Agent.

Morris and Essex, Depot, foot of Barclay St., foot of Christopher St., and Pier 48 N. R.

Newark and New York, foot of Liberty St.

New Jersey Railroad and Trans. Com., 111 Liberty St. and foot of Cortlandt St. A. L. Dennis, President; F. W. Rankin, Secretary.

New York Central, Ticket Office, 413 Broadway. R. L. Crawford, Agent.

New York and Harlem, Fourth Avenue, cor. E. 26th St. C. Vanderbilt, President.

New York and New Haven, Depot, Fourth Avenue, cor. East 27th St. Wm. D. Bishop, President. James H. Hoyt, Superintendent.

New Jersey Midland, 25 Nassau Street.

New York and Oswego Midland, 25 Nassau St.

New York and Flushing, Foot James Slip, E. R.

New York and Philadelphia Line, Passengers leave from foot Cortlandt St.

New York and Washington Air Line, Ticket Office, foot Cortlandt St. W. P. Smith, Gen. Manager, Washington, D. C.

Northern Pacific, Office, 120 and 122 Broadway, N. Y.—*Land Department,* 114 South Third St., Phila.

Ohio and Mississippi, Office 88 Wall St.

Panama, 88 Wall St. David Hoadley, President.

Pennsylvania Central, Ticket Office, 1 Astor House. J. L. Elliott, Agent.

Pittsburgh, Cincinnati and St. Louis, 526 Broadway. J. L. Miller, General Agent.

St. Louis Alton and Terre Haute, Office, 12 Wall St. Charles Butler, President.

Staten Island, Foot Whitehall St. J. H. Vanderbilt, President.

Toledo, Wabash and Western, 254 Broadway.

Union and Central Pacific, 303 Broadway. F. Knowland, General Agent.

Virginia and Tennessee Air Line, 303 Broadway.

West Shore Hudson River, 33 Broad St.

TELEGRAPH COMPANIES,
IN THE CITY OF NEW YORK.

Anglo-American, 88 Liberty St. Principal Offices, London, England. Cyrus W. Field, Director.

Atlantic and Pacific, 33 Broadway. A. F. Wilmarth, President.

Bankers' and Brokers', 16 Broad, and 4 Hanover Sts. Wm. Callow, President.

Erie Railway, Eighth Avenue cor. West 23rd St., and 145 Broadway.

Franklin, 11 Broad St. ☞ Extends from New York to Boston, Mass. George H. Ellery, President.

French Transatlantic Cable Co., (Limited.) "Société du Cable Transatlantique Francais."*

Gold and Stock, 18 New St. Marshall Lefferts, President.

International Ocean, 88 Liberty St. ☞ Extends from Lake City, Florida, to Havana, Cuba. Wm. F. Smith, President.

New York, Newfoundland and London, 88 Liberty St. ☞ Extends from Plaister Cove to Heart's Content, N. F., connecting with the ATLANTIC CABLE. Peter Cooper, President.

Pacific and Atlantic, 23 Wall St.

Western Union, 145 Broadway. William Orton, President; O. H. Palmer, Secretary and Treasurer. This Company reach across the Continent, from the Atlantic to the Pacific Ocean, and embraces every State and Territory in the Union but New Mexico and Arizona. They also connect with the Canada Lines of Telegraph, and with the Atlantic and Cuba Cables—having in use 115,000 miles of wire.

* Merged into the Anglo-American Company.

THE
PENNSYLVANIA CENTRAL RAILROAD,

And Connecting Lines in Conjunction with the

Union and Central Pacific Railroads,

FORMS THE

GREAT OVERLAND ROUTE,

BETWEEN THE

ATLANTIC AND PACIFIC OCEANS.

FOR QUICK TIME, SURE CONNECTIONS,
AND VARIETY OF SCENERY,
THIS ROUTE HAS NO EQUAL,

The Route from NEW YORK or PHILADELPHIA to PITTSBURGH, passes through the finest farming and grazing land of the East, and through the vast Coal Fields of Western Pennsylvania. The Road follows the course of the picturesque Susquehanna, Juniata and Conemaugh Rivers, and crosses the Allegheny Mountains at a height of 2,200 feet above the level of the sea.

Passengers desiring to pass through CHICAGO, the metropolis of the West, will, on reaching PITTSBURGH, take the "Fort Wayne Route" to CHICAGO. From thence to OMAHA, the Eastern terminus of the Union Pacific Railroad, they have a choice of three excellent Routes. From OMAHA to SAN FRANCISCO, passengers will have *but one change of Cars.*

Passengers wishing to visit ST. LOUIS will take the "Pan Handle Route" from PITTSBURGH, and pass through the Cities of COLUMBUS and INDIANAPOLIS. From ST. LOUIS, passengers can take the North Missouri R. R., or Pacific Missouri R. R. to the Junction, with the Kansas Pacific R. W. The Kansas Pacific R. W., connects at CHEYENNE with the Union Pacific R. R. From CHEYENNE to SAN FRANCISCO there is *but one change of Cars.*

PASSENGERS can also connect at St. Louis with the Railroads for Kansas City, and at Kansas City with the *Kansas City, St. Joseph & Council Bluffs R. R.* for Omaha, and at Omaha with *Union Pacific R. R.* for San Francisco.

THE PENNSYLVANIA CENTRAL

IS THE ONLY ROUTE

RUNNING PULLMAN PALACE CARS

FROM

NEW YORK AND PHILADELPHIA

TO

CHICAGO AND ST. LOUIS,

Without Change.

Passengers will please bear this in mind when selecting their Route

ACROSS THE CONTINENT,

AS IT WILL

SAVE THEM THE TROUBLE AND INCONVENIENCE OF SEVERAL CHANGES OF CARS.

THE DAY AND NIGHT CARS

Run by this Line are

THE FINEST IN THE COUNTRY,

As will be seen by a reference to the views on pages 114 and 115.

☞ Each Through Car is in charge of a Special Conductor. Ladies travelling alone, or families, can go through FROM OCEAN TO OCEAN without the least fear of trouble or annoyance.

This Line is in close working order with the NEW STEAMER LINES running between **San Francisco** and **Australia, New Zealand, Japan** and **China.**

112

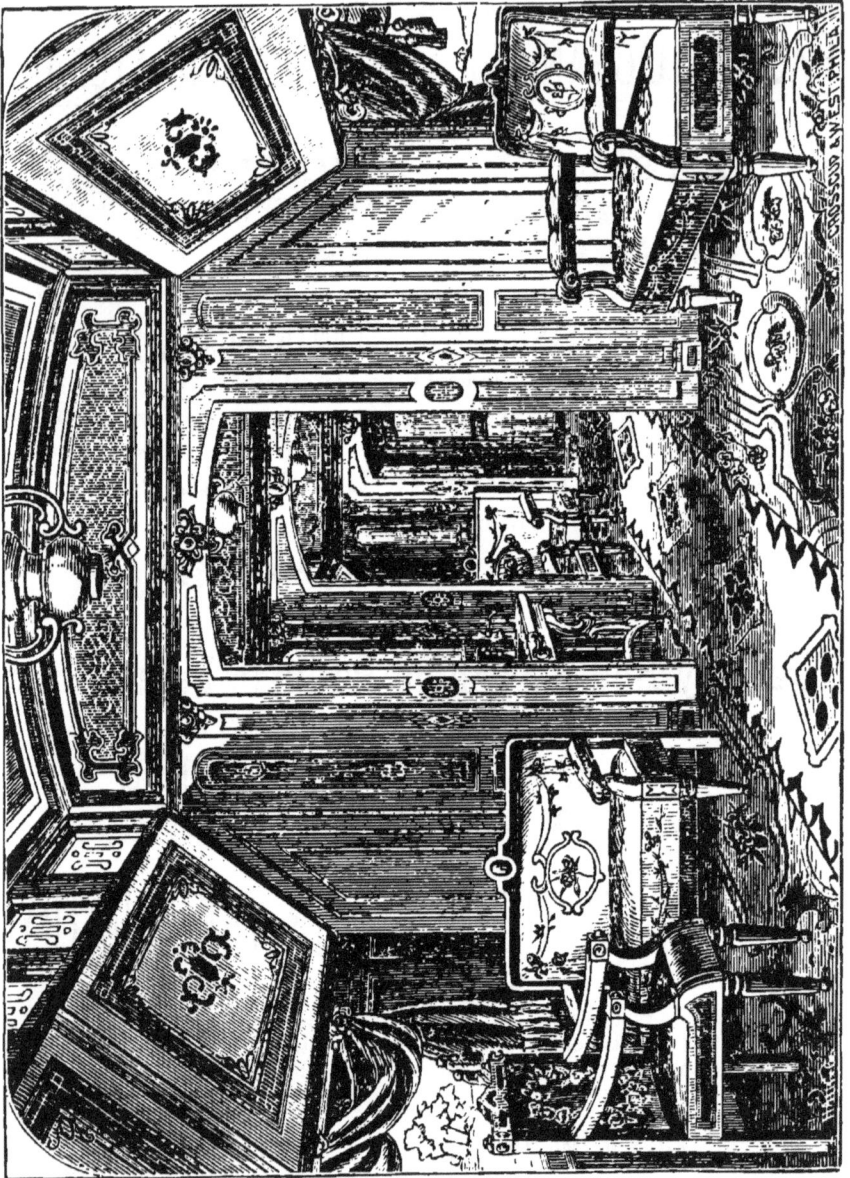

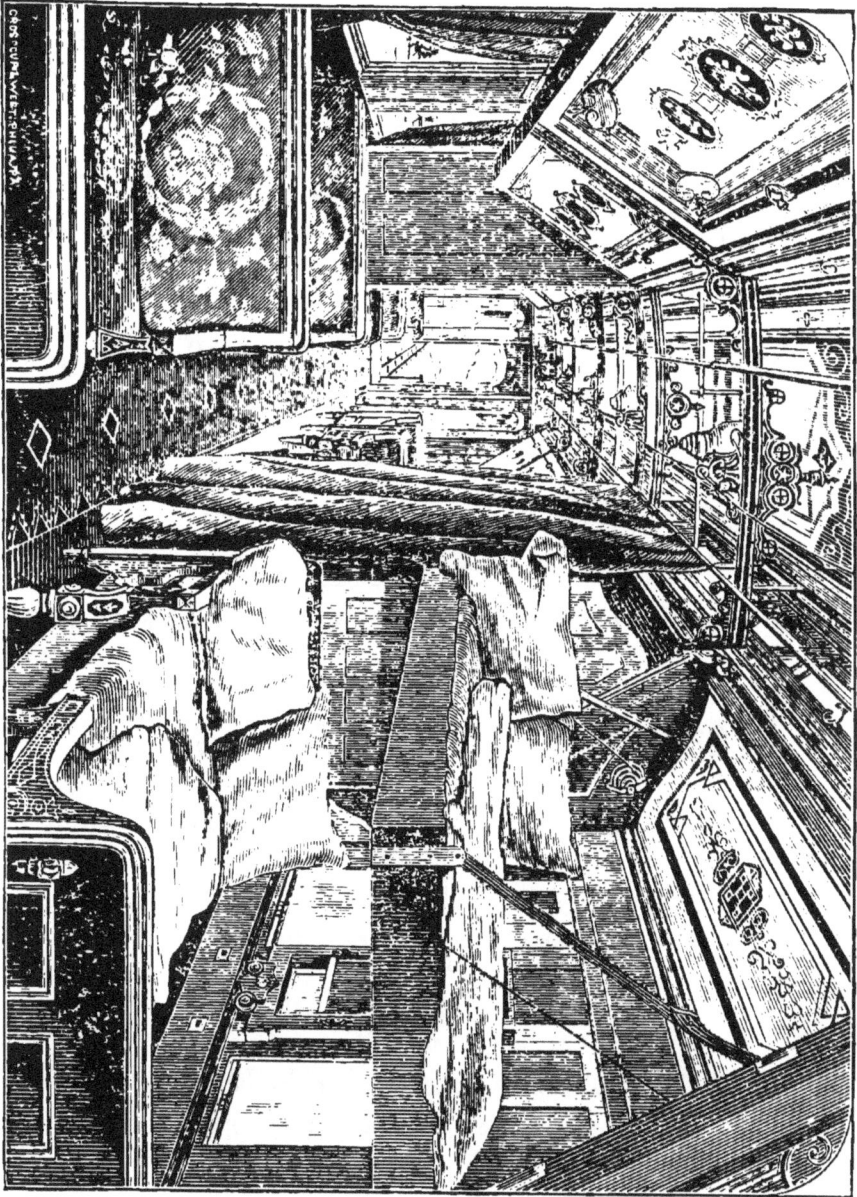

FROM THE

ATLANTIC OCEAN TO THE PACIFIC OCEAN

VIA THE

Philadelphia and Erie Route.

TO PASSENGERS CONTEMPLATING

A PLEASURE EXCURSION TO THE PACIFIC COAST,

THIS ROUTE OFFERS

UNEQUALLED INDUCEMENTS.

PARTIES DESIRING TO AVOID A RAILROAD JOURNEY IN THE SUMMER MONTHS

CAN CONNECT AT ERIE WITH A LINE OF

Steamers for Lake Superior

AND INTERMEDIATE POINTS.

Connecting at **DULUTH**, with the **NORTHERN PACIFIC RAILROAD.**

AT DULUTH, THE HEAD OF NAVIGATION,

Passengers can resume their Rail journey for **St. Paul**, at which point they connect for **Chicago**, via Rail,

OR WITH STEAMER LINES,

FOR

DUBUQUE, CLINTON, ROCK ISLAND, BURLINGTON, ST. LOUIS,

AND OTHER CITIES ON THE MISSISSIPPI RIVER.

116

PASSENGERS, VIA THE

PHILADELPHIA AND ERIE ROUTE,

Can also connect at ERIE with the Lake Shore R. R. Line, via CLEVELAND
and TOLEDO, or with the Lake Shore R. R. Line, and Pittsburgh, Fort
Wayne and Chicago R. W., via CLEVELAND and CRESTLINE, for CHICAGO;
and at CHICAGO with the Connecting Lines of the

UNION PACIFIC RAILROAD.

TO THE TOURIST AND PLEASURE-SEEKER,

NO COUNTRY IN THE WORLD

Offers as Great Attractions as California,

PROBABLY THE MOST NOTED AND WONDERFUL OF THESE ATTRACTIONS IS THE

"YOSEMITE VALLEY,"

The "YOSEMITE FALL," 2,600 feet in height, is the highest waterfall yet dis-
covered in the World. Towering over all, will be seen the lofty summit of
SOUTH DOME, which rises 6,000 feet above the Valley.

ON THE ROUTE TO "YOSEMITE" ARE FOUND THE

BIG TREES OF CALAVERAS,

The largest of these is 320 feet in height, and 90 feet in circumference.

Among the other noted Points of Interest are

THE HOT AND COLD MINERAL SPRINGS.

DONNER LAKE.

SANTA CLARA VALLEY.

THE GEYSERS.

AND

THE NUMEROUS GOLD, SILVER AND QUICKSILVER MINES.

117

FROM THE

Pacific Ocean to the Atlantic Ocean,

VIA THE

PHILADELPHIA AND ERIE ROUTE.

PASSENGERS FOR THE EAST

WILL FIND THIS

ONE OF THE BEST ROUTES.

At CHICAGO Passengers connect with the **Lake Shore Road**, via TOLEDO, for ERIE; or, with the **Pittsburgh, Fort Wayne and Chicago Railway**, via CRESTLINE, for ERIE.

At ERIE close Connections are made with Express Trains for

PHILADELPHIA, BALTIMORE,

NEW YORK, WASHINGTON,

AND

ALL POINTS EAST.

Passengers taking this Route have an opportunity of inspecting

THE GREAT OIL REGIONS,

AND

LUMBER DISTRICTS OF PENNSYLVANIA.

NEW YORK AND PHILADELPHIA RAILROAD.

Depot and Ticket Office, foot of Courtland Street,
NEW YORK,

WHERE THROUGH TICKETS AND CHECKS CAN BE PROCURED TO ALL PARTS OF THE

WEST, NORTHWEST, SOUTHWEST AND SOUTH.

THIS LINE WITH THE

PENNSYLVANIA CENTRAL RAILROAD,

AND CONNECTIONS, FORMS THE

SHORTEST, BEST, MOST COMFORTABLE, AND MOST DIRECT ROUTE
TO

Chicago, St. Louis, Louisville and Cincinnati.

TO ALL OF WHICH PLACES

PULLMAN'S SILVER PALACE CARS

RUN THROUGH FROM NEW YORK WITHOUT CHANGE.

AND WITH THE

PHILADELPHIA, WILMINGTON & BALTIMORE R. R.

AND CONNECTIONS, IT FORMS THE

Great Through Line to the Southwest and South,

NORFOLK, RICHMOND, CHARLESTON, AUGUSTA,
SAVANNAH, FERNANDINA, JACKSONVILLE, CEDAR KEYS, PENSACOLA,
MOBILE, NEW ORLEANS, ATLANTA, MACON, MONTGOMERY,
MEMPHIS AND LITTLE ROCK,

WITH PULLMAN'S SILVER PALACE CARS THROUGH FROM NEW YORK,
WITHOUT CHANGE,

To Baltimore, Washington and Lynchburg.

F. W. RANKIN,	F. W. JACKSON,
General Passenger Agent,	General Superintendent,
NEW YORK.	**JERSEY CITY.**

119

NORTHERN CENTRAL RAILROAD.

FOUR PASSENGER TRAINS WEST AND NORTH.

Trains leave BALTIMORE, four times Daily, for

HARRISBURG, SUNBURY AND WILLIAMSPORT,

TWICE DAILY, FOR

ELMIRA, CANANDAIGUA, ROCHESTER, BUFFALO AND NIAGARA FALLS,

CONNECTING AT HARRISBURG WITH THE

PENNSYLVANIA CENTRAL RAILROAD

FOR

PITTSBURGH, CHICAGO, &c.

The **Northern Central Railroad** affords the Most Direct and Speedy Route from WASHINGTON and BALTIMORE to the

WEST AND NORTH,

Connecting with the **Philadelphia and Erie Railroad**, at WILLIAMSPORT, and with the **Erie Railway** at ELMIRA, N. Y.

FOR TICKETS TO ALL POINTS NORTH AND WEST,

APPLY AT

CALVERT STATION, BALTIMORE.

EDWIN S. YOUNG,
General Passenger Agent.
120

ALFRED R. FISKE,
Gen'l Superintendent.

ILLINOIS CENTRAL RAILROAD.

GOING SOUTH.

CHICAGO to ST. LOUIS without Change of Cars.

TWO DAILY EXPRESS TRAINS, Morning and Evening.

Connecting at St. Louis for Kansas City, Leavenworth, Lawrence, Topeka, Denver and all parts of the West and Southwest.

☞ Fare as low and Time as quick as by any other route.

CHICAGO to CAIRO without Change of Cars.

TWO DAILY EXPRESS TRAINS, Morning and Evening.

This is the only direct route from **Chicago**—it is from 100 to 150 miles shorter, and from 12 to 24 hours quicker than any other to **Memphis, Vicksburg, Mobile, New Orleans** and all parts of the **South.**

ST. LOUIS to CAIRO without Change of Cars.

TWO DAILY EXPRESS TRAINS, Morning and Evening.

This is the only direct route from St. Louis, it is 30 miles shorter and two hours quicker than any other to Memphis, Vicksburg, Mobile, Nashville and all parts of the South and Southeast.

DUBUQUE to ST. LOUIS and CAIRO without Change of Cars.

TWO DAILY EXPRESS TRAINS, Morning and Evening.

This is the only direct route from the North and Northwest to St. Louis, Cairo and all parts of the South and Southwest.

ELEGANT DRAWING-ROOM SLEEPING CARS ON ALL NIGHT TRAINS.
Through Tickets and Baggage Checks issued to all Important Points.

FOR THROUGH TICKETS AND INFORMATION, apply at Chicago, at the Great Central Depot, foot of Lake Street; at St. Louis, at the Company's Office, 102 North Fourth Street; at Cairo and Dubuque, at the Depots.

W. P. JOHNSON,
GEN'L PASSENGER AG'T, CHICAGO.

M. HUGHITT,
GENERAL SUP'T, CHICAGO.

ILLINOIS CENTRAL RAILROAD.
GOING NORTH.

CAIRO to CHICAGO without Change of Cars.

TWO DAILY EXPRESS TRAINS, Morning and Evening.

Connecting at Chicago with all Eastern and Northern Lines for Niagara Falls, Buffalo, Pittsburgh, Philadelphia, Baltimore, Washington, Milwaukee, St. Paul and all parts of the East and North. This is from 100 to 150 miles shorter and from 12 to 24 hours quicker, from all parts of the South, to Chicago and the East and North.

☞ **Only One Change of Cars from Cairo to New York.**

CAIRO to ST. LOUIS without Change of Cars.

TWO DAILY EXPRESS TRAINS, Morning and Evening.

This is the only direct route from the South and Southeast to St. Louis, Kansas City, Leavenworth, Denver and all parts of the Northwest; it is 30 miles shorter and 2 hours quicker than any other.

ST. LOUIS to CHICAGO without Change of Cars.

TWO DAILY EXPRESS TRAINS, Morning and Evening.

Connecting at Chicago for Niagara Falls, Buffalo, Pittsburgh, Philadelphia, Baltimore, Washington, Milwaukee, St. Paul and all parts of the North and East.

☞ **Only One Change of Cars from St. Louis to New York.**

CAIRO and ST. LOUIS to DUBUQUE without Change of Cars.

TWO DAILY TRAINS leave Cairo and St. Louis, Morning and Evening.

Passing through Vandalia, Pana, Decatur, Bloomington, El Paso, La Salle, Mendota, Freeport, Warren, Galena and Dunleith to Dubuque, at which points connections are made with the *Iowa Division of the Illinois Central Railroad* for Cedar Falls, Independence, Waterloo, Fort Dodge and Sioux City, also with Steamers on the Upper Mississippi, for Prairie Du Chien, La Crosse, Winona, St. Paul and intermediate points. The *Lake Superior and Mississippi Railroad* runs from St. Paul to Duluth, Minn.

W. P. JOHNSON,
GEN'L PASSENGER AG'T, CHICAGO.

M. HUGHITT,
GENERAL SUP'T, CHICAGO.

CHICAGO, KANSAS CITY AND DENVER THROUGH LINE.

CHICAGO, BURLINGTON AND QUINCY,

Hannibal & St. Joseph and Kansas Pacific Railroads.

---

64 MILES, THE SHORTEST ROUTE
From CHICAGO to
KANSAS CITY, FORT SCOTT, LAWRENCE, TOPEKA,
AND ALL POINTS IN KANSAS.

The only Route Running Pullman's Palace Sleeping Cars through between Chicago,

KANSAS CITY AND DENVER,
Without Change or Ferry, Connecting with

Denver Pacific Railroad for Cheyenne, Ogden, Salt Lake, Sacramento and San Francisco.

---

70 MILES, THE SHORTEST ROUTE
From CHICAGO to
LEAVENWORTH, IATAN, WESTON,
·And all Principal Points in Northern Kansas.

---

115 MILES, THE SHORTEST ROUTE
From CHICAGO to
ST. JOSEPH, ATCHISON, WATERVILLE,
And all Points on Central Branch Union Pacific Railroad.

Passengers should be particular to ask for Tickets via Chicago, Burlington and Quincy Railroad.

SAM'L POWELL, GEN'L TICKET AG'T, CHICAGO.   E. A. PARKER, GEN'L WEST. PASS. AG'T, CHICAGO.
ROBERT HARRIS, GENERAL SUPERINTENDENT, CHICAGO.

CHICAGO, ROCK ISLAND AND PACIFIC
RAILROAD.

THE DIRECT ROUTE FOR

Joilet, Morris, Ottawa, La Salle, Peru, Henry,

PEORIA, LACON, GENESEO, MOLINE,

Rock Island, Davenport, Muscatine, Washington, Iowa City, Grinnell, Newton, Des Moines,

COUNCIL BLUFFS & OMAHA,

Connecting with Trains on the Union Pacific Railroad, for

CHEYENNE, DENVER, CENTRAL CITY, OGDEN, SALT LAKE, WHITE PINE, HELENA, SACRAMENTO, SAN FRANCISCO,

And all Points in Upper and Lower California; and with Ocean Steamers at San Francisco, for all Points in

CHINA, JAPAN, SANDWICH ISLANDS, OREGON AND ALASKA.

ELEGANT PALACE SLEEPING COACHES
Run Through to Peoria and Council Bluffs, Without Change.

☞ Connections at LA SALLE, with Illinois Central Railroad, North and South; at PEORIA, with Peoria, Pekin & Jacksonville Railroad, for Pekin, Virginia, &c.; at PORT BYRON JUNCTION, for Hampton, Le Claire, and Port Byron; at ROCK ISLAND, with Packets North and South on the Mississippi River.

☞ For Through Tickets, and all desired Information in regard to Rates, Routes, &c., call at the Company's Office,

No. 37 South Clark St., Chicago; or, 257 Broadway, New York.

A. M. SMITH, Gen. Pass. Agent. HUGH RIDDLE, Gen. Supt. P. A. HALL, Asst. Gen. Supt.

125

CHICAGO, ALTON AND ST. LOUIS RAILROAD.

THE SHORTEST, QUICKEST, AND BEST ROUTE TO

JOLIET, BLOOMINGTON, SPRINGFIELD, JACKSONVILLE, ALTON,

AND

SAINT LOUIS,

WITHOUT CHANGE OF CARS OR BAGGAGE.

THE ONLY ROAD BETWEEN CHICAGO AND ST. LOUIS RUNNING

Pullman's Palace Sleeping and Celebrated Dining Cars.

THE ONLY LINE OVER WHICH

THREE THROUGH EXPRESS TRAINS

Leave Chicago for St. Louis Daily,

AND MAKING THE

TIME IN 11 HOURS.

This being the most Direct Route, via ST. LOUIS, to all Points in Missouri, Kansas, South and Southwest, Passengers have an assurance of making advertised Time and certain Connections which cannot be relied upon by longer and more circuitous Routes.

FARE ALWAYS AS LOW AS BY ANY OTHER ROUTE.

BAGGAGE CHECKED THROUGH FREE OF CHARGE.

ASK FOR AND NOTICE THAT YOUR TICKETS READ

Via Chicago & Alton Road—the Short Air Line Route!

Which can be purchased at all principal Ticket Offices in the United States and Canadas.

A. NEWMAN, Chicago, Gen'l Ticket Agent.　　　J. C. McMULLIN, Gen'l Sup't.

127

Chicago & Northwestern Railroad.

Cleveland, Columbus, Cincinnati, and Indianapolis R. R.

IF YOU ARE GOING

NORTH AND EAST,

BUY YOUR TICKETS OVER THE FAVORITE

"BEE LINE,"

FOR SALE

THROUGHOUT THE WEST AND SOUTH.

The Cleveland, Columbus, Cincinnati & Indianapolis Railway, ("Bee Line") extends from Cleveland, O., through Wellington, New London, Shelby, Crestline, Galion, Cardington and Delaware to Columbus, Ohio, —138 Miles; from Delaware, Ohio, to Springfield, Ohio,—50 Miles; from Crestline, Ohio, through Marion, Bellefontaine and Sydney, Ohio, Union, Muncie and Anderson, Indiana, to Indianapolis, Indiana,—207 Miles; Total, 395 Miles.

The Indianapolis & St. Louis Railway, extends from Indianapolis, Indiana, through Danville, Green Castle and Terre Haute, Indiana, Charleston, Mattoon, Shelbyville, Pana, Hillsboro', Litchfield, Bunker Hill and Alton, Illinois, to St. Louis, Missouri,—261 Miles.

These Two Important Railway Lines run THREE EXPRESS PASSENGER TRAINS each way, Daily, with Direct Connections to and from Buffalo, Dunkirk, Erie, Cleveland, Crestline, Pittsburgh, Chicago, Columbus, Cincinnati, Indianapolis, Louisville, Terre Haute, Pana, Mattoon, Alton and St. Louis, and through those places with the entire country—

EAST, WEST, NORTH AND SOUTH.

E. S. FLINT,	S. F. PIERSON,	E. A. FORD,
Gen'l Superintendent,	General Ticket Agent,	Gen'l Pass. Agent,
CLEVELAND, OHIO.	CLEVELAND, OHIO.	CLEVELAND, OHIO.

9

129

BURLINGTON RAILROAD ROUTE.

THE BURLINGTON & MISSOURI RIVER RAILROAD,

Starting from BURLINGTON, Iowa, is a tree whose trunk forks into three branches, for it has three Western termini, each one of which is the representative of a distinctive class of Business, or separate class of Travel. Its first terminus is at

COUNCIL BLUFFS, OR OMAHA,

where it connects with the Union Pacific Railroad, for all points on the Pacific Roads and Pacific Coast, and it is now generally conceded that this is the best Route to these points. Its next terminus is at

LINCOLN,

the capital of Nebraska, fifty-five miles West of the Missouri River, (crossing the River at Plattsmouth,) opening up a rich country lying South of the Platte, where half a million dollars worth of Railroad Lands were sold last summer, and being indeed the only Direct Route thereto. Its third terminus is at

HAMBURG AND NEBRASKA CITY.

At Hamburg, its Passenger Trains, (two each way, daily,) make close connections with the trains of the

KANSAS CITY & COUNCIL BLUFFS RAILROAD,

for St. Joseph, Leavenworth, Kansas City, and all points in the Territories. In this regard it may be truly said that the passenger travelling from the East to Kansas, via Burlington, obtains advantages that he can find on no other Line, for he not only travels over a First-Class Road, splendidly equipped, where he is sure of safety and comfort while *en route* to his destination, but he has an opportunity of viewing the richest portions of Illinois and Missouri, as well as several hundred thousand acres of Railroad Land in Southwestern Iowa, just now coming into market at low prices and long credit.

☞ To passengers bound Westward, for any of these points, no better advice can be given than

"TAKE THE BURLINGTON ROUTE."

130

NORTH MISSOURI RAILROAD.

THE SHORT LINE FROM
ST. LOUIS TO OTTUMWA, KANSAS CITY, ST. JOSEPH
AND COUNCIL BLUFFS, AND ALL POINTS WEST.

EXPRESS TRAINS
LEAVE ST. LOUIS DAILY,
On arrival of TRAINS from the EAST and SOUTH, and from CHICAGO.

CLOSE CONNECTIONS
Made in UNION DEPOT, KANSAS CITY, with all Trains of WESTERN ROADS.

THE ONLY LINE RUNNING THROUGH CARS FROM
St. Louis to Ottumwa, St. Joseph and Council Bluffs.

THE ONLY LINE RUNNING
PULLMAN'S PALACE SLEEPING CARS
FROM ST. LOUIS TO OTTUMWA,
Kansas City, Leavenworth, Atchison, St. Joseph and Council Bluffs,
WITHOUT CHANGE.

Ask for Tickets " Via North Missouri Railroad," which can be had at all Regular Ticket Offices, and in ST. LOUIS at the Offices of the Company,

113 North Fourth Street, (under the Planters' House,)
AND AT BIDDLE STREET, AND NORTH MARKET STREET DEPOTS.
FARE AS LOW AS BY OTHER ROUTES.

JAMES CHARLTON,
General Passenger and Ticket Agent,
ST. LOUIS.

W. R. ARTHUR,
GENERAL SUPERINTENDENT,
ST. LOUIS.

NORTH MISSOURI RAILROAD.

THE SHORT LINE FROM
SAINT LOUIS
TO
KANSAS, COLORADO AND CALIFORNIA,
IOWA AND NORTH.

A CONTINUOUS ROUTE, UNDER ONE MANAGEMENT, FROM

SAINT LOUIS

To Columbia, Mo., Ottumwa, Iowa, Chillicothe, Mo., Lexington, Mo.,
Kansas City, Mo., and St. Joseph, Mo.

THE GREAT IRON BRIDGE ACROSS THE MISSOURI AT ST. CHARLES
Is now completed, making an unbroken Connection by
THIS SHORT ROUTE FROM
ST. LOUIS TO ALL POINTS WEST AND NORTH.

NO TRANSFERS! NO FERRIES! AND NO CHANGE OF CARS!

65 Miles the Shortest Line from St. Louis to Macon.
72 " " " " " St. Louis to Chillicothe.
11 " " " " " St. Louis to Kansas City.
15 " " " " " St. Louis to Leavenworth.
10 " " " " " St. Louis to Atchison.
50 " " " " " St. Louis to St. Joseph,
COUNCIL BLUFFS, AND OMAHA.

ONLY THREE CHANGES OF CARS,
(One at ST. LOUIS, one at OMAHA, and one at UNION JUNCTION, CENTRAL AND UNION PACIFIC RAILROADS) between NEW YORK and all important Eastern and Southern Cities and San Francisco, by this Route.

PULLMAN'S PALACE CARS
Run from NEW YORK to ST. LOUIS, ST. LOUIS to OMAHA, and OMAHA to UNION JUNCTION by this Route only.

JAMES CHARLTON,
General Passenger and Ticket Agent,
ST. LOUIS.

W. R. ARTHUR,
General Superintendent,
ST. LOUIS.

132

PACIFIC RAILROAD OF MISSOURI,

PASSING THROUGH JEFFERSON CITY.

THE DIRECT ROUTE TO

Kansas, Colorado, Utah and California,

CONNECTING WITH THE

KANSAS PACIFIC RAILROAD.

THE ONLY ROAD FROM

ST. LOUIS to ATCHISON and FORT SCOTT,

PASSING THROUGH

KANSAS CITY AND LEAVENWORTH,

WITHOUT CHANGE OF CARS.

Two Daily Trains, Morning and Evening,

LEAVE ST. LOUIS FOR KANSAS CITY, &c.

PALACE SLEEPING CARS ON NIGHT TRAINS.

Ticket Office, 115 North Fourth Street, St. Louis,

AND AT DEPOT, CORNER SEVENTH AND POPLAR.

W. B. HALE,
General Passenger and Ticket Agent.

T. McKISSOCK,
General Superintendent.

NEW ROUTE TO CALIFORNIA,

VIA

KANSAS PACIFIC RAILWAY.

TRAINS LEAVE KANSAS CITY

On arrival of Trains of Hannibal & St. Joseph, North Missouri and Pacific Railroads, as follows :—

	MILES.	11.00 P. M.	9.50 A. M.
Leave **Kansas City**..		11.00 P. M.	9.50 A. M.
" Lawrence	38	1.00 A. M.	11.55 "
" Topeka..............	67	2.30 "	1.30 P. M.
" Wamego..............	104	4.15 "	3.40 "
" Manhattan...........	118	4.55 "	4.23 "
" Junction City.......	138	5.50 "	5.23 "
" Abilene.....	163	6.55 "	6.35 "
" Solomon..............	173	7.20 "	7.00 "
" Salina..	185	8.25 "	8.15 "
" Brookville...........	200	9.25 "	9.00 "
" Ellsworth............	223	10.30 "	....
" Hays City....	289	1.40 P. M.	....
" Carson...............	487	11.30 "	....
" Hugo...............	534	1.45 A. M.	....
ARRIVE AT			
DENVER..............	639	7.00 "	....
Cheyenne	745	1.20 P. M.	....
Ogden..................	1261	1.20 "	....
San Francisco.......	2143	6.00 "	....

Connecting at **Denver** with the **Denver Pacific Railway** for **Cheyenne**, where close Connections are made with the **Union Pacific Railroad** for

OGDEN, SALT LAKE, CORINNE, RENO, BATTLE
MOUNTAIN, ELKO, COLFAX, SACRAMENTO, MARYSVILLE, SAN FRANCISCO,
AND ALL POINTS ON THE PACIFIC COAST.

Making close Connections, Daily, at DENVER, for Central City, Georgetown, &c.; at Kit Carson, with *Southern Overland Mail and Express Co.'s Daily Line of Coaches* for Pueblo, Trinidad, Las Vegas, Sante Fé, Las Cruces, and all Points in Southern Colorado, New Mexico and Arizona.

TICKETS FOR SALE AT ALL PRINCIPAL TICKET OFFICES.

PASSENGER AND FREIGHT RATES AS LOW AS BY ANY OTHER ROUTE.

BEVERLY R. KEIM,   **T. F. OAKES,**   **A. ANDERSON,**
Gen'l Ticket Agent.   Gen'l Freight Agent.   Gen'l Superintendent.

134

1,500,000

ACRES OF LAND

IN

CENTRAL AND SOUTHWEST MISSOURI,

Offered for Cash, or on Seven Years Credit, at

FROM $3.00 TO $15.00 PER ACRE,

—BY THE—

ATLANTIC & PACIFIC RAILROAD COMPANY,

EMBRACING THE

SOUTH PACIFIC RAILROAD.

The State of Missouri, more than any other in the Union, contains the materials that constitute wealth. It is one-and-a-half times the size of the State of New York, and more than eight times that of Massachusetts. It is in the centre of the Mississippi Valley, near the heart of the Continent, and its metropolis, St. Louis, naturally, the half-way station between the Oceans.

The Climate is the golden mean of the Temperate Zone; its salubrity is proverbial—especially in the centre and southwestern portions—where the elevation above the ocean produces all the vitality of a more Northern latitude, while none of the Southern advantages are lost. Consumption and asthmatic complaints seldom or never originate here, but are often cured by this climate.

The Easterly portions of the State, through which the Railroad passes, including the Ozark range of hills, is broken, but of good soil, and has many excellent farms in the valleys, with extensive ranges for flocks and herds upon the higher land. This extends over 100 miles from St. Louis, when small prairies and a smoother country begin to appear.

The Central and Southwestern portion of the State, extending about 150 miles, easterly and westerly, cannot be excelled in beauty and fertility. The

136

dead level of trackless prairies is not found here, nor stagnant creeks and muddy pools. Instead of these are hill and dale and rolling prairies, frequent streams, and rapidly running water, over rocky bottoms, with numerous waterfalls and springs of clear, pure water.

The principal productions are corn, wheat, rye, barley, oats, flax, hemp, sorghum, tobacco, cotton, vegetables, and an abundance of all kinds of fruit.

The Southwestern portion of the State, with its mild Winters, late Falls, and early Springs, is peculiarly adapted to Stock-Raising of all kinds; blue grass grows spontaneously, and all tame grasses rapidly, and in abundance. By the aid of the Railroad, cattle in the Western counties are now worth within four dollars a head of what they are worth in St. Louis.

The production of wool is large, and increasing with marked rapidity. Woolen factories would be a profitable investment upon the water powers now unoccupied.

Missouri can challenge the World in variety, value, and extent of mineral wealth. A long catalogue would alone suffice to enumerate the different metals. They pervade more or less the whole State.

Timber is abundant, and so accessible as not to be extremely costly at any point.

As to Schools, few States are more awake than Missouri, and none more amply supplied with pecuniary provisions.

HOW TO REACH THESE LANDS.

From St. Louis, Southwest Missouri and the Lands offered for Sale, may be reached by the ATLANTIC and PACIFIC, otherwise called the

SOUTH PACIFIC RAILROAD.

☞All Station Agents on the Road are authorized to show the Company's Lands. At St. Louis, Descriptive Pamphlets and all needed Information can be obtained at the Land Office, or received elsewhere, upon request, in letters addressed to

AMOS TUCK,

Land Commissioner, Atlantic & Pacific Railroad Co,,

523 Walnut Street,

SAINT LOUIS, MO.

The Union and Central Pacific R. R. Line

FORMS DIRECT CONNECTION AT

OMAHA

WITH EVERY RAILROAD IN THE UNITED STATES AND CANADAS
VIA

Chicago, Rock Island and Pacific R. R.
Chicago and Northwestern R. R.
Kansas City, St. Joseph and Council Bluffs R. R.
and Burlington and Missouri River R. R.

WITH THEIR CONNECTIONS .

Forming a Through Line of Travel from the Atlantic to the Pacific Ocean.

Passengers will choose their own Route and all Connecting
Lines will receive impartial representation.

ALL FIRST-CLASS PASSENGER TRAINS

ARE ACCOMPANIED BY

Palace Drawing-Room and Sleeping Cars.

Fare $2.00 Each Day and Each Night.

☞ Sleeping Berths or Sections can be secured upon application to the
Sleeping Car Conductor on the Train, at the Railroad Ticket Offices, or by
Telegraph, to

L. M. BENNETT,

General Superintendent Pullman Pacific Car Company, Omaha.

☞ Conductors on this Line are instructed to Telegraph for Sleeping Berths
for Passengers, by any Route they may choose, FREE OF EXPENSE.

138

DENVER PACIFIC RAILROAD

FORMING A JUNCTION WITH THE

Union Pacific Railroad

AT

CHEYENNE,

IS NOW OPEN, AND TRAINS RUN REGULARLY IN CONNECTION WITH TRAINS ON THE U. P. R. R. AT

Cheyenne, for Denver, Santa Fé,

AND ALL POINTS IN

COLORADO AND NEW MEXICO.

ONLY 110 MILES FROM CHEYENNE TO DENVER.

The Road runs along the Platte River at the base of the Mountains, which furnish the grandest scenery on the Continent. LONG'S PEAK and PIKE'S PEAK, 65 miles off the Line, seen so distinctly through the clear atmosphere of these mountain districts, appear to be not ten miles away.

From DENVER, as a centre, the Tourist is able to reach all the Interesting Points in the interior by easy and short journeys by

Colorado Central R. R. and Fast Stages.

Visiting the Mountain Towns, CENTRAL CITY, GEORGETOWN, and also the magnificent NATURAL PARKS, so often described by travellers and writers, who count among the Wonders of the World, the GREAT NORTH PARK, MIDDLE PARK, CENTRAL PARK, SAN LUIS PARK, GARDEN OF THE GODS, and numberless smaller Natural Parks, filled with game, trout streams, medicinal springs, natural groves and pastures,—presenting the richest and most varied scenery. The high-lying valleys of Colorado having an altitude of 4,000 to 6,000 feet afford a climate unexcelled even by Italy, either for a summer or winter residence. This promises to be one of the most attractive districts for Tourists.

Passengers on the U. P. R. R. having Through Tickets, can, on application to the Conductor, stop over at Cheyenne and visit this delightful country.

Passengers or Emigrants wishing to go only to Points in Colorado or New Mexico, should purchase Through Tickets, via OMAHA and CHEYENNE.

The Utah Central Railroad

FORMING A JUNCTION WITH THE

UNION PACIFIC RAILROAD

AT

OGDEN,

IS NOW COMPLETED AND THREE DAILY TRAINS RUN REGULARLY BETWEEN

OGDEN AND SALT LAKE CITY,

ON THE

GREAT SALT LAKE.

Passengers have now the opportunity to visit that

INTERESTING COUNTRY,

Without, as formerly, enduring a tedious Stage ride.

Only 37 Miles from Ogden to Salt Lake City.

Fare $2.00—Time 2 Hours.

Route through Magnificent Scenery and over a good Railroad.

THROUGH PASSENGERS are allowed to stop over at OGDEN for rest, and to make this delightful Excursion to the Capital of Utah, which is the principal city in this great interior country.

THE MOST COMFORTABLE ACCOMMODATIONS

Are Furnished by the Hotels at Salt Lake,

FOR TOURISTS,

As well as for those who wish to make a longer stay in this Curious and Interesting Locality.

THE MEDICINAL WATERS AND HOT SPRING BATHS

OF THIS NEIGHBORHOOD

Are a great attraction to Pleasure-Seekers as well as to Invalids.

☞The Finest Fruits Grow in Profusion in this Highly Cultivated Valley.

140

Northern Pacific Railroad.

NEW 7-30 GOLD LOAN

OF THE ABOVE COMPANY

Secured by First Moptgage on Railroad and Land Grant.

Safe! Profitable! Permanent!

We offer for sale, at Par and accrued Interest,

THE FIRST MORTGAGE LAND GRANT GOLD BONDS OF THE NORTHERN PACIFIC RAILROAD COMPANY.

THEY ARE FREE FROM UNITED STATES TAX, AND ARE ISSUED OF THE FOLLOWING DENOMINATIONS:

Coupons, $100, $500, and $1000; Registered, $100, $500, $1000, $5000, and $10,000.

WITH the same entire confidence with which we commended Government Bonds to Capitalists and People, we now, after the fullest investigation, recommend these **Northern Pacific Railroad Bonds** to our friends and the general public.

GOLD PAYMENT.—Both principal and interest are payable in American gold coin, at the office of JAY COOKE & Co., New York City,— the principal at the end of 30 years, and the interest (at the rate of seven and three-tenths per cent. per annum) half-yearly, first of January and July.

PERFECT SAFETY.—The Bonds we are now selling, are secured by a first and only mortgage on all the property and rights of the Northern Pacific Railroad Company, which will embrace on the completion of the work:—

1. Over Two Thousand Miles of Road, with rolling stock, buildings, and all other equipments.

141

2. Over Twenty-two Thousand Acres of Land to every mile of finished road. This land,—agricultural, timbered and mineral,—amounting in all to more than Fifty Million Acres, consists of alternate sections, reaching twenty to forty miles on each side of the Track, and extending in a broad fertile belt from Wisconsin through the richest portions of Minnesota, Dakota, Montana, Idaho, Oregon and Washington, to Puget Sound.

While the Government does not directly guarantee the Bonds of the Road, it thus amply provides for their full and prompt payment by an unreserved grant of land, the most valuable ever conferred upon a great National improvement.

THE MORTGAGE.—The Trustees under the Mortgage, are Messrs. Jay Cooke of Philadelphia, and J. Edgar Thompson, President of the Pennsylvania Central Railroad Company. They will directly and permanently represent the interests of the First Mortgage bond-holders, and are required to see that the *proceeds of land sales* are used in *purchasing and cancelling the Bonds of the Company*, if they can be bought before maturity at not more than 10 per cent. premium; otherwise the Trustees are to invest the proceeds of land sales in United States Bonds or Real Estate Mortgages for further security of Northern Pacific bond-holders. Also, that they have at all times in their control, as security, at least 500 acres of average
142

land to every $1,000 of outstanding First Mortgage Bonds, besides the Railroad itself, and all its equipments and franchises.

PROFITABLENESS.—Of course nothing can be safer than the Bonds of the United States, but as the Government is no longer a borrower, and as the Nation's present work is not that of preserving its existence, but that of DEVELOPING A CONTINENT, we remind those who desire to increase their income and obtain a more permanent investment, while still having a perfectly reliable security, that:—

United States 5-20's at their average premium yield the present purchaser less than 5½ per cent. gold interest. Should they be redeemed in five years, and specie payments be resumed, they would really pay only 4¾ per cent., or if in three years, only 3½ per cent., as the present premium would meanwhile be sunk.

Northern Pacific 7-30's, selling at par in currency, yield the investor $7\frac{3}{10}$ per cent. gold interest, absolutely, for thirty years, *free from United States tax.* $1,100 currency, invested now in United States 5-20's, will yield per year in gold, say, $62.00. $1,100 currency, invested now in Northern Pacific 7-30's, will yield per year in gold, $80.30. Here is a difference *in annual income* of nearly *one-third*, besides a difference of 7 to 10 per cent. in principal, when both classes of Bonds are redeemed.

THE ROAD NOW BUILDING.—
Work was begun in July last on the
eastern portion of the Line, and the
money provided, by the sale to stockholders of some six millions of the
Company's Bonds, to build and equip
the Road from Lake Superior across
Minnesota to the Red River of the
North—233 miles. The grading on
this division is now well advanced,
the iron is being rapidly laid ; several
thousand men are at work on the
Line, and about the first of August
next this important section of the
Road will be in full operation. In the
meantime, orders have been sent to
the Pacific coast for the commencement
of the work on the western end, in
early spring, and thereafter the work
will be pushed, both eastward and
westward, with as much speed as may
be consistent with solidity and a wise
economy.

RECEIVABLE FOR LANDS.—
These Bonds will be at all times receivable, at 1.10, in payment for the
Company's lands, at their lowest cash
price.

BONDS EXCHANGEABLE.—
The registered bonds can be exchanged at any time for coupons, the coupons for registered, and both these can
be exchanged for others, payable—principal and interest—at any of the principal financial centres of Europe, in
the coin of the various European
countries.

HOW TO GET THEM.—Your
nearest bank or banker will supply
these Bonds in any desired amount,
and of any needed denomination.
Persons wishing to exchange stocks or
other bonds for these, can do so with
any of our agents, who will allow the
highest current price for all market-
able securities.

Those living in localities remote
from banks, may send money, or other
Bonds, directly to us by express, and
we will send back Northern Pacific
Bonds at our own risk, and without
cost to the investor. For further information, pamphlets, maps, etc., call
on, or address the undersigned, or any
of the banks or bankers employed
to sell this Loan.

FOR SALE BY

JAY COOKE & CO.,

Fiscal Agents Northern Pacific Railroad Co.,

114 South Third St.,	Cor. Nassau and Wall Sts.,	452 Fifteenth Street,
PHILADELPHIA.	NEW YORK.	WASHINGTON, D.C.

By National Banks, and by Brokers generally throughout the Country.

143

MAP showing the Route of the NORTHERN PACIFIC RAILROAD and its CONNECTIONS.

TO SEEKERS OF HEALTH AND PLEASURE.

Grand Pleasure Excursion for the Season of 1871

—FROM—

BUFFALO, ERIE, CLEVELAND AND DETROIT,

TO DULUTH AND ST. PAUL,

PASSING THROUGH

LAKES HURON AND SUPERIOR.

To Continue during the Summer Months.

A Daily Line of STEAMERS will run from **Buffalo, Erie, &c.**, to **Saut Ste. Marie, Marquette** and **Duluth**,—Connecting with Cars on the **Lake Superior & Mississippi Railroad**, running to **St. Paul, Minn.**

FROM **St. Paul** Steamers run Daily on the Mississippi River, during the season of Navigation, to **La Crosse, Prairie du Chien, Dubuque** and **St. Louis**,—Connecting with the Lines of Railroad running to **Milwaukee, Chicago** and **Detroit**,—thus furnishing a ROUND TRIP of over *two thousand miles*, by land and water, through one of the most healthy and interesting regions on the Continent.

NEW ORLEANS TO QUEBEC, VIA ST. PAUL AND DULUTH.

This New and HEALTH-RESTORING LINE OF TRAVEL, by means of the **Lake Superior & Mississippi Railroad**, 155 miles in length, Connects the waters of the Great Lakes of America with the noble Mississippi River at the head of Navigation,—thus affording an extended EXCURSION of over *three thousand five hundred miles*, from NEW ORLEANS to QUEBEC, Can.,—passing up the MISSISSIPPI and through the GREAT LAKES to the FALLS OF NIAGARA, the THOUSAND ISLANDS, and the RAPIDS of the ST. LAWRENCE—forming altogether the

GRANDEST EXCURSION IN THE WORLD.

GRAND EXCURSION.

STOPPING PLACES and OBJECTS OF INTEREST IN THE ROUND TRIP FROM

BUFFALO TO DULUTH, ST. PAUL, &c.

DISTANCES

PORTS, ETC.		MILES.	PORTS, ETC.		MILES.
BUFFALO, N. Y.		0	*Ontonagon*	60	1,066
DUNKIRK		42	LA POINTE, Wis	80	1,146
ERIE, Pa	48	90	*Bayfield*	3	1,149
ASHTABULA, Ohio	41	131	SUPERIOR CITY	80	1,229
CLEVELAND, Ohio	54	185	*DULUTH, Minn*	6	1,235
MALDEN, Can	100	285	Lake Superior & Mississippi Railroad.		
DETROIT, Mich	20	305	FOND DU LAC	16	1,251
Lake St. Clair	7	312	(Dalles of the St. Louis River.)		
Port Huron	68	380	*Thomson*	8	1,259
Point au Barque and Light	70	450	June. Northern Pacific R. R	1	1,260
Thunder Bay and Light	75	525	*Hinckley*	53	1,313
De Tour, Mich	85	610	White Bear Lake	65	1,378
CHURCH'S LANDING	41	651	*ST. PAUL*	12	1,390
Sant Ste. Marie	14	665	Lake Pepin	66	1,456
White Fish Point and Light	40	705	LAKE CITY	25	1,481
Pictured Rocks	80	785	*Winona*	75	1,556
MARQUETTE	50	835	*La Crosse, Wis*	40	1,596
Portage Entry	80	915	*Prairie du Chien*	81	1,670
(HOUGHTON, 14 Miles.)			*DUBUQUE* opp. *Dunleith*	70	1,740
Keweenaw Point	50	965	*Freeport, Ill*	68	1,808
COPPER HARBOR	15	980	*CHICAGO*	121	1,929
EAGLE HARBOR	16	996	MICHIGAN CITY, Ind	55	1,984
EAGLE RIVER	10	1,006	*DETROIT*	229	2,213

STEAMBOAT AND RAILROAD ROUTES CONNECTING THE UPPER LAKES WITH THE MISSISSIPPI RIVER.

This GRAND EXCURSION embraces 1,585 Miles of Lake and River Navigation and 628 Miles Railroad Travel.

RETURNING VIA THE MISSISSIPPI RIVER TO DUBUQUE.

RAILROAD CONNECTIONS, &c.

From MARQUETTE the *Peninsula Division* of the *Chicago & Northwestern Railroad* convey Passengers, via Green Bay, to CHICAGO, ST. LOUIS, &c.

From DULUTH the *Northern Pacific Railroad* will convey Passengers to the Mississippi River, 100 miles, there Connecting with a Steamer on the Upper Mississippi, above the Falls of St. Anthony,—making another GRAND EXCURSION of great interest,—ascending the Mississippi to Pocagoma Falls, or descending to the Falls of St. Anthony.

Usual Through Fare $64, from which a deduction will be made for Through Tickets, embracing the ROUND TRIP during the Season of 1871.

DISTANCES FROM EASTERN CITIES TO PORTS ON LAKE ERIE.

CITIES, ETC.	MILES.
Philadelphia to Cleveland, Ohio, via Pennsylvania Central Railroad	505
Philadelphia to Erie, Pa., via Philadelphia & Erie Railroad	451
New York to Erie, Pa., via Catawissa Route	186
New York to Cleveland, Ohio, via Allentown Route	581
New York to Buffalo, via Erie Railway	423
New York to Buffalo, via New York Central Railroad	443
Boston to Buffalo, via Boston & Albany R. R. and New York Central R. R	498

146

SHERMAN HOUSE,

CHICAGO, ILLINOIS.

This HOTEL is centrally located on the **corner of Clark and Randolph Streets**, **opposite Court House Square**; was built, in 1860, of Athens Marble, and has all the modern improvements, including a **Passenger Elevator** to convey the guests to and from the several stories of the house. In fact, it is in every particular, as COMPLETE AND MAGNIFICENT AN ESTABLISHMENT as there is in the United States.

D. A. GAGE,   J. A. RICE,   }
G. W. GAGE,   H. WALTERS, } Proprietors.

TREMONT HOUSE,

CHICAGO, ILL.,

Situated on corner of Lake and Dearborn Streets.

RE-BUILT, re-modelled, handsomely and richly re-furnished in 1867 and 1868. Has had all the modern improvements introduced, including one of

ATWOOD'S VERTICAL RAILWAY ELEVATORS,

for conveying guests to the different floors. Suites of rooms, baths and water connected, and is one of the largest and best appointed Hotels in the West.

JOHN B. DRAKE, Proprietor.

W. FELT, late of Lindell Hotel. }
SAMUEL M. TURNER.

SOUTHERN HOTEL,
ST. LOUIS, MISSOURI.

The Only First-Class Hotel in the City.

Its Tables are at all times supplied in great abundance with the best the market affords. Its Large and Elegant Furnished Parlors, Long and Wide Corridors, and Comfortably Outfitted Chambers and Rooms ensuite, make it the Most Desirable House in the city for Strangers and Families.

N.B.—This Hotel DOES NOT EMPLOY RUNNERS, and travellers are warned against the representations of those sent out by other Hotels.

Western Union Telegraph and General Railroad and Steamboat Office in the Hotel.

LAVEILLE, WARNER & CO., Propr's.

151

GREAT LAKES OF AMERICA

AND THE

Valley of the Upper Mississippi;

GIVING A DESCRIPTION OF

THE OBJECTS OF INTEREST AND PLACES OF RESORT

IN THE

HEALTH-RESTORING REGION

SURROUNDING

LAKE SUPERIOR AND THE UPPER MISSISSIPPI;

FORMING ALTOGETHER A

COMPLETE GUIDE TO SEEKERS OF HEALTH AND PLEASURE,

WITH MAPS AND EMBELLISHMENTS.

COMPILED BY J. DISTURNELL,

AUTHOR OF THE "INFLUENCE OF CLIMATE IN NORTH AND SOUTH AMERICA," ETC.

The great event of the completion of the Railroad between ST. PAUL and DULUTH, Minn., (finished in August, 1870,) connecting the navigable waters of the Mississippi River and Lake Superior, renders the appearance of this volume one of deep interest to the Travelling Public seeking Health and Pleasure—forming altogether a Complete GUIDE through the GREAT LAKES and the VALLEY OF THE UPPER MISSISSIPPI, from ST. LOUIS to the FALLS OF NIAGARA.

Also, the Railroad and Steamboat Route from Chicago to Lake Superior, and the Northern Pacific Railroad Route from Duluth to the Red River of the North.

CONDITIONS, ETC.

A NEW EDITION OF THE ABOVE WORK will be issued in June, 1871, and include the Railroad and Steamboat Arrangements for the Season, Tables of Distances, &c. It will be comprised in about 250 pages, 16mo., and neatly bound in Muslin. Price, $2.00.

☞ ADVERTISEMENTS INSERTED ON REASONABLE TERMS. ☜

NEW YORK, *March*, 1871.

www.ingramcontent.com/pod-product-compliance
Lightning Source LLC
Chambersburg PA
CBHW030556270326
41927CB00007B/941